SECULARISM
in
Afghanistan

SHUKOOR ZARDUSHTIAN

iUniverse LLC
Bloomington

Secularism in Afghanistan

iUniverse books may be ordered through booksellers or by contacting:

iUniverse LLC
1663 Liberty Drive
Bloomington, IN 47403
www.iuniverse.com
1-800-Authors (1-800-288-4677)

ISBN: 978-1-4502-9083-8 (sc)
ISBN: 978-1-4502-9082-1 (hc)
ISBN: 978-1-4502-9084-5 (ebk)

Library of Congress Control Number: 2011900895

Printed in the United States of America

iUniverse rev. date: 07/30/2013

DEDICATED TO:

Shah Amanullah (1892-1960) compiled the first constitution of our country. His work was branded as Communist propaganda by a person called Mullah-e-Shur Bazar.

Mullah-e-Shur Bazar, an Arab immigrant, who lived on tithes and chariti threw the first Afghan National Constitution against the ground.

Shah Amanullah liberated Afghanistan from the tyranny of the British. He gave freedom to women for the first time and provided them with the opportunity to work in different fields. Shah Amanullah converted the Hijri (Islamic) calendar to the Gregorian (Christian) calendar and the Sabbath from Friday to Sunday.

He opened the doors of schools to women and sent them abroad for complementary studies. He outlawed polygamy, prohibited slavery and introduced a secular society. This brave man banned the wearing of the Borqa and eliminated tribal privileges. He changed the greeting Salam-Alaikum to raising hats and asked the people to adopt European style clothes, behavior etc. If they did not do so, they would be fined. Peter the Great (1672-1725) enacted a similar law when he demanded that men shave their beards.

In appreciation of such a brave compatriot and for his outstanding services, I would like to dedicate a token of my thought "Secularism in Afghanistan" to him.

Note: I believe that in appreciation of such a great figure and his memorable services, our legislature should register the Democracy Award in his name. I would be glad to see a movement called the Amani Movement emerging in Afghanistan.

And I'm also asking our reverent intellectual country men and women to come together to form a commitee for fund raising to build a memorial Icon of this great man on a horse in the heart of Kabul.

Reverent King Amanulla is the symbol of democracy in Afghanistan and his icons must be represented in every government's institutions outside and inside the country. Look at the Pakistani people how do they respect their leader Ali Jinnah (1878- 1948).

Unfortunately, the transformation of social reforms of King Amanulla because of the British poisonous propaganda through its agents like Lawrence of Arabia, Mawlawy Najaf Ali from Lahoor and others made the Pashtun tribes in the eastern part of the country to revolt against the king and in the end he abandoned the country.

The movement of secularisation in Turkey, Iran, and Afghanistan during 1923-24 was a great idea. The Turk people got lucky to keep this great development alive, but Iran and Afghanistan the two ignorant backwarded countries because of love of Arab religion (Islam= hollow logy) could not.

The Islam religion on the basis of nine and teen verses in Quran is only for Arab the country which I named her (Muhammadistan) now Saudi Arabia.

King Amanullah loved his country and he wants to speed up the social reforms as much as he could. Therefore, to appease the ulama to get his reforms through, on 5 Feburary 1925 he stoned two Qadiani shopkeepers to death in Kabul.

So much for religious freedom. This witch-hunt was a violation of the highest ideals of the Nizamnama (and Amanullah is said to have personally regretted it) and the only reason was that the government badly needed a scapegoat to distract the attention of ulama and people the Khost crisis – as well as defender of the orthodox faith. An appeal to bigotry seldom fails in any society and the Qadiani paid the price (Islam and politics in Afghanistan by Asta Olesen). It was very difficult for a hard working King like Amanullah in a country full of Ishak-ha to have a horse.

Hello, Hello, Anybody Home?

To the human rights organizations of the U.N. and Arab – Islam League countries!

We neither blame the God nor his paper boy to stone the innocent people rather the Middle Eastern's mythecal Prophets those who were subjected to sickness of paroxysm and convulsion.Evidents telling us that all religions are made by man and the involvement of God to commit savagery especially to stone people is a big accusation.Therefore I ask the bening and good hearted people those who fighting un justice and human rights to do something good to wipeout this religious soiled (Stoning) from the face of the history.

Thank You.

Secularism, religion separate from politics, is a laudable system which embraces freedom and enhances social awareness as well as the rule of law. Secularism is the brilliant thought that helps people to free themselves from the grip of superstitions. Superstitions are metaphysical ideas inculcated into the brain of the gullible people by the hammer and nail.

From the exchange of differences, cultural clashes among the individuals and societies, new ideas emerge. This in turn makes more room for more dialogues, which helps people to differentiate between good and bad in their confrontations.

هر کیرا عشق دین پدید آید   شهــد دنیاش کی لذیذ آید
(مولوی)

The one who become interested in religion
Can't taste the sweetness of this world

We have got to keep in mind that secularism, unlike religion, is not a system of absolutism that forces one to wear cocoons, black or white Chadors, or to cover one's face. Secularism is not perversion or transgression, but one of the most necessary elements of the governing system. It is designed to fight and correct primordial ideas and superstitions like punishment after death.

PROLOGUE

I'm glad to see that based on the research carried out in the field of Natural Sciences, the thoughtful and dynamic human race was able to be relatively successful in finding out the secrets of the universe. On the contrary, gunpowder, lash, sword, bow and bloodshed of innocent people in the way of God could not solve even a small portion of the problems existing in human society over thousands of years .For example jihad (robe the people, kill infidels in the way of God) and directly you go up to heaven and enjoy there with the pure ones.

The reconstructive characteristics of laboratory scientists, relying on reason and rationalism, have made some people impatient. I'm quite confident that the continuation of such research and scientific dialogue will put an end to the Tautology of fundamentalists in the future.

By resorting to expansion of the religion of god, Arabs contrary to verse No. 36 of Al Nahl chapter and verse No. 4 of Ibrahim chapter, Tah 113, Faslat 3, Yusuf 2, Raad 37, Zumar 28, Shura 7, Zakhraf 3, Ahqaf 12, Faslat 44, invaded Iran and Khorasan 1400 years ago in order to gain wealth. Such an invasion only resulted in slavery, destruction and bloodshed of humankind.

The strange and the most contradicting story is that Adam became the noble creature due to his disobedience to God, and also Lucifer (Azazil the closest angel to God) who, didn't worship Adam and convened with Evil (Satan).

1

George F. Will in his book, <u>The Morning After</u>, has written that Archbishop Desmond Tutu is commonly viewed on TV. Andrei Sakharov, however, has never received such attention. Truly, neither god nor humans could balance the weight of justice.

In order to consolidate and prolong the age of the shaky Islam totalitarianism, Omar, an Arab Hitler, expanded Islam's ideology beyond the border of the peninsula in an imperialistic way.

In the mean time, to perpetuate the Islam new born belief, some coward eggheads deliberately established many psychodynamic pillars such as Jihad (one of the tricky religious political element). In addition, some other seducing principles such as threats and fear, blasphemy, heresy, apostasy and the fire of hell were also established. Also, the principle of the inquisitions of two angels by the names of Nakir and Ankir who enter into one's grave and start flogging them if they have had a good time in their lives was also developed.

The question is this if Omar really believed in Allah's commandments which says the Isalm launage and the Islam religion is only for Arab then he should not have attacked other <u>countries.</u>

One can easily recognize the difference between the healthy and unhealthy mentalities of Dr. Nelson Mandela and the fundamentalist Egyptian Physician, Iman Al Zawahiri. The latter isn't aware that he's suffering from a neuropathic illness. His stomach is full of rockets and his brain is empty.

Arabic fox under the Burqa of demagogic (Viziry Jackal Tribes), dragging desert's devil, (Osama Bin Ladan) the canonical god of Patan Omar from one cave to another. Be careful about the Israeli Dr.Baruch Goldstein who will enter the cave after the fox.

در مشـرب زن و از قیـد مـــذاهب بـــگریـــز
عافیت نیست در آن بزم که سازش جنگ است
(مولانا عبدالقادر "بیدل")

Get away from religions and enjoy life. No peace in a society dancing to the rhythm of war (Mawlana Abdul Qader "Bidel")

The current cowardly government of Afghanistan, comprised of such people followers of Taliban (the world conspiracy of laying the eggs which hatched the most repulsive, blandishing, and inflicting Islamic regime in history of Afghanistan) makes me want to listen to the koranic recitation but silences me not to question.

> All religions take care to silence or to excute those who question them (and I choose to regard this recurrent tendency as a sign of their weakness rather than their strength).
> (Christopher Hitchens).

The Islamic mullahs (knots of the sugar cane according to the great poet Bidel) think that the Islam religion is made of cast iron or of a beautiful China or "ceramic wear". This is why in the past 1400 years the Islamic blacksmiths could not dare to use a hammer to find out the nature of the object since there is a big difference between wisdom and practical wisdom. In a free and open society, if you say Friedrich Nietzsche said that god is dead nobody hurts you but in Islam the subject is different. Why? This is because these cowardly people, including Ajams (the Arab's second hand wives and the psychological Muslims) have no guts. Whatever the Penguins say, the beloved consensually go deeper into bed with their lover.

Two Islamic fundamentalists, Faizunisa Ali, and Muzammil H. Siddiqi, in the Textbook for Islamic Education write "Islam is the best." It could not be better written that Islam is the best, but the others are the beasts.

Believing in religion, does not civilize the society or improve the quality of common sense. Imam Hamid Karzai, a non-productive father, in a decade as a leader physically and mentally never changed so how can he change the people of Afghanistan. The previous democratic government in Afghanistan, in a short time completely changed the hearts and minds of the society. Karzai who, carries a praying mat under one arm and the Arabic book under another arm, belongs to the seventh century.

We, the billion Ajams, have been held hostage for more than 1400 years by Arab fairy tales and this is the time to get up and fight back. When I look at the mosques or listen to the bleating of a mullah, I smell blood, war and destruction.

We, the Ajami, never paid attention or investigated why all the religious privileges, command and control were given to Arabs and not to the Ajam who make up more than one billion people. Any word coming out of the mouth of a braggart Arab, you think is sacred and holy. Why don't they say openly to the Islamic world that everybody can translate the Koran in their own language?

In Koran Verse 142 in Sura of cow has said that the holy land is the only public worshipping place, and Muhammad called upon his own people to pray facing towards holy land. If it is so, why has the position of praying been changed to the latter and from one holy land to another holy land. Isn't this plainly some sort of transgression from the commandment of Allah?

سيقول السفهاُء من الناس ما ولهم عن قيبلتم التى كانوا عليها قل لله المشرق و المغرب يهدى من يشاُء الى صراط مستقيم

When the Arabic drum is being played in Egypt or in Palestine, the Pakistani in Pakistan, the Afghanistani in Afghanistan and the Londoni Ajam in London start dancing in the streets. As they do so, they start accusing Israel and the United States for their big faults. I think this is the time for Ajam to take over the Islamic leadership and make the Arabs dance for them. The Arabs destructive idealogy, dignities, and prides have subsisted for the most part on the ignorance of the Ajam people.

Look at the carpenter who for a living makes a beautiful table from an ugly piece of wood. Look at Buddha and ask why he fled from the castle or privileged life.

Buddha was confined inside a beautiful castle and was not allowed to expose himself to the outside. But, he became a different person when he escaped from the castle and encountered a new environment and saw the realities with his naked eyes.

As Christopher Hitchens writes:" Islam is at once the most and the least interesting of the world's monotheisms. It builds upon its primitive Jewish and Christian predecessors, selecting a chunk here and a shard there, and thus fall, it partly falls also."

The inexplicable mystery of intelligent design and the fascinating revelations have been sent from the sky and have confused so many intellectual people.

In his book "Ideas: a History of Thought and Invention, From Fire to Freud" Peter Watson writes that Newton believed that Moses was well aware of the heliocentric theory of Copernicus and his own doctrine of gravity. A generation after the appearance of his famous book "The Principia Mathematica", Newton was still striving to uncover the exact plan of Solomon's Temple, which he considered "the best guide to the topography of heaven." Newton stated a beautiful metaphor "the modern notion of the universe, as held together by gravity".

You, my scientist, brave compatriot! You, *ajami* (non Arab Muslims), will remain in ignorance forever unless you break away from the chain of slavery of nomadic culture, which drags us towards religious perpetual disputatiousness which is a destructive political idealogy. To consolidate the political position, the pedants resort to hadith and verses or other incantatory techniques to usurp political power. Jihad is one of the most deceptive and dangerous techniques which has caused countless innocent people to die everywhere in vain. Now, who is the care taker after you to that will take care of the orphans,widows, and others who have lost their body parts for the Arab paradoxes.

My brothers, sisters, fathers, mothers, and others! Show me what you gained from this sanguinary jihad? Physically and mentally you are broke. Our ignorant stupid mullahs the Arab mercenaries on the bases of this and that Arabic story sacrificed you like animals just to protect the ideology, dignity and pride which are all attributed to the Arabs, the sons of one God. I'm sure and I'm very happy that you got the message and in the future you have to promise to your beloved wives and your lovely kids that you will never participate again in any situation or situations for Arab interests.

You deceived young mujahiddin! Do you hear the voices of your widowed wives or your orphan kids crying on your graves day and night? They are hungry, they are sick, they cannot go to school. Without shelters, they are begging and dying on the streets because you dummy slaves sacrificed yourselves for the Arab fables.

> Strange but true: those who have loved God most have loved men least.
>
> Robert Green Ingersoll.

We need to have a secular society, separate from religion. In order to achieve such a great goal, solidarity and the endless efforts of intellectual men and women is imperative. My country in the course of history suffered too much from tribalism, religion and feudalism. Since Hamid Karzai was brought up in such a sick environment don't you think that the country is left in the hands of a capricious regressive man?

From the view points of fatuous mentality and funny appearances, what is different between the Patan blind Omar and the Patan Hamid Karzai?

"Zardushtian"

Chapter One

WHY SHOULDN'T I GROAN?

In the past, Afghanistan was called Khorasan, a country comprised of several provinces: Bukhara, Samarkand, Taleqan, Balkh, Sistan and Nishapur. Foreigners invaded these provinces many times on their way to the Indian Ocean. Alexander the Great (356-323 BC), on his way to Iran (Persia) was accompanied by a number of botanists and geographers to provide information for Aristotle, the Greek philosopher. He led the invasion of Iran in 356-323 B.C. with 30,000 infantry and 5,000 cavalry. Alexander defeated Emperor Darius the 111th and advanced to India through Khorasan. On the way, his army committed many brutal atrocities and there was widespread killing. Despite these excesses, he succeeded in introducing Greek culture to these areas.

My motherland Khurasan (the Academic land) from the tenth century 998 up to 1993 before the overthrowing of the democratic government by foreigners was a secular state and got to stay secular.

Secularism is a political system of governing and insisting on separation of religion from the state regardless hurting the religion, secularism is not a new phenomenon and goes beyond to the era of Greek and Roman thinkers like Marcus Aurelius and Epicurus;

A muslim Ibn Rushd from the medieval; the enlightenment brave philosophers such as Baruch Spinoza, Voltaire, John Locke, Denis Diderot, Thomas Jefferson, Thomas Pain, James Madison, Robert Ingersoll, and Bertrand Russel and others.

Secularism is a strong social movement to modernize the mass and provide pleasant work environment for everybody and fight the barriers of discrimination, inequality, bias and superstitions.

Religion is not knowledge or it is the product of scientific observations it is a theology of the Middle East mythology, a tree but without fruit.

As Durkheim notes: for society, religion provides a means for social control; it helps support some of the primary societal rules. However, as a glance around the world would reveal, religious beliefs can also be dysfunctional: religious beliefs can lead to discrimination and even to killing those who are not of the same faith.

If we are enough erudite and comprehensive people sure we are able to push aside this ugly commodity and even abandon it for good.

this is the policy of American government and the Saudi together to protract the age of Islam's religion for their own national interest.

If it is right- Jimmy Carter the President of the United State told the Shah of Iran to leave the country and he helped the Khomeini to succeed him. On January 1979 he delivered one hundred and fifty million dollars to Khomeini banking account in Paris and the main time Leonid Brezhnev the leader of the Soviet Union warned Carter if America interfering in Iran situation Russia will attack Afghanistan.

Newsmax.com- Christopher Ruddy Monday, May 13, 2002 writes:

8

With the Shah gone, the whole region was destabilized. The Soviet Union invaded

Afghanistan; no doubt a direct link to rise of the Taliban can be traced to this invasion.

In order to dominate geopolitically over central Asian possessions, America and Saudi (together for their own national interests but not Afghan national interests) created Pashtoon Taliban and their illegitimate government.

Sence Taliban, the religious inexperienced orphans children who do not represent all Afghan people how is it possible for a superpower like America to take advantage of such a shameful and rejected body as an a easy exit to sign up a very vital contract with them to bring natural gas through Afghanistan from the Caspian Sea?

Quote: In 1997, while George W. Bush was governor of Texas, a delegation of Taliban leaders from Afghanistan flew to Houston to meet with Unical executives to discuss the building of a pipeline through Afghanistan and the same day, Unical signed the pipeline deal with Taliban.

Then in 2001, just five and half months before 9/11, the Bush administration welcomed a Taliban envoy to tour the United States to help improve the image of the Taliban government. Finally the illegitimate government of the Taliban under the leadership of Mr. Hamid Karzai was founded in Kabul Afghanistan.

Shame and shame over shame:

{One unqualified minister informations and culture in Kabul has dedicated the year of 2013 to Ghazni the capital of Islamic civilizations. This man does not know what civilization is? It means to pour more salt on the bleeding wounds of the Indian people and the Kabuly brave hero who cut off the head of the Arab invader (laith Bin-e- Qais) now called him the king of the two swords. I hope my senseful country men and women feel themselves responsible to cover the grave of this Arab killer with cow manure.

Thinker Alexis de Tocqueville (1805-1859) says:

"I studied the Kuran a great deal. I came away from that study with the conviction that by and large there have been few religions in the world as deadly to men as that of Muhammad."

I think this invention is very preposterous to call Ghazni the capital of Islamic civilizations rather than the flourishing place for the Khurasanian cultures. This is another example of shame which represents the Taliban Arabised government in Kabul.

If killing, beheading, burning people alive, spraying acid at their faces, cutting off their noses, blinding, blowing themselves up among the people and burying alive the three hundred

Healthy pigs creation of your creator (الله) exploding the Buddha statues are presumably the gift of the Islamic civilization character then undoubtedly this unaware minister should have not called Ghazni the capital of the Islamic civilizations.

Islam, the parochial and a plagirised religion, made by a group of uncivilized illiterate and irresponsible persons, therefore it never became or becoming the subject of a civilized matters unless you get rid of it because the culture of Islamic religious dogma during fourteen hundred years in the past never made headway to improve the human rights situations or intellectualism.

The Pashtoon Taliban the foreigners Islamic foot soldiers, the vicarious shame of Islam the enemy of the beauties and aesthetics blew up the Buddhas the national touristic treasure of Afghan poor people and the person who committed this criminal act got away without punishment.

Zalmai Khalil Zad, the American ambassador in Afghanistan also a Pashtoon, is another Talib according to Dr. Muhaiuddin Mahdi a member of the Parliament in Afghanistan. On February,2013, in Khawaran web writes that Khalil Zad denied the proposal of the Indian ambassador who said that in the National Costitution, Afghanistan might be titled a federalism State like the model of Indian government but he Khalil Zad shut me up he said and told others be careful he horning you.

Training of CIA personal, military soldiers, and Pakistani ISI operatives who would later train the holy warriors in Afghanistan and Pakistan. The CIA undertook a program of recruitment and toured people like Osama bin Laden and Sheik Azzam visiting twenty six states in the United States.

Out there are some people confusing others that radical secularist is very dangerous to Christian rights and national security, but they forgot the evil forces of the Fundamentalist Christians and Fundamentalist Muslims in the past and at the present time such not educational and obstructive ideology by some fundamentalist Christians is a political trick to provoke the Islamic fundamentalists to create a united front to block the progresses and social reforms in Islamic countries.

Religion neither is ideology and nor knowledge, ideology in dictionary: The body of ideas reflecting the social needs and aspirations of individual, group, class, or culture.

Quote: George Holyoake's1896 publication English Secularism defines secularism as:

Secularism is a code of duty pertaining to this life, founded on considerations purely human, and intended mainly for those who find theology indefinite or inadequate, or unreliable or unbelievable. It's essential principles are three: (1)The improvement of this life by material means.(2) That science is the available Providence of man.(3) That is good to do good. Whether there be other good or not, the good of the present life is good' and it is good to see that good.{25}

Today in the world we have the best secular system in India there in India are many religions and India is the most tolerant country in the world, but not Pakistan the Western neighbor there the Saudi oil money converted them the most intolerant and evil people. Diodorus Siculus a Greek historian who accompanied Alexander the Great he called India the most democratic country.

Marvin E. Gettleman and Stuart Schaar in the book (The Middle East and Islamic World Reader) Quoted from Abu al Rayhan Muhammad ibn Ahmad al Biruni, A Muslim Scholar Examines Hinduism (1030)

Al Biruni (973-1050), born in Ghazni in southern Khurasan , because a great eclectic savant who excelled in mathematics, astronomy, natural science, history, and geography. Over his life time he produced more than one hundred scholarly works.

He spoke Arabic, Persian, Turkish, and learned Hebrew, Greek, Syriac, Sanskrit, and several dialectics of India, studying the latter while accompanying Mahmud the Ghaznavid (998-1030) and his immediate heirs on their victorious warring expedition to northern India.

Al Biruni says Hindus entirely differs from us in every respect, many a subject appearing intricate and obscure which would be perfectly clear if there were more connection between us. The barriers which separate Muslims and Hindus rest on different causes.

First .. Hindus entirely differ from us in everything which other nations have in common.

Secondly, they totally differ from us in religion, as we believe nothing in which they believe, and vice versa. On the contrary, all their fanaticism is directed against those who do not belong to them against all foreigners. They call them mleecha, i.e. impure, and forbid having any connection with them, be it by intermarriage or any other kind of relationship, or by sitting, eating and drinking with them, because thereby, they think, they would be polluted.

In the third place, in all manners and usages they differ from us to such a degree as to frighten their children with us, with our dress, and our ways and customs, and as to declare us to be devil's breed, and our doings as the very opposite of all that is good and proper.

I think the Indian people at that time in their judgments undoubtedly were correct to be differed from foreigners especially Muslims a strange people with strange religion to go five times on the roof tops or on minarets howling (holo ,lolo, lala) in the med night and early in the morning disturbing people when they are at sleep and butchering the cows they are very sacred in Hindu religion. The appearance of the Muslims with bushy beards embodies them look like Gorilla and scares everybody, killing innocents people, spoiling, plundering because Allah told them to do so, washing and cleansing of the private places, as part of religious rite sure you are polluting the streams, poles, rivers and drinking water then your heads down and your asses up isn't strange

?Imposing Jazia on Hindus and exempting Muslims for paying taxes, after so many dismay, and despise, and numerous desecrations still you are expecting Hindus to respect you.

Why the Greek historian praising the Hindus and Hindus hate the Muslims so what is the mystery of comparing the love and hate between this two emperors Alexander the Great and Ghaznavid Mahmud the Great? One wanted to introduce the Greek culture in the area and the other one globalizing the Allah's commandments by butchering the people, robbing, converting them in to Islam by sword and make them to flee their homeland.

Sociologist Kingsley Davis says "socialization takes place in stages throughout our lives" and this is what happening to India.

On January 1982 on a taxi from Bombay I was traveling to Pune for practical training in agriculture cooperative, we got out for a dinner the Indian brothers those were traveling together did not let me to pay the bill and they said to me that I'm coming from a poor country.

Today India not only is a prosperous country but a secular democratic supper power too, Pakistan and Muslims as a whole living in a religious isolating environment like Mosques which belong to the seven century.

Somebody comparing secularism to Fascism, Nazism, Stalinism and deadly he or she is wrong. First of all those systems belong to the past secondly they were a militaristic power but not secularism, secularism is against the totalitarian system or over through a secular state and replace it with religious one.

Secularism is not danger as Islam totalitarianism is, first of all Islam on the bases of so many verses in Quran is only for Arab, so why should the Afghans be suffering to fight and retain the Arab paradoxical ideology, and unlike other books how is it possible the Quran becoming the law of the land? First of all Quran is a plagiarized book written in obscurant way by a irresponsible person, and also it is not the original Quran and we got to investigate what happened to the original one? Judaism and Christianity the open minded and resilient religions during the course of history gave way to social reforms but not Islam the uncompromised religion.

The influential monetary policy of the Saudi kings without tactic and without strategy the Arab league as a socio-religious organization did not accomplish anything good for Arab nations. The statical character of the league with conservative- radical agendum isolating the Muslim communities from each other because on top the Saudi Arabia blocking the movements of socio- cultural and socio-political reforms in Islamic countries.

In year 1962 the league was used by Saudi to fight secularism, and leftists in the middle east even in other Islamic countries this is why I asked those countries which Islam religion has imposed on them to emancipate themselves from the Saudi hegemony policy otherwise implementation of any socioeconomic reforms and cultural diversifications in those countries are impossible .

Practically Islamic scholars unlike other religious scholars are not enough brave to bring profoundly changes in their communities. According to Professor Esposito "Since family law was regarded as too sacrosanct to eliminate, it was reformed but not replaced". Therefore in such a dogma situation Islam could not take advantage of social and scientific revolution in Europe like the 14th century renaissance which gave more freedom to the women, industrial revolution 18th century, gave birth to capitalism, French revolution, enlightenment 18th century, and October revolution in Russia and without passing this life stages I doubt Islamic countries could become a modern state, on the other hand the American supper power with the help of NATO and Saudi oil money under the pretext of their national security disappearing the secular states in Islamic countries because this two countries fear of the establishments of social democratic, secular or leftists government there and they of course prefer the theocratic governments over democratic the most and this is why the United State of America does not want to destabilize the theocratic regime in Iran and in Afghanistan.

Islam from its inception was political and religious power to kill and robe the people but Christianity in fourth century, when Rome adopted Christianity as its official religion, Christian too has been political.

When I say secularism it means that religion cannot play any rule in the government otherwise it is not free from religion to become a secular state. What does it mean some Muslims say they like to join in the political process, freedom, rule of law but not for a totally secular state? I think such people got to go back to school, because fear and ignorance infatuate them to separate themselves from religion like Rajab Tayyab Erdogan the prime minister of Turkey who says secularism is a lie and secular person is not a Muslim shame on you Mr. Rajab I'm very proud of a very brave and outstanding Turk person like Mustfa Kamal Ata Turk who slapped the Bedouin's religion Islam very hard and this is the right time for progressives , leftists and other freedom lovers to come together and build a strong united front to face the political religions.

Religions and Prophets both are a fascinating discovery or Muhammad was a merchant and it is a big lie when he dies he left behind only a white mule. Or Saeed Jamaludin Afghani was a brilliant person. No he was the British spy. Around 1870 he being sent from Kandahar to the Middl East by English to stir up the Arabs against the Turk Empire.

Quote: Abdul Hamid 11or khan Ghazi 1842- 1918 was anxious to appear as a religious champion against Christian encroachment. He encouraged the building of the Macca railroad to make Islam's holy places more accessible. He subsidized the pan-Islamic of Jamal-ud-din al-Afghani, whom he invited to Istanbul but virtually imprisoned there,and encouraged widespread support for himself as the head of the caliphate.

He the Jamaludin was an English representative and spy. His goal was to make Arabs revolt against Turks and this is why he is very famous among the Arab people.

Rethinking Islam and Secularism by John Esposito Professor of international Affairs and Islamic Studies at Georgetown University:

Saudi Arabia and Turkey reflected two polar positions reflecting the relationship of religion and secularism to the state. Saudi Arabia established as a self proclaimed Islamic state based up on the Quran as its constitution. At the opposite end of the spectrum, Ata Turk (Mustafa Kamal) created a secular Turkish republic.

The vestiges of the Ottman Empire the Caliph/ Sultan, the Sharia, Islamic institutions and schools were replaced by European inspired political, legal, and educational systems. And this is a clear attesting credit given to a Hero like Kamal by Professor John L.Esposito.

Mustafa Kamal Ata Turk the hero

Firmly I believe that the October revolution's impact on the rise of secularism, crushing Islamic fundamentalism, and dismantling colonization was very great so the creation of Saudi, Pakistan, and Israel was the invention of the West to block the influence of Communism in the world of Islam especially in the Middle East.

Deepa Kuma in her essay International Socialist Review outlines the particular historic conditions that have enabled the rise of political Islam. These include the active role played by the U.S. in posing Islam and Political Islam as an alternative to secular nationalism and the left; persistent imperial intervention and domination; internal weakness that led to the decline of secular nationalist and various left parties, creating an ideological vacuum that Islamists were able to occupy; economic crises and its exacerbation under the neo-liberal era, which present an economic opening for Islamists and their charitable networks.

From research we found out that some young Muslims the Muhammad lovers believe that the Western influence is negative and inevitably tries to force their agenda upon them. To me this young fundamentalist Muslims do not know to explain how the militaristic and political Islam comes into being? This young checks still are not aware that there in Kuran there are nine verses that say Islam is only for Arab (Saudi Arabia).

When the Khalifa Abu Bakr passed away, Omar the butcher told the soldiers we could not have anything to eat except grass if we do not attack Iran. If the culture of the West is not pleasant to you to changes why should the Muslims flying like flies to the West?

Now they are brook and disappointed and this is why they are appealing to the West to respect all religions. We know that the Islam religion historically is a dissociating absolute organization but not socializing school or product of scientific observations to be respected. Religion is biased to democracy but secularism helps democracy to flourish.

Mr. Ali Dashti in his book 23 years of Prophecy writes: Judge Ayaz, the lover of Muhammad a Poet and traditionalist in Indalucia Spain in the med- Hijree 5-6 in his book الشفاء "The Healing" writes that the Prophet house keeper Om- Yemen was suffering from some sort of stomach sickness and he ate something by- product of the Prophet and he got well. Now I do not know how this young fundamentalist Muslims the Muhammad lovers discern on this historical event? I think in such a sick society secularism is the very cured medicine for Muslims all over the world?

Ph.D.Pervez Amirali Hoodbhoy, a brilliant Pakistani physicist, criticized the backwardness of the Muslim world in every aspects of life especially in science, technology, trade, and education. Pervez is pushing his agenda for a secular Pakistan and personally, I ask the Pakistani devoted intellects young generation to escort Dr. Pervez the Great in this dangenerous journey.

The rise of secularism globally is good news for secularists. The secularism is a very strong movement and already disturbed Vatican and saying it was unknown to humanity.

Arianne Gasser of Canton, Ohio says "People just think that we are evil, God hating. We are just people. We just don't believe that something happens to us after we die".

BBC- The First World War a collapse of the old order across Europe, and in Wales organized Christianity went into a long decline. The word of God was no longer unchallenged at a popular level, in Denmark and Sweden, fever than 5% of adult is in church on a typical Sunday. Posted on 12/25/ 2010 by Ipetrich In much of Europe,

Canada, Australia, and Japan, the fraction of worshippers has dropped to 5-10%.

The guardian-Rising atheism in America puts "religious right on the defensive"

Paul Harris in NEW York the Observer, Saturday 1 October 2011- about 400 people are preparing to gather for a conference in Hartford Connecticut, to promote the end of religion in the US and their vision of a secular future for the country.

Why is secularism on the rise in America - A recent trend I have noticed is that Americans are becoming more and more secular in. their belief system says Steve. Around 45 million Americans live apart from church going. Editor, Gustav Broukal Press.

How do we bring reforms in a fundamentalist society like Afghanistan which intentionally been made fundamentalist by CIA, ISI, Saudi Arabia, and others? The system of education in Afghanistan in a religious environment lack of freedom to express your wishes freely is a big concern.

I think education in a rugged and mentally absolutism society that you cannot express yourself is not education. Freedom in education to express and criticize absolutism is the most important necessities for reforms and mental developments.

It is difficult to abandon your own way of life for another because people being resisted by the force of changes all the time then in light below efforts may be we are able to some degree to bring steadily healthy changes in to a very misogynistic religious back warded society like Afghanistan.

1- Intend to fix the schools curriculum close to the schools curriculum of central Asian countries, and India.

2- Having a strong central democratic government to implement the constructive educational programs by force, and make narrower and narrower the environment for the religious activities. As Durkheim says a social fact is to be recognized by the power of the external coercion which it exercises or is capable of exercising over individuals, and the presence of this power may be recognized in its turn either by the existence of some specific sanction or by resistance offered against every individual effort that tends to violate it.

3- Unisex schooling system is more beneficial for poor country like Afghanistan because we are not merely closing the gap between the genders but socializing the students, and this process slow down the temptation, improving the skills of our kids for better understanding, this program should be applied by force and the coercion force keep going on until the old habits being disappeared.

Inclusive environment to reflect all is the nature of school structure to guarantee to keep the balance of education equal for all. Ensuing a performance, as a drama and other intertaniments to make schools more attractive and pleasant place for the society which is the main principal targets of educational system.

4- Women freedom in Afghanistan: the women there for half of a century enjoyed the taste and the beauty of freedom but the evil powers on the top Saudi Arabia took away this fruitful institutionalized opportunities from Afghan's brave ladies now they have the right to kick out the Arabs from Afghanistan in order to get their freedom back.

ایران تو ، با نام دین زن را به زندان میکشد   من تاج را تقدیم ان بانوی برتر میکنم
دوکتور مصطفی بادکوبه ی

Your Iran under the pretext of religion impreson lady, but for her highness I offer her the Crown.

Anyone worried about the revival of the Taliban ought to be hoping for the revival of the communists.(Stephen Gowans) 9 August 2010

I'm sure that Stephen Gowans, Michael Parenti, John Ryan, and others sharing the same thoughts are right to with hold from deeper sinking in to the Afghan quagmire. To get rid of the stupidities of Hamid Karzai and his friends Taliban and the theocratic absolutism government there the United States on the bases of regional sensitivities and tentions have to revive the previous friendly democratic government in Afghanistan.

When I started to write the next paragraph below:

5- To teach the kids to say no to Taliban, no to terrorism, no to gun, no to religion, and no to the evil person who on Dec 15, 2012 in Connecticut Newtown Sandy Hook School

Massacred twenty beautiful little kids and a number of others decent hard working people.

When I was busy with the above story how to reform the Afghan fundamentalist society and how to educate the Afghan little children in a peaceful secular environment and speed up the freedom movement for the women there suddenly I heard this shocking news and it scared me to death and I was shaken to hear such a exploding news.

I said to my self- in a beautiful and dreaming country how could a vicious thing happen and it saddened me and my family the most because these happy little children died untimely, they lived too short and couldn't make it to see another day and it was a very painful incident.

The flow of the sorrow's tears on every faces, the grief of this bleeding wound and the unforgettable memory impelled me and my family to express our deepest condolences to those who lost their loved ones in this despicable tragedy. To overcome this agony is not easy, but I hope you innocent wounded people will get your strength back and we would have a better tomorrow.

We have an example in Persian says:

"Human being is harder than stone and softer than flower".

Thank you...

Answering to your comments:

1. My historic information about Alexander is based on National Geograhphic Maps, Washington, D.C. December 1991. I want to make a point that my country, now Afghanistan, has been invaded many times by invaders from the Greeks to the Arabs throughout history. My main sources of information are Compton's Encyclopedia; Sociological Footprints (Jeanne H. Ballantine and Leonard Cargan from Wright State University); newspapers like theWashington post; television; internet and the seventh edition of the Western Experience (Mortimer Chambers, Barbara Hanawalt, Theodore K. Rabb, Isser Woloch, Raymond Grew).

2. I'm not a politician but I think the environments developments, injustice and group interaction behavior impels individuals to make a jugement or a point. Abraham Lincoln did not go to law school nor had access to computers and the internet but he was a great politicion who abolished slavery.

3. In the case of Abdul Rahman: The combination of a good education and the association with good people helps you become an understanding person. In addition, no one can take advantage of you and you will not become the target of a stereotype.

4. Constantine the Emperor who gave freedom of religion. Freedom is the natural right of every individual to express his opinion without fear or restraint.

5. I do not consider religion a natonality because you change your religion but you cannot alter your nationality, like African Americans. We cannot form nations under religion. For example, Judaism, Christianity and Islam are Abrahimic religions but they never form a united nation.

6. Clumsy Monsters (Taliban and Mujahiddin) the creation of the world's conspiracy and intelligent Monster (a person with the iron fist).

7. About my biography: I have already published 3 books in my own language, Farsi. By the name of Hindukush, my country and children religion or children manner and two more to be published – (I Have Been Deceived and the other one is On the Bank of the Black Sea)

8. Shah Amanullah (1892-1960) is the founder of Secularism in Afghanistan and he was the first person who compiled our constitution.

9. From its oil income, Saudia Arabia spends billions of dollars annually on Islamization all over the world. But Yemenis, Jordanians and Palestinians also need economic assistance.

10. In the case of Constantine Roman Emperor: I mean how important is the freedom?

Freedom is the condition of choices to express your opinion publicly.

11- God is not Great (Christopher Hitchens, 1949- 2011). Christ you are the Great we lost you prematurely but your beautiful and historical thoughts stay with us all the time.

Professor Richard Dawkins called him Great orator, Great atheist, Great thinker, Great intellect and the day he passed away called it a very sad day.

The Greek civilization flourished there in Athens 750-500 B.C. Bactrian coins has been discovered in Balkh, providing evidence for the existence of Greek civilization during that period. As Socrates said, "trading grain and raw materials became very popular, such as artillery and metals" and a middle class emerged. This newly-emerged middle class strived for political power and, once that was accomplished, they changed the oppressive regime to a democracy.

In the third century, during the Hellenistic era, the Greek culture flourished in Egypt and welcomed foreign sages. Foreign sages such as Iranian magi, the Indian gymnosophistai, and many others were welcomed because of their spiritual curiosity and even more so because of a kind of religious starvation. There were many good Jews but also other Orientals, Syrians, Arabs, Mesopotamians, Persians, Bactrians, Indians and Africans (such as the Sudanese, Somalis, and the Ethiopians). The orientalizing Greeks, unlike Arabs, were opening their hearts to the Great Mother of Phrygia, to Mithras and or to the gods of Egypt (especially Isis and Osiris).

From the purely cultural point of view, the most pregnant (an argument of proof) elements in that mixture were the Jews (next to the Greeks). During the whole Hellenistic age, there flourished in close rivalry three kinds of popular religions: First, the old Greek paganism; Second, Judaism; and Third, various Oriental mystery cults such as the cults of Mithras, Cybele and Attis, Isis and Osiris. (George Sarton)

The fall of the Hellenistic age brought irreparable tragedies to many countries. The great glory land of Khorasan and the great civilizations of the Greeks in Egypt were later ravaged by the invasion of the Arabs. With them, they brought an unnecessary new religion known as Islam (uncompromising ideology) to these areas.

Genghis Khan, (1162?-1227), the Mogul Emperor, invaded Iran and Khorasan and captured this territory, spanning an area as large as the lands occupied by Arab nomads. These two empires, Arab and Mogul, were both founded by invading, ravaging, and pillaging, and neither empire introduced civilization or reconstruction to the territories. On the contrary, civilization was brought to the occupiers by the occupied.

Mawlana says to the Arab invaders:

که عزم صد سفر ستم ز روم تا سوی شام   زبان نبود زبان تو ما زبان کردیم

My 100 trips between Byzantine and Syria
It was us who developed your language

Shuja-Aldin Shafa wrote: "the difference between the repetition of history in the 7th and 11th century in those two empires was that one of them used the sword to kill in the name of religion and the other did it for the sake of the sword itself."

The two different ideological movements of imperialist Turks and Moguls towards Iran and Khorasan dethroned the Caliphs and the Arab Empire. The Turks were mainly Christian but became Muslims out of expediency and massacred people in the name of Islam, the Great Sultan Mahmud (971-1030), in Ghazni, Seljuks and the Ottomans in the Middle East and in the Balkans. According to Professor Enayatollah Shahrani, the Great Sultan of Ghazni belonged to Qurliqu tribe of Turkic Uighur. Uighur was a Turkic speaking tribe dominant in Mongolia and eastern Turkistan from 8th to 12th century. They are now inhabitants of northwest China. Sultan Mahmud can be called the Great since in spite of his cruelty and mass killings, had contributed a lot towards development of the Persian language.

The Ghazni Empire sacked the wealth of India and became rich. The poems and poetry of that period spread fame all across the world. The poems of the Empire were mainly eulogies, flattering to the Empire, with the exception of the eulogist, Abu Rayhan Biruni, who committed perfidy in the trade of Ferdowsi's Shahnameh. About to be executed, he was saved and released due to the efforts of Abu Nasr Meshkan, the Sultan's clerk. Avicenna and Abu Sahl, a Christian, rejected the idea of joining the Sultan's court and fled into hiding in order to elude Sultan Mahmud's conspiracies.

All of the Islamic Empires, whether Arab or Turk (non-Arab), were of a religious or a military nature. This still holds true and applies to the emergence of the Taliban, for example, led by Al Qaida (Al Bana).

The Arab Sheikhs, possessors of the Black Gold, are so powerful and they want to re-establish the Arab Empire, a desire that was further intensified by the collapse of the Soviet Union. They wanted a balance of power, not one dominant power.

In 711 AD, the Moors, Africans who had converted to Islam conquered Visigoths at the battle of Guadalete. They used to rule in Cordoba for over 700 years which is considered as one of the most glorious periods of the Arabic dominance. The Arab fundamentalists are pursuing their dream of Arabic dominance and in achieving this goal they can't tolerate Jewish to be on their way, neither they like Iran since they are not Sunnis. This is the same with Islam Karimov, President of Uzbekistan.

If it weren't for the Americans, the collapse of the Marxist Regime by a few Mujaheedin would not have been possible. But the Taliban (Saudi Arabian Army) accession to power, helped realize an Islamic Empire in Afghanistan as a result of the fact that Al Qaida, in their charter, called it the land of immigrants. But the Taliban had adopted a different policy from their superiors. It was Osama bin Laden who dispatched his 19 terrorists to fly hijacked passenger airplanes into the World Trade Center in New York and caused the downfall of terrorist Arabs and the wandering Taliban. This horrendous act (9/11) is the incessant tradition of the 7th century which took place in modern history of mankind.

Alas! The wounds from the Islamic swords are burning my flesh and bone but I'm numb and can't feel the pain because I'm an ignorant bullying Afghan.

This short essay is the start of a foundation of modern principles for the life of a newborn society which is overwhelmed by old fashioned ways of thinking and absurd beliefs which have blocked people from perceiving modern life. It is believed that Afghanistan's people belong to such a group. Too much blood has been shed for the reconstruction and modernization of the country. The leaders were assassinated or forced to leave and, unfortunately, the Great Abdul Rahman was not around to fight such backwardness (both tribalism and adversity).

Only as a result of severe and cruel punishment such as cutting off fingers and stoning did people fall in line and obey the religious leaders. The Presidential Palace of Hamid Karzai is filled with horrible religious beliefs, such as evils and devils.

Emile Durkheim, a great philosopher like Plato and Aristotle, believed that any kind of social movement or enthusiasm stems from the very existence of humans. Actually, if something stems from a human being, then how can it be derived from a supernatural power? As the great poet Mawlana Jalaludin Rumi says:

من محو خدایم و خدا آن منست   هر سوش مجوید که در جان منست
سلطان منم و غلط نمایم به شما   گویم کسی هست که سلطان منست

I'm lost in God and he exists in me
I'm the God, don't look anywhere else
I'm the king but by mistake
I'm telling you there is someone who is my master.

Monotheism: If you are infatuated with the belief of the only creator without any opponent, than he is not the only superpower but also a dictator. He does not care about war and peace, a displaced one, without personality has no power to bring justice to the world.

Philosphers showed an increasing concern with religion during the first centuries of the Christian era. Prominent Roman philosophers including the poet Lucretius 96?-55B.C an Epicurean, who was antireligion, and the Stoics Epictetus (A.D.60?-130?) and Marcus Aurelius (121-180).

The scientists believe that the domestication of plants and animals took place 14000 years ago or less. 12000 years ago, the earth started to warm up, the ice age came to an end and began the stabilization of weather.

The transition between the two stages of Pleistocene and the Holocene (the geologic time) is the most striking transitional evolution in the history of earth and mankind which intelligent designers (Gods) were created.

Islam and Christianity, together, brought great plague (fundamentalists) into Afghanistan to take revenge on the democratic government there.They taught them the Martial Arts and how to kill, burn, rootout the trees and commit genocide.

The wrong policy, from bad politicians, made the mercenary soldiers turn their guns against their own unskilled masters.

The U.S. governments' Air Force destroyed the Wahabis Taliban only when Al Qaida drove them to the extremities. We (immigrants) are thirsty for freedom and we desperately hoped for a progressive regime to succeed the autocratic religious regime of the Taliban and other Mullahs, however, our hopes have not been fulfilled. The Ethnocentric policy, resulting from all of those clashes and conflicts, came to rule as a result of unavoidable circumstances. The politicians taught political rule to the Mullahs who slipped towards fundamentalism, not democracy. And finally, the next Taliban on the top (Hamid Karzai) succeeded to power to destroy the remaining infrastructures of the country because Mr. Khalilzad, and alike him does not want to concede the Pashtons dominance special advantages to others in Afghanistan.

Tony Blair, the British Prime Minister who in his recent visit to Washington (5.17.07) said, "I believe that we will remain a staunch and steadfast ally in the fight against terrorism."Thanks a lot, anybody who created the clumsy Monsters now must create the intelligent Monster.

Great Britain got a lot of experiences how to use the Islamic backwarded idealogy when its interests are at risk, and we are the witnessing of such imperialistic operations inside of Aghanistan in the 19th and 20th centuries.

Under the pretext of Islam is endanger the British government with others antagonistic forces, awakened the dead Islam worldwide especially in Afghanistan.

Sir Martin Ewans, writes "Sebghatullah Mujadidi, an orthodox Islamic teacher". 1- He should have written, that this Mullah and alike him is the enemy of science and social devolpments, 2- religion "hollow-logy" being considered not knowledge, but the stories of the widows circling around us for thousand years. Mujadidi, like other pusillanimous fundamentalist Mullahs during the reverent <u>President Daoud's</u> social reforms fled the country, but he and his colleagues including Pashton, Hamid Karzai the most submissive student to Sebghatullah became a lucky stars when the democratic government in Afghanistan was over thrown by the triangle plane, and based upon some considerations, or appeasement policy, the foreigners installed the most fundamentalistic Islamic regime there, because the players of the Great Game, knew that national unity among the Afghanistanis has always been weak and only the bonds of Islam, makes them to unite together therefore, the anti-democratic elements always prefer religion over intellectualism movements but I my self always prefer colonolization over the religionism.

Note: A conflect attributed to the fake name of Afghanistan now going on among the intelligentsias there inside and outside of the country, and this issue still weakening the bonds of Islam amongst them. Because they fought more than twenty years together pro dear Islam religion but not pro freedom, and in the end the seventh century religion emerged there by Taliban.

I attest that such an Islamic unity among this people in the future is not any more issue of national unity, but it further more pushes the country towards disintegration and disunity unless a strong, comprehensive, and relenting leader took over there, other-wise the animosities between Northen Alliance, and Pashtons never go away therefore, the national unity to form a stable government there in Afghanistan, is not imminent.

Sir Martin Ewans added: Both the Tajiks, the Hazaras and the Nuristanis have in the past been the victims of Pushtoon expansionism, and these and other antagonism persist to the present day.

Some may say that children fly kites over the roofs of mosques in Kabul, however, this was not allowed under the Taliban. Perhaps, now this will be seen as a sign of democracy, brother! Although, there is a proverb, which says, "One swallow does not make a summer". Over the past 1400 years, Arabs-led tyranny and oppression have had such a shocking impact on our people; it seems as if our population has been in a coma (a deep, prolonged unconciousness, usually the result of injury, disease, or poison).

This is why I seek the assistance of scholars in all fields such as the Social Sciences, Psychology, Economy and others to help us find a cure together for such ailments in society. Being exposed to Arab cultures hasn't satisfied our peoples' needs in different aspects of their lives over the past centuries. The bloody and shameful events of September 11th, 2001 are evidence of the bizarre philosophy of these people.

An intellectual posed the question about why some values flourish or why some are threatened. Obviously, due to certain considerations, some values are not supported by countries. However, a backlash due to the application of political techniques can result in the aggressiveness of fundamentalism and can slow down the reconstruction process. We should not forget the overreaction to certain cartoons published by Danish artists that resulted in extreme reactions being encouraged by religious fundamentalist Mullahs, and resulting in chaos in some Islamic countries, including Afghanistan, a model democracy, created by the President of the United States George W. Bush.

زیان کسان از پی سود خویش   بجویند و دین ارند پیش
(فردوسي)

Those who are fearful of sustaining a loss
Resort to religion

"I'm proud of my religion" said John Edward former Presidential candidate.

Human beings are extremely complicated. Our eyes see objects in different colors; our brain thinks and, sometimes, works in a satanic way. One part of the brain may be in this world, the other part could be seeking another world. He worships a shadow, I resort to knowledge... Someone may build a nice house, but it may be destroyed by his pride and snobbery.

> There is a play called The Cloud, composed by Aristophanes, features a philosopher named Socrates who keeps up a school of skepticism. A nearby farmer manages to come up with all the usual dull questions asked by faithful.For one thing, if there is no Zeus,

who brings the rain to water the crops? Inviting the man to use his head for a second, Socrates points out that if Zeus could make it rain, there would or could be rain from cloudless skies. Since this does not happen, it might be wiser to conclude that the clouds are the cause of the rain fall. All right then, says the farmer, who moves the clouds in to position? That must surely be Zeus.not so, says Socrates, who explains about winds and heat. Well in that case, replies the old rustic, where does the lightning come from, to punish liars and other wrong doers? The lightning, it is gently pointed out to him, does not seem to discriminate between the just and unjust. Indeed, it has often been noticed to strike the temples of Olympian Zeus himself. This is enough to win the farmer over, though he later recants his impiety and burns down the school with Socrates inside it.

(Christopher Hitchens)

After thousand years to day we have the same confrontations with the Islamic mulahs, and imams who follow the lugubrious path of the Greek old rustic farmer.They resist rational, changes, and opining that what is right is now wrong. What is wrong is now right.

As a Great poet "Bidel" with his beautiful condensed language says:

A person, who is deprived of the light of knowledges, he lives in a state of nihilism which he even can not see the existence of the sky. He says that muslims to-day have every thing but faith.

پیش چشمی که نور عرفان نیست   گر بود اسمان نمایان نیست

بیدل امروز در مسلمانان   همه چیز است لیک ایمان نیست

On July 3. 2007 Maulana Abdul Aziz Ghazi head of the Seminary school of Lal Masjid in Islamabad Pakistan declared Jihad and establishment of "Shariat Coutr "in Pakistan and threatened to resort sucide attacks.The Pakistany government asked Ghazi to surrender to security forces but he did not yelde to the order.

On July 8, 2007 the Mosque was stormed Abdul Aziz was arrested dressed in Burqa . Now the poem of the poet above is correct that Islam got every thing but faith.

Similar incident happened in Waco Texas by David Koresh. On Feburary 28, 1993 the government of the United Sates, cut off the head of the snake but the Pakistany government failed to do the same.

Psychologist, Dr. Sigmund Freud (1858- 1958), says: "The conflicts resulting from the demands of living and repressed desires and experiences stored in the subconscious were the cause of mental disorders." He denies the involvement of god in these situations and said that god was an illusion.

Some Muslims perform Hajj even if their son is sick and they have no money to buy medicine or their daughter doesn't have proper clothes. Children do not attend classes. Someone carries a bomb under his showe (full-body cloak) in the name of Allah, and another blows up a passenger plane. Some troublesome Imam instigated action by provoking some idlers on the streets to take futile actions which resulted in violence, destruction and human fatalities. Violence does not represent tolerance or leniency.

As Rumi said to an agnorant person:

اي خواجه زهر خيال پر باد شوي   وز هيچ ترش شوي و دلشاد شوي
ديدم كه در آتشي بگزاشتمت   تا پخته و تا زيرك و استاد شوي

The eunuch, your head if filled with dreams .You become happy or sad out of nothing, I saw you burning on fire and left you there alone untile to become mature and wise.

If the actions of that so-called Imam could have prevented the provocative drawings of 12 Danish cartoonists, then a group of conservative Catholics "Opus Dei" in Italy on April 16, 2006 wouldn't have distributed a cartoon of a prophet in hell.

Poets such as Dante Alighieri, 1321- 1265, and Virgil, 70-19, the greatest Roman poet, were looking at the divided existence of the prophet. In this Conservatory, Virgil asked Dante that isn't (…). And he replied yes, he's been, because he created the division in society. Extract from *The Sunday Times*, April 16, 2006.

When philosophies of separation, ambition, massacre, looting, Jihad, and more are used to pave the way for Arab Imperialism and such ideas are raised from an altar (Mehrab, which means the place of war in Arabic), then it becomes obvious that the method is atrocious and lacks any logic. This explains why people get furious and condemn such ideology.

Fear, ignorance and humiliation are the three main factors which Muslim theologians couldn't explain the touchy and ambivalent issues from Quran and, inevitably, other theologians took up this task to try to clarify what Islamic scholars couldn't clarify with footnotes and annotations for 1400 years while still running in circles. This has caused jealousy amongst Islamic fundamentalists, especially Arabs and Pakistanis in London.

Imams in places of worship and teachers in classrooms wouldn't have talked about it, if it was not stated in the Quran (Verse 65 of Baqarah) that God turned the Jewish people into monkeys on Saturday.

ولقد علیمتم الذینَ اعتد وا مینکم فى السبات فقلنا لهم کونوا قیردَ ة خاسین.

35

However, I believe it is impossible for human to physically turn into an animal or to be turned into an animal. If we consider the role of biology, biochemistry, physiology, anatomy, ecology (which discusses the natural relationship between organisms and the environment in the process of life and the different stages of genetics and its role in heredity and in the formation of organs) and all natural factors (made by nature), then such things cannot happen at all. According to Darwin's theory of evolution, all living creatures evolve and life is an evolution. Maybe monkeys are transformed into humans in the process of evolution but we cannot say that humans can be turned into monkeys or pigs. If it is correct, why are Arabs and other poor muslims rushing to come to Europe, America as well as Australia to live amongst pigs and monkeys?

According to Karen Armstrong, one of the most sympotetic and not to say apologetic analyst of Islam, the Arabs of the time had a wounded feeling that they had been left out of history.

God had appeared to Christians and Jews, "but he had sent the Arabs no prophet and no scripture in their own languge." (Christopher Hitchens).

I think what Armstrong wants to tell is that some jealous sect or a group of people in the peninsula tried to find a person to claim the Prophecy and tell the stories of Moses, Abraham, Jesus and others through him in an inconsistent and contrasted manner.Like the advent of the Messiah, a believe that Christ's second coming and the end of the world near at hand.So for this was the believe of the Jewish guardians who protect the temple at Mecca, prior of Muhammad.

I am sure that the view points of Karen Armstrong regarding to the establishment of the Islam religion is very logical. Disappointment and emulation made someone in the Arabian Peninsula to create their own faith.

If Greatness of personality is the result of seizures and epileptic sickness, then we would have countless numbers of such perspiring Prophets all over the world.

Religion, in its nature, is a funny staff as it has always been in the service of corrupt political organizations. In 1990, for instance, King Fahd asked the Imams of Al Azhar to issue a verdict for the deployment of US troops on sacred land in order to save his country from the danger of Saddam Hussein.

In World War II, the churches in Europe did the same thing. They took sides with Hitler and Duce Mussolini to crush Semitism and Communism. At the end, by the generosity of the Catholic Churches, Duce Benito became Italian Ayatullah.

In Afghanistan, to defeat the democratic government, the politicians washed their feet and hands then they entered the Mosques for help.

I hope that someday, the brave Iraqi people would have conquered Saudi Arabia because today's Iraqi miseries and destructions attributed to the retainment of the Saudi kingdom.

With the sudden death of the Prophet in year 632, Islam (as a new borrowed religion) was in a dissolution stage. On the other hand, the Prophet did not leave behind any instructions because he thought that his mission was accomplished or maybe god told him not to turn in anything to anybody.

According to many Verses in the Koran, Islam was reveled in the Arabic tongue only for Arabs. But the Prophets soldiers, standing by their camels, demanded from the Caliphs the provisions for their physical necessities or otherwise they would revolt and there would be no more Islam.

So, the Caliphs left with no other choice except to resort to Jihad. Under the pretext of Jihad Omar, the Caliph behaved barbarically against humanity. He pillaged, plundered the countries and imposed the Arab religion on other nations. In this manner, he could keep the soldiers satisfied with spoils (sifted wealth) and stabilized the shaky and questionable Islam religion.

Mullahs and other Imams! Can you shed more light on the veracity of the incident stated in Al Ahzab chapter, verse No. 37, about the pitying act and the suppression of women's and men's rights. I've been puzzled by the verses of 51 and 52 of the same chapter.

گویی که ترا شیطان افگند در این ویران   خوبی ملك دارد شیطان خراباتم
(مولوي)

Please look after your beautiful wife and young daughter and the other person who actually caused all the disgrace and scandal in the family. Quibbling amongst some wise Muslims who mastered the teachings of the rightist philosophers, accused Arabs of being narrow-minded and conceited people.

Fawaz Turki, a journalist living in Washington, wrote an article in the *Washington Post* on April 15, 2006, "Never mind a society that remains broken in body and spirit more than a half-century after independence – it needs very much to engage in serious self-assessment and to promote an open debate in the media, among intellectuals, academics, political analysts and others about why Arabs have failed all these years to meet the challenges of modernity." Fawaz who used to publish the Saudi news in English, wrote that Saudi officials didn't allow issues such as blatant abuses in an Islamic country to be brought up in the news.

I ask all young Muslim intellectuals, from every group, not to endanger their lives and the lives of their families because of some invidious, hateful and provocative statements made by some hypocrite Imam or leader. (Learn first, and then try to teach).

Are we amazed by the preaching of an (intellectual) Mullah or by the large dams that are constructed by engineers to bring water to parched lands? Are we amazed by the ideology of a righteous politician or by a farmer who plants a tree, a teacher who leads students on the right path, a surgeon who operates on you and then stitches you up, by an economist who tries to create a better life for people, a scientist who invents something to benefit our lives, and so on?

Look at the Russian Ice Breaker with a displacement 23000 tons, 75000 total horse power, and Hoover Dam in America.

The superficiality and dauntlessness of politicians and religious people in the world is shown regarding the collapse of the former Soviet Union, which held the most barbarian Islamic parties (Al Qaida, Al Taiebeh Army, Mujahideen Al Badr, Hezbullah, Hamas) and others, and which endangered the safety and security of earth, water and space, as in the Tobeh Chapter, verse No. 73, "O Prophet! Strive hard against the unbelievers and the Hypocrites, and be firm against them. Their abode is Hell – an evil refuge indeed."

يا يها النبى جاهيدالكفارَ و المنفيقِنَ و اغلظ عَليهم و واهُم جهنمُ و بئس المصير

However, Ferdowsi is opposed to the above as exhibited in the following poems; and he states that knowledge and wisdom are much preferred to war and violence when solving the sometimes complicated issues of life.

کنون جامهٔ رزم بیرون کنید   با سایش ارایش افزون کنید
کسی کو خرد را ندارد ز پیش   دلش شاد گردد از کردهٔ خویش
نخست افرینش خرد را شناس   نگبان جان است و ان را شناس
خرد چشم جان است چون بنگری   تو بی چشم جان ان جهان نسپری
سپاس تو گوش است چشم و زبان   کزینت رسد نیک و بد بی گمان

Over a thousand years ago, Mansour Abolghasem Ferdowsi, teacher of elocution, considered wisdom to be a valuable component of fortune, peace and prosperity in society. He suffered from war and violence which cause destruction and bloodshed. It is clear that this Persian scholar prefers peace and comfort based on knowledge and wisdom. These two factors are solutions to the complex issues in life. By killing, threatening or sending a hypocrite to hell, or dissolving the body of Patrice Lumumba (1925-1961) in concentrated sulfuric acid one can't construct a society or a country, but through education we can train people and overcome the ever-increasing adversity in our society.

In the autumn of 1973, I was traveling by taxi from Kabul to Parvan in the north. There were three passengers in the back seat of the taxi, two of them were Sikhs. Later, a bearded man, about 30-35 years old, carrying a box, flagged down the taxi and sat next to me in the front seat, which was against the rules. Now there were two of us sharing the same seat and I was very upset because I find such behavior backward.

The bearded man was a member of the court in Gharabagh and people thought that he had attended the theological seminary of Kabul. During the drive, he saw a woman wearing western-style clothing, a teacher walking to school. The man was so upset by what he saw that he turned to me and said if she were his daughter, he would have killed her. As an educated cosmopolitan, I simply could not accept what he had said and felt compelled to offer some input about his narrow and bigoted way of thinking. I told him that before this road had been paved no taxis could use it, only carriages. But now that the road had been paved, taxis were able to use it. People traveling on the new road could bring the fruit of their orchards to sell in the marketplace and earn a living, someone could be taken to the hospital in an emergency, and others could get to work on time.

Using a tractor plowing the land on the other side of the road as an example, I told him that a tractor can plow several acres of land in one hour and that this task would have been impossible in the past when we depended on horses. We also saw a farmer spreading fertilizer on his crops and I informed him that it would triple or quadruple his yield of fruit. I finally asked him if he thought such blessings in our lives were good or bad. I went even further and told him that if he were to badmouth the leader of the Sikhs, Babah-Nanak, those sitting in the back would speak up to defend him. The two Sikhs in the back of the taxi nodded their confirmation.

Nowadays, due to the hue and cry about establishing democracy and deploying troops to bring democracy to our country, those Sikhs are no longer able to speak out in Kabul. I asked the same man "was it a sin if our teachers dress nicely to go to school in order to teach our children?" The teachers should smell good and dress well in these modern times.

The taxi stopped and a good-looking man wearing a silk turban, an Iranian ascot, and a military winter coat, exited the taxi. He saluted me and told me that everything I had said was true and that I was a good and honorable man. He prayed for me and went off, quoted from my book, My Homeland (Nawaby, 1998). Changing a society is a rigid process, but age and new environment are very important weapons to the socialization.

You, my compatriots – Women fighters, revolutionary scholars, girls and boys from this country's good families, farmers, widows and all others, what have you learned from this writing so far? There is no sword or stick in this dialogue. My arguments, simply based on social facts and my academic field, could defeat the enemy and that is why the two Sikhs and the other good-looking landowner supported me. A philosopher once said "An individual who has a specific talent but does not care to apply himself will probabl accomplish little.,"

The most outstanding Afghan's Professor Ghulam Ali, Ayen writes:

> Somewhere, there occurred a horrible flooding and
> a smart monkey climbed on a strong tree and from

there looking down he saw a big fish in a small pond struggling for his life.

The monkey felt bad about the fish so he came down from the tree and pulled out the fish from the murky water and set it on dry land. But after a few minutes, the fish died.

Now, how do you resonate the monkeys' discernment in this case? Was he a good designer and if not, what would have been the right way to save the life of a dying fish?

1. The monkey thought if he pulls the fish out from the water, the fish will survive.

2. He thought in this way, he can prevent the fish from more suffering.

3. If the monkey really was intelligent enough, he could have released the fish back into the river.

4. Maybe the monkey thought that the fish cannot survive in the murky water or the fish suffers more than ever back in the river?

5. You might think that the feeling of the monkey is stronger than his sensing.

6. Maybe neither of the above.

We, as a mammal, make mistakes all the time. When you want to correct your mistake, it is too late. Religion, from the beginning, was a mistake which we cannot correct now because we cannot efface the holy scriptures (the words of god).

Anyhow, the sympathy and the kindness of the smart monkey attributed to the poor fish always being appreciated because in such a dangerous situation he did not remain indifferent like mullahs who said that "On Saturday, the human changed into a monkey."

I saw a young patriot named Khaled Hosseini at the end of 2005. He was giving a speech at a conference about his book <u>The Kite Runner</u>, to be broadcast on the "Ketab" TV channel. I was so moved at seeing such passion and compassion in this young man who was obviously an observant and caring human being. He did more than just repeat old writings to no avail, nor did he practice sophistry. I wish that my other compatriots would exhibit the same courage as this young man and use their powers to enlighten our youth, so desperately in need of such valuable guidance. I wish that they would work on revealing the facts behind the social backwardness, poverty and illiteracy of our people.

The valuable book, <u>Children's Manners</u> (ائین کودکان) the revered writer شکیبا نورو

hakiba Naurau and the ideology of others of the same ilk could totally change the attitude of our backwarded people. Therefore, I respectfully ask all of our writers, artists, poets, politicians, instructors and others to join together to work on finding a solution that will help release our patriots from 1400 years of oppression and aggression and serve their compatriots in this way.

ز هر دانش چون سخن بشنوی   از آموختن یک زمان نغنوی
" فردوسی"

"You should gain knowledge about every science and never stop learning."

(Ferdowsi)

I visited my homeland at the end of 2004 and stayed through September and October. I traveled to Kabul, Polkhomri, Bandar Heyratan, Mazar Sharif, and Andarab. Throughout the country, the so-called "Jihad" had inflicted immeasurable damage, whether financially, physically or mentally. It reminded me of a meaningful saying from one of our country's outstanding figures, the blessed Mr. Roshandel Roshan in Pishavar, who once said that people should pray that the Mullahs never gain political power. Due to the authoritarian behavior of a few revolutionary youngsters, he was sent to jail in Polcharkhi for 18 months by Hafizullah Amin, the faithful student of Noor Mohammad Taraki, the genius of the East for no plausible reason. Roshandel Roshan died on December 17, 1984 in Pishavar due to cardiac malfunction. He has left behind some of his writings in the form of several books, namely: <u>Eighteen Months in Polcharkhi Prison, Betrayals of Russia</u> and <u>Mujahideen Uvali.</u>

Parallel to the statement of the late Mr. Roshan, a patriotic and aware woman, Melali Jouya, in the National Congress (øÛDiÛDÊlÜëDØÛ) said that the Mujahideen had played a major role in the destruction of the country in favor of foreigners, especially the Wahabi Group. She also called for preventing the latter from attending the National Congress for the crimes they had committed against Afghans (refer to the Constitution and Parliamentary Election Law). Whereas the middlemen and fundamentalists, Hamid Karzai, Sebghatollah, Abdulrab Rasul Sayaf, Burhanuddin Rabani and their followers had already compromised by establishing an Islamic regime and even Mr. Zalmai Khalilzad, the US Ambassador to Kabul, had affirmed their policies.

This was a collusion just to appease the Taliban's prelate, but it was a very wrong collaboration because in the end the country fell into the hands of fundamentalists.

Unfortunately, Melali Jouya's request and the warnings of other world politicians that Afghanistan should not be taken over by the fundamentalists were ignored and instead of religious reform, we saw more fanaticism. On the other hand, it must be recognized that the policies of Mr. Khalilzad resulted in bringing bearded fanatic people to power to provide more wool to keep the Kabul Wool Factory in operation. During fighting, the factory was short of wool. So the bearded people were a helpful source of wool to keep the factory operating. (This is a joke in Kabul!)

Malalai Joya called the Parliament of Afghanistan, a stable. Because of that, one member of the Parliament said "grab her and rape her". Now, can we call the Parliament of Afghanistan an organization of Jack the Ripper?

Malalai Joya is a new face from the oppressed new generation. She is a very young, brave and talented revolutionary lady who is also a member of the parliament. She accused the other members of the parliament "that they are not mujahiddin, but killers and criminals" and asked the justice to punish them in the court of law for the crimes that they have committed.

Academically, I found her to be the most enlightened and openminded lady. Much more so than the fundamentalist Hamid Karzai and his cabinet members.I personally congratulate her for her bravery and her talented show and I wish her to become the next president of the country.

I'm not a constituent of Rawa's movement, but I'm certainly a supporter of Malalai Joya, and of what she said. I'm opposed to the political behaviours of groups and individuals who parody and desecrate others.

Great Afghan ladies! I know as do other peace loving countries all over the world how much you have suffered from the interpretation of Arab religion. Taliban God's commanders, a vicious powerful foreign army furnished by the outsiders to destroy the country mentally and physically have disgraced, killed and raped you. Now, the time has come to stay shoulder to shoulder for the cause of freedom and justice. I ask all of the brave, intellectual Afghan girls and boys, men and women, young and old (like myself) to come together to support the great universal movement of "Joya" and to fight the fundamentalists and their supporters, the Arabs.

The museums of medieval Europe, from Holland to Tuscany, are crammed with instruments and devices upon which holy men labored devoutly in order to see how long they could keep someone alive while being roasted (Christopher Hitchens).

I'm sure that the Karzai fundamentalist government would have done the same thing to Zalmai Ghous (who translated the Koran in to Farsi language), Parviz Kambakhsh and Abdul Rahman (who recently converted from Islam) if they did not fear outside reactions.

As early as the 14th century, however (Wycliffe John, 1320?-1384). The "morning star of the reformation" an English priest and teacher at Oxford University, declared that people had the right to read the Bible and interpret it for themselves.

Despite protests by the church, followers of Wycliffe translated the Bible from Latin into English in 1382 and carried copies throughout the country side.

In 1377 Wycliffe was brought to trial before the archbishop of Canterbury and the bishop of London. A crowd of his supporters came to his rescue. They raised such a commotion that Wycliffe was allowed to go free. I do not know why the Master does not allow us to translate the Koran in our own language?

The emergency meeting in Germany in December, 2001 did not take into consideration the professional and academic background of Mr. Hamid Karzai, a tribal man with a feudalistic background. He was elected for the top position as leader of our oppressed people. It would have been necessary to give such a position and honor to an experienced thoughtful individual, someone who was knowledgeable about Afghanistan.

Many suffered physical and mental abuse at the hands of the Mullahs. For example, during the invasion of foreigners (Taliban) in 1996, the Kabul people fled to Pakistan and the Pakistani officials told them you are Tajik, go back to Tajikistan. Why? Because General Masoud was a Tajik. Finally despite efforts of world relief organizations they were placed in the worst camp called "Jalghuzai" where, as a result of the negligence of the Pakistani authorities, their beloved children died in the flood.

On January 29, 2006, Dale McFeather, a columnist for Scripps Howard News Services of Washington, commented that the radical group Hamas won 76 seats out of 132. In his commentary about the elections in Palestine, he continued on saying that the problem with free and fair elections was that there's always a chance the wrong people would win. The political win of Mr. Hamid Karzai (the Taliban ilk, a debauchery movement) could certainly be categorized this way. Most of Mr. Karzai's officers are sympathetic to Pakistan and the Mullahs of his entourage who flatter him every day.

Mr. Karzai was only familiar with religious issues and not any social, economic and political affairs. He has given religious affairs advantage over other social development issues. As theorists have stated," Religion is a system of thoughts about a specified object. What makes us rich does not add to our knowledge."

When Taliban (Saudi Arabia Corps) banned flying kites and attending schools, Hamid Karzai was cooperating with them. Flying kites is a sport which refreshes body and mind of our children and they enjoy doing it freely, without having any fear.

Hamid Karzai required all the officials to take an oath to Quran which was totally a new practice throughout the history of Afghanistan. This is a clear example of his religious characteristics. Afghanistan is called an Islamic state in the constitution which is a disgrace. Karzai's new invention is not even in line with his fake democratic mottos. As a matter of fact Secularism which was one of the best ideas for reconstruction of Afghanistan by the Great Amanullah, should be implemented, otherwise the efforts of international organizations to make a developed Afghanistan will all be in vain.

Due to devastation and political turmoil, religious people took over the country and our kids lost their playgrounds. The only sport allowed there is kite flying, which had been banned by Taliban.

During the 1970s, I used to live in Kabul in the neighborhood of Ghalaeh Shadeh (near Sarai Ghazni). One day, when I was busy at home, I heard something fall outside.

I looked through the window and saw a little boy on the ground; he was unconscious and not moving. I hurriedly ran to my wife, Maryam Nawaby; who later died in 1976 of cancer, and yelled that my son had fallen from the roof.

I rushed out and saw that it was not my son but the neighbor's son who had been flying a kite and had fallen into our yard from the roof which was 4 meters high. My first thought was that he was dead because his head was flattened. My wife checked his pulse and said that he was still alive. I lifted his head and manipulated it until it was back to its normal shape. The boy started to come around, opened his eyes and when he saw us, he climbed over the 2 meter high wall and ran away. The fact is that flying kites in our country, like games played in other countries, is a joyous activity, however it is very dangerous from a physical point of view. Flying kites in Kabul and other cities is a form of amusement for young people. During the period of Taliban rule, this sport was banned in addition to the senseless closing of public baths.

Flying kites is great fun for young boys and children. It became more fascinating after the downfall of Taliban. During my visit, I noticed that children were flying kites with great enthusiasm. While staying in the north of Kabul I personally observed, on one occasion, that the string of a kite caused a nasty cut on the nose of a passerby, causing him to bleed all over. I reached the boy who had been flying the kite and asked him if he could play somewhere safer. He politely replied that Kabul was full of houses and that there were no open playgrounds in which to fly kites. Kabul is surrounded by mountains and there is only one park called Zarnegar, built for the purpose of relaxation and leisure; some business-minded, ambitious person bribed the Taliban and built a mosque with a huge dome on top there which did not fit into the area and also restricted people's freedom, leaving less room for relaxation. To my surprise, on top of the dome, I saw a child flying kites. I'm much happier about the freedom being enjoyed by our people at the moment because flying kites was impossible not so long ago, during the Taliban regime whose war machines operated on gas provided by Saudi Arabia and were driven by Pakistani military men.

Barefoot children get so excited about flying kites that they could inadvertently and unknowingly run into barbs or thorns. The day after my visit to the park, I heard the news that a child, Parviz Yazd, had fallen from the dome and had died. His father was already suffering since his left leg had been injured during a bombing in Kabul and he still limps to this day. His poor sister, Sarah Yazd, lost her mother in a car crash in Pishavar, Pakistan; she was yelling and weeping over the dead body of her only brother. She had hoped that he would grow up to become a doctor. She was saying that Parviz loved his father, Jamshid Yazd, so much. Following the way of our ancestors, we are taught to cherish our parents, because their warm and comforting embraces teach us to be proud and how to live life. Parviz and his sister, Sarah used to wash the bloody clothes of their father and hung them up to dry.

The Parviz family, like other families with disabled family members, lived a hard life. The incompetent government in Kabul could not arrange any relief organization to help these families, although there is a so-called "Relief" Ministry in the cabinet. Ministry of Border-Tribal and Ethnic Affairs is serving the interest of a special ethnic group and is neither necessary nor has a national value but hatred. Therefore that should be dissolved. The same routine should be applied to the Ministry of Haj and Islamic Affairs, since they are serving to prolong the prides and dignities of Arabs tradition.

Wouldn't it be more humanitarian for the government's budget to be allocated for disabled compatriots and other needy people, who, although poor, will hold Arab dignity and pride high, rather than used for ineffective rubber-stamp ministries?

The story goes as follows: The other day, Parviz had challenged another boy to a kite-flying competition. Other children gathered at Zarnegar Park to watch the competition and were enthusiastically waiting to see the kites flying overhead. Parviz was on the top of the mosque's dome and was preparing to fly his kite. On the other side, was Parviz's rival, Darius, who flew his kite next to Parviz.

Both kites had colorful patterns; they were flying high and low, left and right in the blue sky of Kabul. People and onlookers were cheering for their favorite. The cheering encouraged the two young men and added excitement to the competition. Parviz shouted at Darius warning him that the string of his kite was rubbing against his kite's string and in response; Darius yelled back that Parviz should be careful not to fall off the dome. Soon enough, Parviz's superior kite-flying abilities were proven when he cut off the string of Darius's kite. People were crying and shouting in excitement. Parviz was so energized that he jumped high in the sky, but was unable to retain his balance and fell headlong from the dome. Onlookers ran to him where he had fallen, still clutching the string of his kite, but Parviz was already dead. Darius, who had been the one to challenge Parviz to this competition, bent over his rival's dead body, weeping and mourning. People were looking at him sadly. A middle aged man holding Rumi's Masnavi, from amongst the crowd, said that emotions resulting from happiness or outrage could be self destructive.

I asked myself, how can emotions cause injury? To find my answer, I consulted a book to find the definition of emotions. Human beings are obscure creatures. They can rationalize, memorize, learn and create ideas by using their brains. They are able to lead the way for a cause. In other words, human beings can be inspired through reasoning and sagacity. Therefore, encouraging factors for human beings could be desires, wishes and other perceptions. These perceptions differ in intensity, sometimes called excitement. It is called "movere" in Greek, which means move on. But such emotions are not the only factor behind inspiration. All individuals should fulfill their basic needs in order to live. These basic needs are logical ones.

Aristotle, 384-322, points out the fact that there should be a distinction between having a good life for an individual which is truly good or seemingly good. Such a distinction is reasonable, to which he successfully applied alternation. When sensations come in to play, they take the individual from a logical level to an illogical level. Nevertheless, this doesn't mean that all sensations are negative or in contrast to logical thinking. From this viewpoint, sensations should enhance reasoning. Someone who has special talents but is indifferent and does not apply them properly accomplishes little.

Paying attention to, and being ambitious towards, appropriate sensations can strengthen talents, and could lead individuals to accomplish tremendous tasks.

Definition of Sensations

Even the top-ranking scientists do not completely know how the brain works. What is it and what is the source of sensations? The brain is one of the physical organs in the body. It is an organ of thought and sensations are a name for special reflexes and the definition of senses. It is not precisely known which part of the brain stimulates sensations. Maybe it… is more related to the balance or imbalance of chemicals.

Sensations are also related to distinctive characteristics of humans called willpower and the freedom to choose. The abstract terms related to sensations are love, hatred, fear, happiness, perplexity, anger, willpower and dislike.

Those who were carrying the coffin of poor Parviz, the young kite flyer, were chanting "Down with Taliban", "Down with that greedy businessman", "Down with the uncaring engineer" who built that mosque in such a critical spot. Someone in the crowd named Shirjan told people that the kite flyers had submitted a request to the government asking that the mosque be bombed or demolished since it greatly reduced the parks area and space available to those people who came for leisure and enjoyment. He then commented that the purpose of having parks in the cities is to provide people with places for leisure and relaxation, not prayer, politics or business; he continued that if the mosque and its dome had not been constructed there, Parviz would still have been alive.

It was generally thought that the incompetent government was not taking any measures to deal with the valid concerns of the population and youth, in particular, so Shirjan asked the compatriots and kite flyers to form a committee to gather and present all of their needs, requirements and concerns to the government. These concerns included the creation of a safe place for sport, in order to ensure the safety of youngsters who enjoy this sport.

When writing this book, I saw "The last of the Summer wine" comedy show, written by Roy Clarke and designed by Alan J W. Bell, on the MPT channel on January 31, 2006. I thought to myself that flying kites is not only a game enjoyed solely by Afghan children; it's really a universal game. In this comedy, Howard could not steal a kiss from Ms. Marina.

Bayla Singer wrote that thousand of years ago, in Asia, kites had religious significance in honoring gods and heroes. We, modern people, might wonder why it took Europeans such a long time to discover the kite, since it had been known in the Islamic world since at least the ninth century. It seems odd with all communication between the Islamic and Christian world in those years, the Kite comes to Europe via China rather than from the Middle East or even from Muslim Spain.

Parviz, instead of immediate sending him to the hospital to be examined, people instead just gathered around the body and started to mourn.

Some elderly people who saw this felt that it was a disgrace and they felt badly about Parviz's untimely death. They said that Mullahs who had neither defended freedom nor the motherland, but had supported Arabs and their cause, had totally destroyed the country and ruined peoples' lives. They added that they would never again retreat in the face of the Mullahs, because such Mullahs like Hamid Karzai (who deifies Mullahs) are the cause of our lack of progress in all aspects of our civil life and liberty.

Mohammad Din, a young man said to some of the other youngsters that if they didn't stand up against the Mullahs who were anti-human rights, the latter would tyrannize the nation. Have you forgotten the wrong doings, the tyranny, oppression, torture and the severing of hands and legs committed by these people? Have you already forgotten that they whipped your wives in front of you? That bloody whip is still hanging above Judge Fazl Hadi Shinvary, representative of Mullah Karzai. He used to teach religion in the Avicenna school, whose principal was Hafizullah Amin. That dogmatic Shinvary used to call those who wore ties infidels.

Shinvary and Amin had ties with the ruling regime and, although they may have had differences in ideology, both of them were enemies of social justice and equality. People still resent the old Shinvary Mullah who remains on the tribunal. They are right. Amin, who pursued his higher education at Boston University, became the principal of Avicenna School when he returned to Afghanistan. Through students specifically of his own tribe, he organized sectarianism and nepotism, and as a result of repressive acts committed by these students, a number of Hezarah, Uzbek and Tajik students were expelled from the school.

One of the ejected students was my friend Khan Mohammad Siyah who was the top student of the school. He became a victim of Amin's conspiracy, since he had refused to join Amin's group. In those dark days, Amin, who was from Pashtun, spared no effort in promoting and preferring his tribe. Such an act of sectarianism was rooted in the behavior of ruling officials such as Mohammad Davood who was then the Prime Minister as well as some of his ministers including Ali Ahmad Popel, Minister of Education. Because of this unpleasant behavior, Hafizullah Amin was called a hero by Mohammad Davood.

These two factors (tribe and language) social fascist malfunctions, inherited from Nader Shah, one of the former kings of Afghanistan, still exist in our society. A counter-national method was used to pave the way for some other incompetent officials to impose oppression on other tribes which Amin was one of them. I believe that the majority who hold a position of power over other minorities use repression to such an extreme degree that they only end up causing resentment from the latter.

My friend, Dr. Razagh Andarabi who was a student of Avicenna School at that time, wrote a note about Amin's discriminatory behavior some 45 years ago. He read the note to me over the phone from Idaho State, in December, 2006. The note read, "During the winter holidays, students used to return to their homes. The Government used to provide transport for this purpose. Amin, the school principal, would give priority to students from the Southeast territories and send them home first. He wanted to ensure that they would arrive home before any of the other students. Professor Afzal Banuwal who taught at that school and opposed the insane methods of Amin, asked him in a ridiculing manner when would the "Black students", a metaphor for the non-Pashtuns, arrive home. However, I should add that instead of buses, Amin provided some cheaper type of transport for the other students. The minority students, however, didn't keep quiet about this situation and they resorted to violence to express their anger about this discrimination of language and tribe.

As a result of this unrest, a new political party emerged: "Hizb-e Setam-e Melli" led by (Tahir) Badakhshi, who disappeared during Amin's reign. People accused the party of being separatist so what is the Afghan Milat party? I believe that if such false accusations are not expeditiously corrected in the short run, more concerns about separatism and physical violence will be raised in the longer term and will result in damaging all of the parties. If the minority acts responsibly towards the majority, then the former should be running the country, but we can clearly see that is not the case; the feasible action of a group or an individual towards progress, civil society, social justice, etc. can be more constructive than the majority and minority. Honest people have been trapped by illiterate and cunning politicians. This group cultivated darkness in the minds and thoughts of our populace. It is the responsibility of considerate and compassionate scholars to help protect our people from old-fashioned thinking, tribalism, illiteracy, and obscurity.

The late scholar, Abdul Vahab Fanaie, upon returning to Afghanistan soon after completing his studies in the U.S., in one of his meetings, asked people if it wasn't possible to build a public bath instead of so many mosques, since this would enable men, women and children to take a bath at least once a week. But instead of considering his comments, people called him an infidel. This great scholar had a long history of cardiac disease and passed away in January of 2005. May his soul rest in peace.

I am really thankful to young Mohammad Din. On the sad day when Parviz died, he was talking to the crowd about the lack of freedom in society. One of the kite flyers asked him about the meaning of freedom. Mohammad Din took out his dictionary and read a few sentences in English. "The condition of being free of restraints, liberty of the person from slavery oppression or incarceration, political independence, possession of civil right, immunity from the arbitrary exercise of authority." The youngsters asked Mohammd Din to talk about freedom in their own language since they didn't know English so he explained freedom in their native language and in terms that they could understand.

Toriali added that, yes, it was true that they didn't have any kind of freedom. Mullahs and those conceited people (Mujahideen) had deprived people of their rights by relying on and resorting to old legends and narratives. Mullahs had prevented us from flying our kites simply by declaring it a sin. But when there is a public dog fight, one of the crueler and bloodier "sports", they abandon their prayers and can be found standing in the first row to watch the "fun" of dogs tearing each other apart.

Our people of Afghanistan, forced to endure the tortures of these fundamentalist Mullahs for the last 30 years, didn't cast their votes for the Mullahs during the shameful elections but are still trapped by these fundamentalists. We and the free world, we who were hoping for a democratic regime to take power, were disappointed. Bear in mind that ineffectual policies, whether from abroad or from inside the country, intended to positively determine the future of our political system in Afghanistan, only resulted in strengthening the solidarity between the Afghan fundamentalists and Ikhvan Al Muslimin rather than with the free world, the U.S. and others.

An Islamic regime in Afghanistan is obviously a concern to democratic countries in Middle Asia. However, there is still time to believe that an Islamic regime is not yet cast in stone and that the Mullahs do not control democracy. Mr. Hamid Karzai, Washington's man, supports religion at each and every conference in the name of culture but he is unable to distinguish that religion is the substance for culture, not culture itself and it will change under different conditions in favor of development and a better social life. As a diplomat, he should use diplomacy to make peace and, if necessary, follow the example of King Hassan of Morocco. Otherwise, he should act responsibly and resign from his post.

The Islamic Conference of 2003 was held in Malaysia in October of that year. The Malaysian Premier, who chaired the session, stated that Jews acted as America's proxy and declared that they had invented communism, socialism, human rights and democracy and therefore they shouldn't be prosecuted and should enjoy human rights equally. The way this religious man talked was not much different from Mahmoud Ahmadi Nejad, the Iranian President. Heads of State and leaders of Islamic countries including Hamid Karzai, President of Afghanistan, applauded the Malaysian Premier, not realizing that Jewish-American soldiers were responsible for the safety and security of Hamid Karzai in Kabul.

Such conferences and the Non-Aligned Movement lack national and international credibility and are of no value. Arabs are the main organizers of such shows that are created and staged for world consumption. If I were Hamid Karzai, I wouldn't participate in such conferences due to the fact that Osama bin Laden, Iman Al Zawahiri are such blind "Omar" of Muslims, those who destroyed the World Trade Center in New York and the Pentagon and killed thousands and thousands of people in the heart of the democratic world, the US.

Arabs arranged for the killing of Ahmed Shah Masoud; Kandahar Muslims destroyed Buddha statutes in Bamian; the killer of Theo Van Gogh was an Arab youth; those who massacred children and students at the Beslan school in Russia close to Chechnya were also Muslims.

The Afghan people lost Amanullah, their progressive and democratic king, in 1929 because of nonsensical and erroneous beliefs. His successor, Nader Khan the Gestapo placed restrictions on the freedom of our people, and again made women wear the chador, following Arab culture, as well as insisting that schoolgirls be dressed in black. If, in reality, our people liked Mullahs and Arabs, a poet wouldn't have written this poem.

چشم کورش در کفن   یک ملا بود در وطن

A Mullah in my homeland should lie down blind in a shroud

During my visit to Afghanistan I went to see a friend of mine who was one of the instructors at the Poly Technical College in Kabul. This college, previously so unique in all of Asia, now appeared devastated and in real need of major renovations.

Coincidentally, I came across a religious man and I told him about a trite religious subject that my friends and I used to joke about some fifty or sixty years ago. The religious man became very angry and started using phrases in Arabic (atheism, paganism, heterodox) and in different Egyptian and Saudi dialects. His young son, who was sitting next to him, interrupted and asked me if I believed in the Quran. Other students who were around laughed at the question, however, the instructor would not allow me to argue or discuss the question with the religious man. Later, the instructor told me that in order to dethrone the previous regime, Afghans had used Saudi money provided by foreign intelligence agencies and that they were taught to replace good for bad and bad for good. Based on such damaging religious teachings and with the support of the nomadic Arabs and in the belief that communism was an enemy to Islam, they were able to overthrow the democratic regime. Such mercenaries not only preserved the reputation of the rival powers but also put an end to their concerns about the future. As a result the democratic regime of Afghanistan and the USSR Empire were overthrown. They killed three birds with one shot! They celebrated this great victory, not knowing that the successors were much worse than the Communists. They leveled the beautiful towers of New York. Remembering that scene is not only painful but very shameful.

Flawed political thinking during the overthrow of the young regime of Afghanistan resulted in the killing of many innocents by sinful Muslims, and will only end in a huge crucial financial situation in the long term. Furthermore, this would allow the opportunist fundamentalists to take advantage of the gaps and create trouble, an example of which could be those Danish cartoons about Mohammad in 2005. Muslim fundamentalists, both Arabs and non-Arabs took advantage of it and created such an insane and shameful scene, the most bloody of which was in Afghanistan, since it's an Islamic country. It should be noted however that two Algerian journalists, Kamel Bousaad and Bouderbala, from Journalists without Borders, who were living in Paris at the time, also printed those Muhammad cartoons. A similar cartoon was drawn by a Muslim cartoonist in Harat, Khorasan in 1436. In this cartoon, Muhammad is riding on a Pegasus with a human head, and Gabriel is drawing Muhammad toward the sky The original cartoon is kept at the French Bibliotheque Nationale. It is surprising why Muslim fundamentalists didn't resort to violence back then. Although this drawing was on most walls in the street, the Shiite Muslims never protested at that time.

Cartooning or drawing is part of aesthetical industry. A cartoonist as a prophitionalist has the right to sketch humorous or satirical figures of a caricature a comic just to make people laugh therefore no one has the right to deprive or punish her or him for their passion and love. Art is our traditional treasure which we inherited from the past. Therefore, morally and legally, we have the obligation to protect, preserve and flourish the beauty of this precious wealth.

Drawing is Art and also the litmus test for the physiognomy of all living staff. Art is love and beauty. Art in the dictionary is the human effort to imitate, supplement, alter, or counteract the work of nature.

I hate Islam, says Geert Wilders a rising politician in Holland.

In 2008 he then called for Koran "Alfitna" means division and stirring. In Iran, Afghanistan, Pakistan people gone crazy but not the Saudi people where Islam was born, because the Arabs are smarter than Ajam.

Don't blame the person, but the story. What would have happened if Wilders would have replaced "Alfitna" with the word of "Almakaar" which means tending to deceive.

"Almakaar" is one of the 99th names of Allah.

What are the causes and motives behind such troublemaking?

1. Perhaps the understanding and moral criteria of the former Muslims were more advanced than the modern ones.

2. The Muslim population in Europe was small at the time. The high population growth in the Muslim population since that time is due to Europe's tolerance and generosity.

3. Political developments in Afghanistan and Iran have made Muslims so irreverent. The more you push them, the more they pull you.

4. The Internet, television and international travel are current methods for spreading all kinds of messages throughout the world.

5. There are high unemployment rates and a lack of large and small industrial manufacturers. (Satan infiltrates the minds of unemployed people).

6. The key behind troublemaking is the religious gangs of the Saudi Kingdom. They spend millions and millions of dollars of public funds to build mosques and to promote Islam everywhere not in benevolent manner or useful. I'll quote some examples from the book written by Laurent Murawiec called Princes of Darkness, translated by George Holoch. There are 50,000 mosques in Saudi Arabia, one place of worship for every 100 people, and 50,000 Imams, leading people in their religious practice.

The Saudi kings make billions of dollars by selling oil. They have bought and corrupted countries, people, political parties, popular figures and mercenaries. They play a key role in the corruption of the Middle East. They know how to strengthen their power outside the Islamic countries. They transferred their assets to Europe and to America. In 1973-74 and 1978-79, by raising oil prices, the Saudis were able to place billions of dollars in the banks, nearly 80 billion dollars. This Islamic country has turned into the most destructive organization in modern times and this increase as each year passes. The wealth generated through selling oil has enabled them to buy influence in many countries including Pakistan. Thousands have become Haji using Saudi's money. However, it should be labeled illegal pilgrimage. General Shah Mahmud, one of the aides of General Zia Alhagh of Pakistan, once said that if it were possible, Zia Alhagh would have moved the sands of Saudi to Pakistan.

During the term of Tarki Al Faisal, Information Minister of Saudi Arabia, 15 million dollars was spent on buying advanced artillery for the Taliban (including rifles, binoculars, infrared viewers and more). The Taliban (Saudi heroes) have secured a special place in the hearts of Saudi kings and fundamentalist Arabs.

King Fahd of Saudi Arabia and his propaganda organizers, General Zia Alhagh, then (President of Pakistan), Mujahedin and illegal Hajis and Hajias (women) should all be held directly liable for damages done to our country with either physical or mentalconsequences. They should be the sole country to make compensation for all losses.

Chapter Two
WHO DEVIATED RELIGION?

According to the journalist Ahmad Rashid, Saudi Arabia supported the Islamic party of "Golbodin Hekmatyar" which had close ties with Mowlavi Modudi as well as Abdul Rab Siyaf, who, along with others like him, put millions of dollars of Saudi aid money into their own pocket.

Thomas Woodrow wrote that Prince Sultan, the War Minister of Saudi Arabia, paid a visit to the uranium enrichment facilities in Kahutah, Pakistan, where ballistic missiles are being manufactured. He also participated in the testing of atomic bombs and the launching of a new missile. Saudi Arabia has spent a fortune to pay the Chinese government to transfer technology to Pakistan. Right now there are many Chinese scientists in Pakistan. Pakistan and Saudi Arabia enjoy close ties. Pakistan will transfer missiles to Saudi Arabia whenever the latter asks for it, due to the fact that the Saudis have spent a wealth of money on atomic projects in Pakistan. Saudi Arabia just needs to transfer the missiles and atomic warheads.

Saudi kings could gain the political and diplomatic support of world organizations such as the High Commissioner of Human Rights, UNESCO and others, simply by funding their needs. Saudis are using this support to cover up their crimes. They supported terrorists in Uzbekistan who were indirectly connected to Saudi Arabia and directly connected to Al Qaida. They compared the Uzbek president to Hitler.

It isn't just that Saudi Arabia fits in with the neighboring countries because it is an Islamic state. The huge oil revenues are used by the Saudi kings to stay in power and to spread their Islamic interpretations and ideologies. Physical and mental problems and other social backwardness of neighboring countries require assistance for improvement but are of no importance to Saudi kings.

The Saudi kings and other reactionary followers of Muhammad only know how to spread their own interpretation of Arab ideology and their language; the hatred of Jews and western civilization or their economic and social cooperation, innovations and other services aimed at benefiting society and human beings. Here are some examples from the curriculum of elementary schools in Saudi Arabia:

1. The knowledgeable Allah orders us to continue war between Islam and Judaism till the Judgment Day. (I'd like to respond that perhaps there are blind and deaf Muslims that obey your baseless, hollow and invidious orders like Indonesians who used to worship rice, Pakistanis who recently converted to Islam, or the Hamas Group, but not me).

2. Hadith proclaims that with Allah's help, Muslims will gain victory over Jews. (Which Hadith is Mullah Al Sadayes talking about? Those which Rumi called immature? If one of them is not real, then all of the others will become non sacred. For example, if a drop of milk is poured into a glass of water, it will change quality and quantity, color and taste. Therefore, I call upon Mullah Al Sadayes not to misguide people anymore with these verses and traditions. Nowadays, most Muslims believe that there are thousands of untrue Hadiths and this belief has been extended to verses as well).

3. Jews and Christians are our enemies. They are not sincere in their dealings with Muslims, therefore we should be cautious in our relations with them. (In April 2002, Sheikh Abdulrahman Al Sadayes, the Imam of Mecca Jame Mosque said that, "Jews are the leftovers of mankind; rats on the earth, killers of Mohammad, they are pigs. He asked for all who pray to God to destroy the Jews. However, extensive research has also connected Afghans to Jews. If Sheikh Abdul Rahman, knew the story of the sons of Abraham, to whom he is also related, he wouldn't have used such indecent words about his ancestors.

The Al Azhar University of Egypt, founded in 971 by the Shiite of Fatemi, is now attended by Sunnis and supported by Saudi Arabia. One of the lessons taught in this university is that no one can donate his/her organs, because the very existence of mankind belongs to God. Whereas the Arabs had bought so many kidneys and poor people had to sell this organ, in order to make some extra cash. In Islam there is no distinction between moral principles, good and bad criteria, correct and incorrect viewpoints and the law; in the philosophy of Georg Wilhelm Friedrich Hegel, 1770-1831, such characteristics are part of philosophical logic.

In the western world, mankind and animals both have the right to live... especially dogs, as they are a part of family but we don't see such generosity of spirit in other parts of the world.

The other day, I was passing by the ruins of a house when I heard a dog barking. In our country, people build walls around their houses or orchards for protection. My brother, climbed to the top of the wall and looked over. After passing a few other ruined houses and destroyed walls, he finally found the dog. He quickly came to me and said that he had found the dog. The poor dog was still barking. I felt pity for her. I saw three little boys who had a bag full of stones. They had tied the dog to a tree and were throwing stones at the dog. The poor defenseless dog paced back and forth but was unable to escape and could only bark at its tormentors.

We tried to find a way to quickly access the orchard. My brother said that there was a canal which could get us into the orchard. It was fall but the weather was still mild and we could cross the canal. As soon as the dog saw us it started barking again. The children looked around and when they spotted us they ran away to leave the dog to its fate. As we got close to the emaciated, thin, and bony female dog, she crawled towards us on all fours and wagged her tail. I was very upset about what it had been through, but also happy to see that the poor dog was no longer being tortured by the children.

I managed to find the children and told them that this poor animal was very much just like us, and that although she couldn't talk, by barking she was begging the children not to hurt it by throwing stones at it. Then I pointed to the many bleeding injuries on the poor dog and told them that tying an animal to a tree and stoning her was a great sin. They were quiet and looked down at the ground. I asked them how they would like it if they were to be tied to the tree and be treated the same way as they had treated the dog. I asked them about their school. A look of shame crept across their faces. They told us that due to religious wars, all of the schools had been destroyed and many children were now orphans and homeless. These must be the worst maladies existing in religious communities. This great sin is directly attributable to those who have instigated such destructive religious wars in our country.

It is not right to tie up any animal and throw stones at her but there is a cause and effect for everything. Those who brought into power the traitor Mullahs and countries fostering them for their own ideological and financial benefit, were responsible for helping these Mullahs destroy our peaceful country; they ensured that the only outcome would be unemployment, wrecked schools, throwing stones at animals and the like. Any sin, murder, robbery or misdemeanor in our country has been brought on by the greedy traders from Pakistan and it's their crime and sin, not ours.

The imported Mullahs with imported ideas never told us that throwing stones at an animal or a dog was a sin. They carried out the plans of foreigners because their pockets were filled with bribe money. Such traitors didn't have any desire or wisdom to defend the physical and moral values of our country. Their one and only cause was to destroy the country and to build mosques.

For example, wife of Mr. Khalilzad, Ambassador of the US to Afghanistan, spent thousands of dollars for maintenance of a mausoleum which doesn't worth a dime, while the basic requirements for living such as having schools are ignored.

Mercenaries bought by foreigners blew up the electricity power grid towers of Suruby, the towers that had been built using the taxes of orphans, widows, grandmothers and grandfathers. This thoughtless, destructive act left the population in the dark for many nights and weeks and uncooked food remained on cold stoves.

One of those children, whose name was Mirza Baig, told me that he had a neighbor Arash and a sister Maryam. When those bastards blew up the towers so that they could make a forged movie for millions of dollars, Rials, Maryam, who was three years old, used to cry "no electricity".

Religious youth and crazy Mujahedin (who are simply bodies without any soul), sold their faith, conscience and even their country, which is like our mother, to the Arab politicians and their ideology.

We couldn't do our homework due to the power failure. Because of the ignorance of Afghans who sold themselves to Arab Sheikhs and western politicians, and followed their orders to destroy the economic and social infrastructures of Afghanistan, our teacher sighed over this in such a way that it upset all of us.

One of the students, Hares, had written the following note for his teacher, Ms. Torpikai, in the darkness of night. "Last night my mother was in the kitchen, frying onions when the power was cut. She began to tremble with fright and all of the family slept hungry that night. This morning I grabbed a piece of bread and came to school. I'm sorry that I couldn't do my homework, please don't blame me."

The students handed in their homework, on which they had only written their names with the date, for the young intellectual teacher, Ms. Torpikai. I handed mine in too. The teacher looked at my homework and said that I had written a nice note and thanked me for it. My note said that "Last night Kabul was in the dark because thieves were afraid of the light. Gullible enemies who receive orders from foreigners make a lot of trouble for us". Ms. Torpikai read my note once again and put it in her bag.

A week later, on Monday, Ms. Torpikai told us that Babrak Karmal, Afghanistan's President would visit our school. She asked us to attend school in proper dress since the leader of the country was coming to visit. The students were so happy that the president wanted to visit our school. I went home full of pride and as soon as I arrived I started to shout with excitement and hugged my mother. My shouting frightened her and asked me, while combing my hair, what was it that had made me so crazy since I would usually sit off to the side, on my own, and wouldn't even talk to my father.

Hares told his mother that the same night the thieves destroyed the power towers of Saruby, not only did they go to bed hungry but they couldn't finish their homework either. And the day after, he wrote the note to his teacher on a piece of white paper. Hares thought that maybe his note had encouraged Babrak Karmal to pay a visit to their school. His mother said that Babrak Karmal didn't have time for such visits due to the fact that the Pakistanis were creating unrest and chaos in the country. Hares said to his mother that Ms. Torpikai, his teacher, had read his homework and then put it away in her own bag. She is affiliated with the ruling party and she is powerful. He convinced his mother that the visit was actually going to take place and she asked him to go to the market to buy an oil stove since they couldn't rely on the supply of electricity. She added that helicopters were flying in replacement power towers to Saruby and that this was a major expense for the government and compensation for damages in that area would be difficult to make. Managing that part seemed beyond the power of any empire, but in fact this was true and the history of our country is full of such stories.

We saw my father in the city. He was the manager of a food distribution company. He was so concerned when he saw us that he asked my mother if something bad had happened. My mother told him that she wanted to buy an oil stove and why, and she asked if he had seen the helicopters transporting the power towers. He acknowledged that he had seen them and added that such a despicable act carried out by traitors impacted everyone. People were cursing them. Life had been improving everyday and would have continued in that direction if only such traitors did not exist in our midst. My father went on to say that if the enemies thought we were the servants then they had made a terrible mistake since being a servant in your own country is better than being a servant of foreigners against your own in other country on enemy's soil. I was proud of my father's statement and understood that freedom has different faces.

زیان کسان از پی سود خویش   بجویند و دین آرند به پیش
(فردوسی)

My father gave my mother some more money to buy the best stove possible and she thanked him. We bought an oil stove (China), a few candles, some other items and returned home. That night my mother cooked a truly delicious meal. In the morning, she placed a large pot full of water on the stove. The boiling water filled the room with humidity.

I took a bath, put on clean clothes and, smelling good, headed towards school. City buses were very crowded because all of the drivers were party members and they gave priority to students. The bus stopped near the school and the students rushed out. They saw the police and security guards all around the school. Teachers guided the students to the meeting area. Our principal, Mr. Jooya, a handsome and well-built man, told the teachers to ask their students to put their books on the tables and to stand in three orderly lines in the school yard.

A few yards away, two motorcades stopped behind our school with President Karmal riding in the third car. The left door opened, he exited the vehicle and was quickly surrounded by his bodyguards. Beautiful girls from the school, dressed in traditional dress, offered him floral bouquets. He patted the girls on the head and expressed hope that one day they would make their country proud, just like Queen Soraya. He condemned the negative reactionary role played by the Saudi kings in restricting women's freedom and called King Fahd the evil of the Mujahideen.

President Karmal kissed and embraced the school principal, Mr. Joya, a friend of his, and shook hands with all of the school teachers. The girls and boys all appeared clean and nicely dressed, lined up in three orderly lines. The choir sang "*I worship my homeland*" to the applause of teachers and students alike and Karmal patted the choir members on their heads and rewarded them with small gifts.

We looked up and saw the helicopters airlifting the power towers to Saruby. Karmal explained to the students that imperialists and fundamentalists were fearful of the victory of our small country's revolution; that our country's enemies, including Arabs, Ajams and the British, saw their defeat in the solidarity of the working class, and resorted to any solution in order to safeguard their interests, and therefore bowed to China, the second labor pillar in the world, whose ideology is not much different from ours.

He added that "you boys and girls" are powerful pillars of our democratic society and that we have an endless struggle ahead of us, because if we or our friends were defeated in this crucial and dangerous path, or killed or imprisoned, then we would be left to continue the struggle and we shouldn't let mercenary fundamentalists celebrate victory on our graves.

Mr. Karmal continued by saying that a sweet life is one that is achieved by living in abstinence, as the Greek philosopher Epicurus said, 341-270, "Real pleasure comes from practicing abstinence." This is supported by philosophers, Sir Thomas More, 1478-1535, Rumi, 1207-1273, Francois Fourier, 1772-1837, Saint Simon, 1760-1825, Karl Marx Heinrich, 1818-1883, Vladimir Ilyich Ulyanov Lenin, 1870-1924, Avicenna, 980-1037, Ibn Rushd Abu Walid Muhammad, 1126-1198, Muhammad bin-e- Zikrya Razi,825-925, and Ferdowsi, 935-1026, king of the Persian language who completed Shahnameh in 35 years and died in poverty. This is revealed in his poem:

نماندم نمکسود نه هیزم نه جو   نه چیزي پدیدست تا جو درو

These historical heroes lived in piety and many died in poverty gaining personal satisfaction through the interests of the human race living well and in peace. President Karmal told the students that he was proud of himself if he could sit in darkness yet light a candle for students.

Mr. Karmal looked at Ms. Torpikai; she took the note from her blue file and brought it to the podium for the president. He unfolded the note and said, "Dear Hares, not only have you written a good note, but also you have chosen a good name for yourself since it ends with an S and not with th." Karmal said that he wanted to talk to the young man. Students looked around at one another and wondered, what was this all about?

Hares exited his line and walked over to the president. Karmal, the students and teachers all applauded him enthusiastically. The girls and boys were chanting "Hurray" and the anti-revolutionaries, who couldn't understand the meaning of the slogan, looked very jealous.

President Karmal appreciated Hares' sincerity shown in the note and asked all of the students to write down their ideas on how to improve the revolutionary regime, and to do so without fear. The students were also encouraged to inform their teachers about their social problems, in the same way that Hares had brought up a very important issue. Mr. Karmal then read a piece from Rumi's poems that taught fortitude and patriotism and deflected the evil will of those thieves who had robbed the power towers of Kabul.

چون شهسوار فارسي خر بندگي تا کي کني
ننگت نمي آيد که خر گويد ترا خروار کش

President Karmal told his audience that Hares' note was given to him through the party secretariat. The message had been delivered to him while he was having a conversation with the Indian Ambassador. An hour after that meeting, the Indian Embassy donated a power generator to Hares' school. It would be installed in the school and the students would be able to complete their homework there. President Karmal acknowledged the generosity of the Indian Ambassador and his country. The students and Mr. Karmal applauded in order to recognize the support and generosity of the Indian Ambassador and his country. The president continued by adding that not only students of Hares' school, but also students of other schools could do their homework at this school with the light created by the Indian generator. In this way, we would meet new friends and such interaction could bring us all closer and also help in bringing political stability that was being sabotaged by foreign enemies.

Babrak Karmal was indeed a democratic and pious man, who supported equality of the masses. He despised discrimination, disunion and regionalism. The writer of this book was Karmal's classmate in 1958, 47 years ago in the School of Precautionary Bailiffs in the Bala Hesar region of Kabul. I think he was in the 6th group and I was in the 7th group. I used to stand behind him when we lined up in the school yard.

There was a student named Amin in my class who was so lazy in marching, I used to kick him. He would turn around and blame me. One day while lining up, I said something to him and he became angry and called me Panjshiri. I reacted and told him that his mother was a Panjshiri. President Karmal, who was standing in front of me, turned around and asked me what was wrong with a Panjshiri? I was so ashamed of using such a word and said he should ask Amin who had gone to Law School. He added that unfortunately we didn't have enough knowledge about masses and how we could bring them closer. Our teachers lack knowledge about Anthropology, Economics, Geography, History, Political Science, Psychology and Sociology and the role they play in social development. However, this negligence is not of our doing, but that of the Ministry of Education, which should be held responsible for this oversight.

Therefore, we should educate those kind, sincere people and try to avoid labeling each other because such behavior could destroy our unity and solidarity. The point is that we cannot compare the butcher Hafizullah Amin and his followers to Karmal who respects knowledge and piety. Amin had spent much more time in the U.S. and had completed his higher education there. Even such an education could not alter his naïve, racist attitude and his intolerance and hatred of other races.

Oh! I've been distracted from sharing my memories by mentioning a story. Anyway, the bruises on that poor dog had me very concerned about its well being. She was lying on the ground, digging with her paws. Obviously, she was trying to tell me something - that she was hungry and thirsty. I asked the children if there were any grocery stores or restaurants nearby. They said that there was a restaurant and a bakery not too far from where we were. I gave them some money to buy some food for the tortured dog and for themselves, but they continued to gaze at me. My brother understood what was happening and told me that the children were asking for something else. One of them whose name was Tughral asked for some more money for a kite and said they wanted to perpetuate the sport which had taken the life of Parviz Yazd.

The children were so happy about what had happened. Tughral, a sharp boy, started saying good things about dogs. He said that once he had heard about a child at a hospital who was in coma and doctors were unable to cure him. It happened that one of the doctors had asked the parents of the child that if they could bring the child's dog to the hospital. They brought the dog in and the doctor called the dog by name. When the child heard the name of his dog, he opened his eyes.

Tughral then joked and said that if there was a dog at the house, there was no need to wash dishes. I asked him to elaborate his point and he said that during a hot summer day, a stranger was passing by their neighborhood. He became thirsty and knocked on a door, asking for some water but when they brought him water, he refused to drink. He went to another house and asked them for water and there he drank the water and thanked the landlord. The landlord asked him why he didn't drink the water of the neighbors and the man replied that their jar was not clean. The reeve then told him that they didn't have a dog at house.

Tughral continued that in ancient Egypt, where imperialist Arabs destroyed the Egyptians civilization, dogs were so highly considered that the Egyptians made the head of their God Anubis to look like a dog's head.

The children not only prepared food for the dog, but they also promised that they would never again hurt any other dog or other animal and they pledged to fight such bad behavior from then on. The poor hungry dog, which had not eaten anything for days, ate the food very quickly, constantly looking around, on the alert for other dogs that might try to steal its food.

Seeing the dog so obviously hungry brought back a long forgotten memory. It seemed just like only the other day that I had been in Kiev, Ukraine and at that time I was terribly hungry. I rushed into a restaurant named Metro, on Chrischiatic St, grabbed a tray and stood in line. We Asians like rice so much and sometimes we like to eat it with our hands. I saw the rice, chose a bowl and a handful of different foods, found a cozy corner and pulled up a chair. Seated at the table, I began eating when I spotted several black specks in the rice that looked like small black seeds. I picked one out and squeezed it with the fork and noticed it was a mouse dropping. I was about to throw up but managed to control myself.

I took the dish of rice to the cashier and asked her who had cooked the rice. She asked me what was wrong with it and I told her that I just wanted to speak with the cook. She led me to the kitchen and I entered carrying the dish of rice. Several beautiful blonde girls, all wearing white hats and gowns, were surprised at the intrusion. The reader should bear in mind that women in Russia are very sociable and hearty; they approached me with smiling faces and asked me what was wrong. I asked which of them had cooked the rice and they pointed to a very beautiful blonde girl. She came to me and asked if something was wrong with the rice. I pointed to the black "seeds" and she suggested that this might also be rice. The other young ladies were standing around, watching. I told the beautiful blonde that these were, in fact, mouse droppings. She covered her beautiful face with her hands and seemed almost ready to faint. Back then every shop had a log in which the behavior of shopkeepers was recorded. If I had recorded the complaint about her she could have been fired the same day. On the other hand, they weren't familiar with rice and this was the very first time that she had ever cooked rice; she had honestly thought that it was some kind of black rice. The ladies apologized and were ready to prepare a whole new tray of dishes but I had lost my appetite and just wasn't hungry anymore. I thanked them for their offer of restitution, politely declined it, and left the restaurant.

According to the writings of one of our knowledgeable compatriots called "The Jihad + Dinar", protection of the Arab tradition has made it a tradition to become powerful worldwide. For more than 30 years there was an ongoing war on the southeast border of Afghanistan to protect Islam and all physical and intellectual achievements sustained a terrible loss due to Afghan's negative characteristics. Such tyranny, encouraged by evil-intentioned foreigners led to forced migration and homelessness. It was the reason behind the untimely death of our children and youth who were forced to travel long distances. Hunger and poverty on one hand and breaking-up of family relations, disappointment and frustration on the other hand, all of this just to keep up the Arab tradition.

A scholar once said that we should consider the application and usefulness of every phenomenon in our lives based on the political, economical and moral values which are fundamental to a civil society. From the viewpoint of economics, politics and social sciences, these factors are the most valuable. Building a fanatic society like Al Qaida and the like has caused Islam to gain disrepute in the world. Our children are afraid of these bearded, hairy and foulmouthed Mullahs.

I wonder how the British people and government tolerate these Muslims of the new era who create verses and hadith and translate as they like.

It was King Fahd, the Saudi king and other universal traders who destroyed our country for their own corrupt interests. They were the ones who said that flying kites was sinful. By the order of these "outsiders", they suppressed every new idea and freedom which are the fundamentals of mental and physical progress of human beings. Not only did such misfit efforts bring Al Qaida but also resulted in the monopolistic world filling the Mullah's pockets with Rials and Dollars and "Israfil's blow" to their bodies.

The Arab-worshipping traitors used force and violence against our youth based on the religious policies of Saudi Arabia and their belief that the very existence of the dictatorship-kingdom could have been threatened by the intellectual youth. The capitalist Arab sheikhs and puppet Imams prevent expansion of free ideas and thoughts in the world of Islam. Mullahs are continuously speaking about heaven and hell. Instead of such rhetoric, it's much better to preach about morals, good manners and being kind to other human beings and animals and generally enjoying a better life.

When I was about 11 or 12 years old, we used to have a wolf-like dog at home. Our neighbors used to call her by our family name. The heads of the family were ashamed of this and ordered that the dog be killed. She was wrapped in a rope and her four legs were tied tightly together; she was then thrown into the river. But the loyal dog returned home a few hours later. The children were so happy but the family elders were very angry and wanted to take revenge. This time they tied her very tightly and she was never seen again.

Abu Taliheh referred to Hadith No. 539 in the fourth volume, stating that "if there is a dog at home, angels will never enter the house, therefore dogs should be killed."

In the past 1400 years our people have been physically and mentally tortured like animals to embellish the Arab ways. Slaves (non Arab Muslims) who have been held prisoners in the five pillars of Arabic hell for more than 14 centuries, serving just a religious political plot to prolong the age of Arab traditions which are based on uncompromised and intolerance facts. It's impossible, therefore, to believe that these people and their traditions could possibly incorporate any kindness whatsoever towards mankind and animals. In recent times we have seen the inhumane treatment based on these traditions and carried out by the order of some evil Imams who have incited fellow Muslims to behead other human beings as if they are beheading camels.

I was drowning in thoughts that the country's youth was no longer on the correct path, and I was about to leave when a door opened and an average looking man with a colorful tie came out. He asked me not to get angry because he didn't greet me in Arabic (asalamalaikoom) since he felt that the greeting related to Arab imperialism and therefore did not use it. He felt that I was an educated person and I confirmed that. His name was Jamshid and he used to teach Sociology in one of Kabul's universities.

This happened when Kabul was in the middle of major political change. Jamshid continued, saying that if something is meant to happen, it will happen. Perhaps our people needed such a change to help them to progress towards a better life. But, unfortunately, we failed to keep the old regime, and now we should strive to retain the new system. I don't want to see our youth dying once again due to the instability of this regime that our foreign enemies are trying to destabilize and topple.

I believe that, in the name of democracy and freedom, the world will prepare enemies of mankind such as "Ikhvan Al Muslimin," a Muslim movement that hopes for the big Islamic Caliphate, we know how the Ikhvan were successful to win the big war in Afghanistan.

Professor Jamshid held my hands and wept while saying goodbye. He told me that ignorance was the worst social disorder. After I left him, a man who was standing nearby approached and told me that the professor had lost his son Parviz while kite flying, just a few days ago.

I found Professor Jamshid to be a smart and knowledgeable man. I was hoping that if there were more such individuals in my country then we could prevent the collapse of the existing regime. The predictions of Professor Jamshid proved to be accurate because Afghanistan's regime was supported by the Soviets and, as a result, the West started to call Afghanistan a communist country. Never before had the regime called itself a communist system and, in order to defeat communism, not for the freedom of Afghanistan, the West severed the lifeline of the Afghan people, meaning that dear Islam became endangered.

Huge sums of money and a large number of personnel were directed towards this goal. Primary financial and physical support came from the Saudis, Arabs and universal Ikhvan Al Muslimin, USA, Britain, Pakistan and others, who provided them with military training. All these efforts resulted in the collapse of the government in Afghanistan. Pakistanis cooperating with Afghan mercenaries spared no effort to destroy Afghanistan.

The small country of Afghanistan has suffered greatly from the naïve, destructive and religious policies of Pakistani Mullahs, Pakistani ISI and Arabs Ikhvan Al Muslimin and others. We've seen how these Mullahs have multiplied like mushrooms and how they have violated freedom and human rights.

Now the opportunist fundamentalists gained fame in the West. The generosity of the free world opened a new door for Ikhvan Al Muslimin and they shifted their centers from Egypt, Chechnya and Uzbekistan to London and Pakistan. My Christian brothers, defend yourself, do not wait to turn the other cheek. According to these naïve Imams and their gunmen, our poor and frustrated people, particularly our younger generation, should remain subjects of slavery. They don't understand the value of a social, political, economic, artistic life and, most importantly of all, freedom.

Professor Jamshid was correct in saying that if the Americans and others hadn't used Muslim fundamentalists in Afghanistan to take revenge on the USSR, they wouldn't have had become so bold and rude.

The Great Abdul Rahman, the iron man who developed Afghanistan from 1880 to 1901, was an enemy of the Mullahs. He described these freeloaders as the most destructive of people. He wrote that every priest, Mullah and tribal head called himself a king and no king had tried to restrict their independence over the past 200 years. The Great Abdul Rahman couldn't tolerate the kind of torture and oppression these Mullahs imposed on the people. He called one of them the Mouse of the Universe, the worst insult. He further added that the Mullahs represented ignorance which is totally true.

"Mouse" Mullah Ghalazi proved his ignorance by announcing "Jihad" which cost thousands of lives of my compatriots in 1879 by Lord Roberts of Kandahar.

Professor Jamshid added that, "Our unpretentious people have been deceived by the erroneous preaching of Mullahs resulting in their wives becoming widows, their children becoming orphans and their cities being destroyed."

Professor Jamshid said to the Khorasani and Kabulestani people that: Remember the day the Arab spears landed in our hearts, remember the army of children who searched for their fathers' bodies, remember the poor widow who wept over her dead husband, remember the aggressive Arabs who beheaded people with two swords and remember your brave brothers who groaned from the wounds caused by the aggressor, looter, oppressor and cowardly enemy. Remember the ruins, the homeless people and the holocaust caused by nomad Arabs. I was an innocent. I had the right to defend freedom, achievements, homeland and our women and children. I was not another Zaid bin Hareth to offer my wife (Zainab) to another man. Look at other animals to see how they react in such special cases.

I can say that I'm Pakistani, Khorasani, Uzbek or Iranian but I'll never say that I'm an Islamistani, since it does not help the recognition of my national identity and is not even considered as tribal pride. The democratic and free world encouraged Ikhvan Al Muslimin to topple Afghanistan's regime, taught them war techniques and how to have a political organization, as a result of which the US global interests incurred losses due to Ikhavan Al Muslimin's operations. However, even if these Arab terrorists led by Osama bin Ladin, wouldn't have leveled to the World Trade Center towers in New York in Sept. 11, 2001. Would the US still want to take revenge on the terrorists who caused damage to US interests across the world.? The hasty and deadly terrorist attacks by Bin Ladin which indicate agitation, failure and weakness, not only dragged the US into a war but also made it an Arabic war. We shouldn't attribute the policy of Islamization and Islamic extremism to Osama bin Ladin, but rather to Prince Faisal and his agenda in establishing the Islamic Conference against Jews and the West, and Prince Fahd who expanded the agenda throughout the world.

The religious policies and Arab Nationalism could take advantage of Islamic countries and all others, including Moscow, using bribery and the name of Islam. They succeeded in establishing religious academies and centers, Quranic Schools which promoted Wahabi tradition and the Arabic language. Prince Fahd, King of Saudi Arabia, resorted to conspiracy by encouraging Arabs to emigrate to Europe and the US to marry Western girls so they could promote Islam. King Fahd used public funds to buy Heads of States as well as powerful elites such as politicians, university instructors, landowners, etc. He is using millions and millions of Dinars every year to attract people for Haj which I consider unlawful. And this, while his own people are illiterate and cameleers. The younger generation in the peninsula try to topple the Saudi Royal family and its dictators, but they are killed and hanged. These youngsters are the real martyrs.

Prince Mohammad Al Faisal (brother of Prince Al Taraki) chaired the Islamic Bank from 1975 to 2001 in Geneva. One of the main duties of this bank was inviting people to convert to Islam. The US seized some of the financial assets of the bank. The Islamic World Charity Organization contributed millions of dollars for terrorism including USD 500 million spent for Palestinians to plant bombs and paid USD 1000 to the families of suicide bombers.

The Rebat Conference, established in 1969 through the initiatives of King Faisal of Saudi Arabia, was a response to the conspiracy of Jews since the latter wanted to destroy Omar's mosque in Jerusalem. As a matter of fact, King Faisal declared Jihad against the Israeli government.

King Faisal wanted to create solidarity among the members of the Conference, so the Muslims were asked to protect sacred places, support the Palestinian uprising and strengthen the world of Islam. The fact that such attempts were very similar to the international communist agenda (Commintern) in the former USSR should be mentioned here.

The Assembly of Muslim Youth whose head office is in Riyadh, has 450 institutes in 34 countries. They promote the real ideology based on Towhid (Unity) to expand Wahabism. This means shut non-Wahabi Muslims up. They want to strengthen the relations between Muslim youth and the Muslim Youth Organizations universally. What's meant by stating the above facts? After the first attack on the Word Trade Center in Manhattan, New York, in 1993, a bomb-making manual was found in the house of one of the terrorists, printed by the Muslim Youth Organization of Saudi Arabia.

Investigation teams discovered that 4 of the terrorists engaged in the attacks of Sept. 11, 2001 had contacts with office of the Muslim Youth Organization in the US which is not far from Washington and, more amazing, was that Abdullah bin Ladin was the head of such organization. Islamic jurisprudence (Fiqh) is the logic behind all such conspiracies.

The NGOs established by the Saudi Royal family are busy with their own sabotage. The murder of Jamal Abdul Nasser, the Egyptian President, was arranged by the Saudi Royal family and carried out by a Syrian. President Nasser was harsh with the leaders of Ikhvan Al Muslimin in 1950 in Egypt which resulted in such leaders fleeing to Saudi Arabia and other countries.

Between 1973 and 1993, the Propagation Organization of Prince Fahd, had contributed 5.5% of it's GDP to universal propagations. The financial support of Saudis increased from Rials 2 billion in 1974 to Rials 6 billion. Such financial assistance is given to certain countries whose representatives to the Human Rights Commission, UNESCO, etc. defend the political and diplomatic interests of Saudi Arabia in the UN. Billions of Rials spent by Prince Fahd converts to billions of Dollars and is quite remarkable. Saudi Arabia has 220 Islamic centers, 500 mosques, 220 intermediary schools and 2000 primary schools worldwide.

The semi official gazette of Saudi Arabia "Ain al Yaqin" mentioned some of the Saudi Propagation Organizations in the following cities which are totally supported by Saudis: Malaca, Toronto, Rome, Brasilia, Rio de Janeiro as well as Gibraltar, Mantes-La-Jolie, Edinburgh as in London, Lisbon, Vienna. In Geneva, Brussels, Madrid, New York, Zagreb, Australia... Or N'Djamena in Chad, Khartoum in Sudan, etc.

Shiite and Sunni groups in Nigeria are jointly managed. It's a country in which religious battles between Muslims in the north and Christians in the south of Nigeria is ongoing. There are Islamic centers all over the world, Asia, Japan, Indonesia and Maldives, in America the Islamic Centers of New York, Washington, the Chicago grand mosque, the Fresno mosque, the Islamic Centers of Columbia, Missouri, New Jersey and New Brunswick, the Islamic Center of

Virginia, the Albanian mosque in Chicago, Tida in Maryland. An Islamic Center in Toledo of Africa, Tanzania, Burkina Faso, Gabon, Senegal. The mosques built with Saudi support are prominent. Examples: Lyon, which cost USD 3 million. USD 15 million in Chad, King Faisal university in Guinea, USD 14 million, Grand Mosque of Senegal, USD 3 million, Faroue mosque in Cameroon, USD 4 million, Zanzibar mosque, USD 2 million, Bamako mosque USD 5 million, Yaounde mosque and bridge in Nigeria, total USD 5 million, USD 5 million for renovations in Al Azhar University in Egypt, Belal university in Los Angeles, Omar bin Khatab university in Jerusalem, Brent Central in London, Calgary, Quebec and Ottawa universities in Canada, millions and millions dollars were spent. Millions of dollars were spent in Europe, USD 5 million in Brussels, USD 5 million at the Islamic Center of Geneva, USD 5 million at the Islamic Center of Madrid, USD 6 million at the Islamic Center of London and USD 5 million in Edinburgh.

And from his personal account, King Fahd donated USD 5 million to the Islamic Center of Rome, including a mosque rivaling the Vatican. Although, in Saudi Arabia, it is not permitted to build a church or offer services for other religions than Islam.

Islamic academies supported by Saudi Arabia are spread all over the world. The Islamic academy opened in 1984 in Washington and had 1,200 students, most of them Saudi nationals.

King Fahd's Academy had 1,000 students in London and another one was opened in Moscow in 1995. This academy included a mosque and cost about USD 7 million. It had 500 students whose responsibility was to promote the Arabic language and Islamic culture and fight against the use of non-Islamic words. Another academy was built in Bihas in Bosnia-Herzegovina to promote Wahabism in the Balkans.

Shaw University in North Carolina and Syracuse University in New York are the propagation centers of Saudi Arabia. The prestigious Duke University in Durham, North Carolina has been receiving donations from Saudi Arabia since 1977. It's the only university with Saudi guests. Potentially, it is the southern branch of the Saudi Embassy which carries out tasks such as Information Bureau, General Communications, Consultations and Propagation. Professors of this university mainly protect Arabs interests and huge corporations.

Georgetown University in Washington trains politicians in addition to other professions. The faculty of Arabic Language and Literature flourished with the generous donations of Saudi Arabia, Egypt, U.A.E. and Oman to the Contemporary Arabic Studies Center.

A former British Diplomat, John Kelly, says that existence of such a large number of Islamic academies is just a cover. Saudi kings hold honorary seats in western universities. King Abdul Aziz was given an honorary seat at California University in Santa Barbara in 1984, King Fahd holds one at Harvard University, at the East African Studies Center in London. and at the Persian Gulf University.

Other Islamic Centers in Japan, Indonesia, Djibouti, Mauritania and Ras Al Khema are supported by Saudis. Other centers are Arabic Islamic Institute of Du Monde in Paris, the American University in Colorado, Harvard University in Washington, The Arabic History and Islamic Science in Frankfurt, the Middle East Institute in Washington and many more which are supported by oil-rich Arab countries to promote Arab pride and dignity.

John Esposito a scholar who converted to Islam, defends Arabs against the western extremists and says that the former call Arabs terrorists whereas their own university is a center for propagations in favor of Arabic extremism. Martin Kramer who has always criticized Saudis, says that the Islamic centers in the US, such as in Berkeley and Harvard, should be the last ones to be criticized. They never talk about anti-Saudi movements.

Saudis resorted to all sorts of bribery, giving away gifts, etc. in order to buy Mullahs. Mohammad Jalal Kishk is one of these Imams at Al Azhar university. He had given many speeches on Wahabism. He received a USD 200,000 gift from King Faisal which encouraged him to write a book on Wahabi traditions. He received USD 850,000 from King Faisal for his book. In order to save his country from the danger of Saddam Hussein, in 1990 King Fahd asked the Imams of Al Azhar to issue a verdict for the deployment of US troops on the sacred land.

I believe that such efforts to keep the Saudi Royal family alive will end soon. As soon as the US abandons her interests in Saudi Arabia and leaves behind those who believe in Allah to worship their God as much as they want.

Thanks to Ferdowsi, the King of the Persian language, who had never used Allah in Shahnameh. Laurent Murawiec in his book Prince of Darkness, translated by George Holoch into English, has written that Ka'ba, originally built on a Black Cube, was worshipped by millions every year, is not Ka'ba in fact but it is "cubes" or "cube".

If the respected readers think more deeply about this religious competition, anti-Judaism, fighting against civilization and other poisonous thoughts of Saudis, they will find out that there wasn't really a true cause for their donations, whether in Dollars or in Rials. Such money was not spent for real economic, artistic or social reconstruction, with the exception of a bridge constructed on the river of Nigeria.

I found Professor Jamshid to be a civilized man and asked his opinion about Arabs, especially Saudis. He replied that useless and groundless efforts of Saudi Imperialism in the world are to cover up their kingdom and not only people of the same peninsula but the whole Arabic and Islamic world will soon face the consequences. I asked him whether there was any solution or not? He replied that the answer to this question was not easy. Since cooperation between this oil-rich country and the world, especially through Aramco, (the Arab oil cartel) with the US and their usury has not only violated the people's rights in that peninsula, but also has promoted Wahabi ideology through religious centers worldwide and billions of Dollars have been spent on this cause. This is the motivation for the anger and outrage of Saudi Arabia's intellectual youth whom we call "terrorists".

The true motivation behind attacking New York's twin towers and massacring thousands of innocent people comes neither from Sharon or Saddam Hussein, but from the Saudi kings. In November, 1979 some people from Libya, South Yemen, East Germany, Palestine (PLO), those who were trained in Iran, Egypt, Sudan, Kuwait and Iraq, occupied the Jame' Mosque of Mecca.

"Johamein Al Tayebi" leader of the rebels from the Shamar Harb tribe, the revolutionary family whose grandfather Al Tayebi was killed 50 years ago in a battle against Ibn Saud, called himself the last "Imam Mahdi".

However such a retrogressive movement without any special formula for social existence and freedom of rights, not based on democratic rules would embrace a horrible destiny for the people. But if a pioneering and more humane movement which holds itself responsible to the rules and regulations of the UN, could take the lead in toppling the Saudi Royal family, it would work as a national liberation body.

However, such an underground movement is now active within Saudi Arabia and some countries call it "terrorism". I believe that giving such a name to such a political cause is unfair because they are fighting against the tyranny of the kings in their own country, not against the free world, the US or the Israeli government. If someday their cause is realized, the income from selling oil will not only be used for homeless Palestinians, to provide them with houses, etc. but also will help develop poor Arab countries.

Laurent Murawiec in his book Prince of Darkness, suggests dividing the Saudi Empire into five instead of four meaning Ibn Saud, Saud bin Abdul Aziz, Faisal bin Abdul Aziz, Khaled bin Abdul Aziz and

Fahd bin Abdul Aziz. This kingdom will collapse after the latter's death and his successor would be the last king.

I asked Professor Jamshid what will happen if the terrorists whom you call the "liberation movement" get into power. Maybe they will act worse than the Saudi kings due to their religion and nationalism. He replied that predicting such regimes is not easy, since the emergence of different thoughts and ideas would cause conflicts, which in turn, will cause their downfall or separation. On the other hand, they are not kings who eat and sleep together under one roof. National and international responsibilities, liberalism and pressures of the outside world will force them to act in a synchronized manner in accordance with modern demands. Or, it could be even worse than we think. The founder of historiography and modern Sociology, Abdu r-Rahman bin Khaldūn of Yemen, 1332-1406, who died in Cairo, mentioned that Arabs are the uncivilized people on the earth in his writings about the Nomads and their empire. Al Qaida is an unsystematic Arab movement and Ibn Khaldun was right about them 700 years ago, as what's going on in the Arab world now (Palestine and Iraq) is a good confirmation of his statements. In the last report of the 9/11 commission on Al Qaida it was stated that "the enemy is not just terrorism but some generic evil".

Arabs lost their empire but in no way are they ready to surrender their religion which is considered to be their dignity and pride. This is why Saudis have intoxicated Muslims and others with the smell of oil.

Arabs don't believe in Mohammad's Quran. They only believe in a Quran by Mohammad bin Abdul Wahab who called himself the leader of the Islamic Society and declared Jihad in 1787 against the Ottoman Empire. The 12000 Wahabi troops set Karbala ablaze in 1802 and Imam Husayn's Mosque (Mohammad's grandson) and massacred 4,000 people. They killed pregnant women and pulled out their fetuses. The dead bodies were covered with blood. Such atrocities and the like well explain the patience and endurance attributed to Islam.

Maybe you remember that a Danish cartoonist drew a cartoon of Mohammad in 2005. Arabs created such a riot in 2006 and certain Islamic extremist countries, including Afghanistan, followed them. During these riots a few crazy people died. The February 2nd, 2006 issue of the France Soir newspaper wrote, "Yes, we have the right to make a cartoon of God". A cartoon was printed in this newspaper, showing Jews, Buddhists, Christians and Muslims above the clouds, the Christian was saying, "Hey Mohammad, don't complain, they also drew cartoons of all of us". .

A great sculptor, Adolph Weinman, made a sculpture of Mohammad which has been placed in the US Supreme Court. Sculptures of other figures have been made worldwide. Many outstanding Muslim scholars drew cartoons of Mohammad in the 14th and 15th centuries and nobody issued an order declaring their infidelity. Some of these imaginary drawings of Mohammad in 1436 in Herat of Khorasan exist in a book. In this book, Mohammad was pictured riding a horse with a human head and Gabriel is drawing it towards heaven and hell. However, it is so amazing that such artistic works have never been mentioned in the Quran as infidelity, except in the Quran of modern worshippers.

Kamal Nawash, head of the Muslim Union, says that there is no reason to condemn the Danish cartoonist.

Fanco Farattini, the European Union Commissioner and former Italian Foreign Minister, in an interview with the Daily Telegraph, stated that millions of European Muslims have been hurt by such acts. He asked the journalists not to provide these opportunists with this type of opportunity to play politics. He admired the religious sensitivity, however, which didn't prioritize among the various religions.

In April, 1803 the great Saudi King entered Mecca and ordered all the houses built on the grave of the prophet's family to be destroyed. They robbed the jewelry of Mohammad's treasury. They even disinterred Mohammad's grave in 1810 by the order of the Saudi Imam, sold the jewelry and distributed it among the Wahabis.

In 1808, Wahabis and Saudi forces occupied most of the Arab Islands and advanced towards Syria and Iraq, surrounded Basra and penetrated Palestine. A large number of their troops had almost reached Damascus. At this time Napoleon Bonaparte's troops were deployed in Egypt to assist the Ottoman Sultan, ordering Mohammad Ali to cause to surrender the impudent nomad and take back the sacred shrines and the two sacred cities. At this point the arrogant son in Cairo launched his attack.

He cut off the ears of 4,000 Wahabi soldiers in 1812 and sent them to Istanbul. In 1813, the Saudis lost control of Jeddah and Mecca. The great Saudi King lost control of Hejaz, Oman and Bahrain before his death. In 1816 and late 1818, Al Daira the first capital of Saudi Arabia was occupied and its people were scattered. The Wahabi Imam "Abdullah", chained and shackled, was exiled to Istanbul and hanged there. His body was ripped apart by dogs. Eighteen family members of Saudi King were killed in this battle.

Ibrahim Pasha, executed his special torture on Suleiman bin Abdullah, the grandson of the founder of Wahabism. Before execution, he forced Suleiman to listen to the blasphemy order played by Robab (a type of violin) because Wahabis hate any kind of music. This was the first Saudi Empire to be destroyed by the Ottomans.

Abdul Aziz bin Faisal bin Al Saud was born in 1880. His family were driven out of Saudi Arabia by Al Rashid and he lived in Britain in exile. In 1887, the second Saudi was born. In 1893 he earned the support of Sheikh Al Sabah of Kuwait and 30 years later he became the new Saudi King in 1932. This evil family has set the world on fire. I wish Ibrahim the King would be reborn and oust such a stubborn family.

The social revolution in Afghanistan couldn't improve the economic, cultural, political and artistic life of the people due to the fact that efforts by the Saudi family and others, regardless of Social anthropology, ethnology and ethnography, turned the country into a bloodbath. It is because of this fact that the religious revolution has been imposed on the modern society of Afghanistan.

In Asia, in Kabul a young guy named "Abdul Rahman" was converted to Christianity in 2006. Mullahs strongly resisted such a practice.

During Babrak Karmal, President of Afghanistan, I was invited to a conference of the Village Development Directors in Kabul in which brother Ghader Behyar also participated. The Village Development Director of Baghlan Province, whose name I can't remember, told us a story about religious passion and the sensibility of people in one of the villages of Ghour province. He told us that a few tanks had entered the village and people were fighting against the tanks with bats and flint guns. Two brothers in their 60s, one of them holding a sword and the other holding the sword's cover ran straight into the tanks. The one holding a sword, hit the tank and his sword was cut into two pieces. The other one holding the sword's cover attacked the tank with the cover. Finally the tank's operator came out and told the two brothers that fighting a tank with sword was impossible. The fundamentalists should be warned that freedom tanks are rolling down every corner in Afghanistan and couldn't be defeated by swords. We know this sort of emotion comes from a complex and usually strong subjective response, it is love and love is fair. Such a response involves physiological changes as preparation for action, a choice determined by emotion rather than reason.

Today, Tuesday, March 28, 2006, the ABC channel announced that 10,000 Afghans have converted to Christianity. The religious regime of Kabul couldn't come out with any answer to the international community. In order to find a way out of the crisis, they announced that the very healthy Abdul Rahman was insane. Wouldn't it be wiser if Hamid Karzai did the same as the Azizudin Ahmad, Secretary

General of the Youth Congress of Malaysia did, and confess that the reason for those who convert from Islam to other religions is to seek freedom. Meaning that there was no freedom in Islam…

The Islamic philosophers such as Ferdowsi, Mowlana Jalaludin Mohammad Rumi, Abu Zaid, Ibn Khaldoun, Abdul Rahman Yemeni, Avecinna, 980-1037, Abu Walid bin Rushd, 1126-1198, Mohammad bin Zikria Razi, 865-925 (who is also called Hakim Jalinus), Abu Yousuf Yakub bin Ishaq Al kandi, 801-803, Omar Khayyam, Hafez Shirazi, Nasser Khosrow and thousands of others had warned people about the uncivilized and barbarian culture of Arabs. Unfortunately, my compatriots didn't pay attention and not only suffered the consequences, such as being disabled and homeless, but have also turned into beasts and ignorant psychopaths (like Taliban, the Beard Designers, creations of the Intelligent Designer). They are a vicious sect who denied every right of human autonomy and freedom, especially womens rights.

Poisonous Arab propaganda spread by agents of the Saudi Kings are not only causing disunion but have also misled Muslims and continuing in this manner will turn them into puppets in the hands of their Arab owners.

Intentional lies and labeling by Muslim Imams in Arab and Ajam in (non-Arab Muslims) countries of about 15 million Jews who would finally take control of hundreds of millions of Muslims, had created such a hatred, pessimism and disunion among Muslims. These brash Mullahs and their followers ignore their unpleasant behavior and sermons about Jews and Christians and ask the U.S., the Jews' ally, to help them in overcoming poverty and adversity. On the other hand, the fundamentalists who can't practice their "destructive ideas" in their own countries,escape to the heavenly U.S. and Britain.

They have caused many problems for their hosts. In the mosques in Europe and US, the Saudi Imams bravely criticize and attack Jesus Christ and Moses in their speeches and disrespectfully place their religion, based on Allah and Mohammad (Islam), above other religions.

Abdul Rahman, as a hero and based on an in-depth and stable assessment on beliefs and thoughts, ran away from Olympia Zeus to seek freedom due to the fact that he opposed the spread of knowledge, insight, art, etc.

Hey Khorasani! Believe in God, in prophets and their books. So, based on which reasoning and rationalization, do you as a Mullah prevent people from converting to Christianity, Judaism, Islam, Buddhism, Hinduism or not having a religion at all?

By taking advantage of peoples' ignorance towards principles of peaceful coexistence, the tempting and misleading propaganda of Saudi Kings and using such phrases as "protecting sacred places", "protecting the rights of the Palestinians" and the "dignity of Arabs" mobilized over one billion Muslims against 15 million Jews.

زیزدان پرستنده بیزار گشت   از او نام و آواز تو خوار گشت
(فردوسی)

Chapter Three

BEING DELUDED IS THE WORST SOCIAL DISASTER

Suzanne Fields is a famous columnist who writes about other peoples' lies about Jewish conspiracies. Any darn thing happens in the world, and they attribute it to the Jews. From the 4th century when Christianity became the official religion of the Roman Empire, the anti- Jewish movement remained powerful until the 16th century. In 1021, when Rome was destroyed by earthquake and storms, Jews were blamed. Some of them were tortured, some confessed and some were burned at the stake.

When an epidemic disease (Bubonic Plague) in the 14th century claimed the lives of millions people including Jews in Europe, Jews were blamed for such a disaster. Henry Ford blamed the Jewish capitalists in World War I for taking advantage of all the parties engaged in the war. Charles Lindberg claimed that Jewish riots caused World War II.

The rivals of Franklin Roosevelt called the New Deal the Jewish Contract. Arabs blamed World War I on Jews and not only this, but also the October Revolution, September 9th Tragedy and, moreover, they believe that the Shiah faction is the product of Jewish conspiracy.

In the Quran, verse No. 95 of Baqarah Chapter, reads that God changed Jews to monkeys. Not only Adolf Hitler but Mel Gibson and Mahmud Ahmadinejad were hard on them.

Arkady N. Shevchenko in his book, breaking with Moscow wrote: Gregory Morozov, a Jewish scientist, married Stalin's daughter, Svetlana. Stalin slapped Svetlana and asked her why she couldn't find herself a Russian husband and forced her to divorce Morozov. Stalin had never met his son in law and even deposed him. Sometimes constraint, sometimes hatred and pessimism are hard on an individual's destiny.

I remember a story about a man who carrying a sheep, and he encountered a few trickeries who wanted to deceive the poor man. So all of them in their turn told him what a nice dog he had and asked him whether he wanted to sell the dog or not? Finally, the poor man was convinced that he had a dog, not a sheep, and he left the animal behind.

In 622, Muhamad moved out from Mecca to Yathrib (now called Medina). Then on the Diffusion of jealousy and hatred toward Jewish people strengthened first among Arab and then among Ajams.

Jalaludin Muhamed Rumi, an outstanding Muslim philosopher, condemns this disrespectful behavior about the Jewish people and expresses his sorrow to them with this poem below:

همـچون جـهودان می زیبی ترسان و خواران و متهم
پس چــون جـهودان کن نشان عصابه بر دستار کش
یــا از جـهودی تــوبـه کن از خاک پای مصطفی
بـــهر گشاد دیـــده را در دیـــدهٔ افـــکار کش

You live like barred Jewish, frightened, despicable and accused
So when you show connived like Jew put on your cane and turban
Or repent from being a Jew by drawing in the soil on Mustafa's feet
With your wide vision see the ideas and opinions

The combination of a good education and the association with good people helps you become an understanding person. In addition, no one can take advantage of you and you will not become the target of a stereotype.

Religious ghastly sermons, lack of freedom and joy, repetition of lies, deceptions and fear in the course of 1400 years turned the Afghanistani people into stone. Abdul Rahman is the only patriot and free thinker in the history of Islam to publicly convert into Christianity.

In my neighborhood lived a blacksmith called him Mr. Janggy. His house was about 50 meters away from the Mosque but he never prayed at the mosque. One day, the Imam of the Mosque together with his Taliban entered his house and dragged him out. They whipped and flogged him almost to death then threw him into the water. Mr. Janggy was crying like a dog but no one could dare free him from the tyranny of that Imam. This poor man, Mr. Janggy, was in a bed for four weeks. When his injuries healed, he sold off all of his belongings and fled to a more peaceful place.

In the end of 2004, I went to Afghanistan to visit my birth place and asked the people about the situation of the mosque which is adjacent to my previous home. They laughed and said now we are very happy because we don't have any more Imams and Taliban. I asked them what happened to those people and one of them jokingly told me that they fled to America.

They were joking but I think that they were right because there is an Arab Imam in New York City who wants to build a huge isolating institution (the Cordoba Mosque). He is doing this to refresh the past glories of Arabs in Spain and the joys with the blond ladies.

First of all, Cordoba is not the property of Arabs nor is it located in an Arabic country. Also, isn't this some sort of plagiarism or thievery for Arabic pride?

1. What would be the reaction of the Spanish government about this sensitive issue in the future? Shame on this fundamentalist Imam who plays a dirty trick while he says if we moved from this place, the Islamic world would rise up. This demanding Statement from a strong position is a direct provocation.

2. A black President with Islamic roots is the wonderful motivation for this fundamentalist Mullah and his entourage to build such a huge mosque in a nucleus state like New York City.

In sura the immunity verse? 29. Says: "kill those that believe not in Allah". In a deceiving way, the English translator translated the word of killing to fighting (this is the very tricky policy of the Egyptian Islamic brotherhood). The policy uses lies and deception to penetrate the world of christianity in the West. We must fight them face to face because through this tricky policy, they are still making the kuran very fabricated.

Speaking of conscience in Emile, for example, he issues the reproach that 'Fanaticism dares to counterfeit it and to dictate crime in its name.'2 In the draft "On the Social Contract", the so called Geneva Manuscript, he refers to 'the furies of fanaticism,' which if unrestrained by 'Philosophy and laws,' would cover the earth with blood and destroy the human race.3

Quote:

The U.S. Costitution may insist on a separation of church and state; that is, there is a right to religious expression but no religion is guaranteed favored governmental dominance. This insurance, however, does not mean that religion is not involved in the political institution.

The above definition is a great incentive to all religions all over the world to come to America and make America a more religious country. Who knows if Abraham Lincoln believed in God or if he was even a Christian? The same thing could be said about Dr. Martin Luther King. In 1960, I was a student in the Soviet Union (Kiev Ukrine) and I found that the Russians branded him a communist. They believed that socialism ideology played a persuasive role on the civil rights movement in America. There was also a rumour that Joseph Stalin (1879-1953) expected the emergence of a black Communist republic in the South of the U.S.

A few days ago, I emailed a short note to Mr. Glenn Beck of Fox News about the Cordoba Mosque. I wanted to find what his reaction to the topic and related issues would be. The next day, he was talking on Fox News about something very strange: moderate muslims? Such a comment from an opportunist person who wants to take advantage of a sick environment infers his mockery and his egotistic attitudes. Maybe something is worrying him? Something like disestablishment and disendowment?

Americans never understood Islam because they are not born in Islamic countries and were not raised in one. What does moderate muslim mean? Islam has one thousand faces. If a Muslim says Allah is not the only God and Muhamed is not the only Prophet, as it mentioned in Sura 23 Al-Najm in the Koran: And certainly the guidance has come to them from their God, another God prior to Allah.

وَلَـقـد جَـاۤءَ هُـم مِـن رَبِهِـمُ الـهُـدای

Also, in sura omran or amran in the Koran verses 3 and 4 says:

نَزَّلَ علیک الکتابه بالحق مُصدِقا لِما بینَ یدیهِ و انزلَ التوراتة و الانجیل .
من قبلُ هُدّی للناس

3. He has revealed to thee the book with truth, verifying that which is before it, and he revealed the Torah and the Gospel.

4. Aforetime, a guidance for the people. So why do muslims repudiate the other gods, the other books or the other Prophets?

Ibn Khaldun (1332-1406), Arab historian and sociologist on the bases of above two sura and three verses attested that the muslims god is different from the other gods.

Ibn Khaldun is the only intellect and gallant person amongst Arabs and Ajams who witnessed Polytheism. Furthermore, he writes that the invaders (Arabs) are naturally wild people and instinctively unreluctant to looting and pillage.

Then, he or she as a moderate Muslim can erase this below Verse 286 of Cow from the Koran (Arabic Parochialistic hollowed Book) which says:

انت مولانا فالنصرنا على القوم الكفرين

Oh God succeed us over the infidels.

Now, can the moderate Imams or other moderate white capped muslims delete this harsh tongue from the face of the Koran? Mr. Glenn Beck, if muslims believe in creation, then why do they hate pigs, Jews and Shiah people (products of a Jewish conspiracy, according to Arabs)? Since the Shiah are more intellegent and more open minded people than Sunni fanatics.

With Shiah societies, may we have a chance at a more peaceful and more prosperous world but not with backward Sunni people. As a result, this is the time for the free world to support and strengthen the movement of Shiahesm globally against the Sunniesm.

In sura Al- Omran 28 in Koran says:

لا يتخذ المومينون الكفرين اوليا ء من دون المومينين

Don't take infidels as a friend. Any one that does is not a Muslim.

The point is this, why do Muslims fly like flies to "infidel" countries regardless of Allah's commandments? Wake up America to evils you know why because the caterpillars like soft tree.

To me, moderate muslim means a person without courage. Being a moderate is a weak position because he or she is located between the two strong polar opposites of extreme and excessive.

If muslims have faith in verse 23 of Sura Al-Najm which says: "And certainly the guidance come to them from their God", apparently this verse rescinds the authenticity of----------. لا اله الا الله محمد رسول الله

There is no god but only Allah and Muhammed is the only Prophet. Therefore, years of researching by Leone Caetany attributed to the Koranic issues one hundred percent is correct.

In the above Sura, Allah plainly confesses from the existence of another God.

A Poet (Bidel) said: "Today muslims have everything but faith".

بیدل امروز در مسلمانان   همه چیز است لیک ایمان نیست

Abdul Rahman was a symbol of democracy. He wasn't insane. Imposing ideas, forced migrations, standing against social, political, economic and cultural injustices rising from vain ideologies, led him to a confrontation of philosophies. Not as an Afghan but as a liberal and brave individual, he popularly declared in the court that he converted from Islam to Christianity.

پسندیده باد آن نژاد و گهر   همان مام که چون تو آرد پسر
چنین گفت که از مام و پدر   یکی شاخ شایسته آمد ببر
(فردوسی)

Abdul Rahman is a symbol of freedom and he risked his life. He characterizes an outstanding and revolutionary hero.

The willpower, decisiveness and stability of such a hero in changing the 1400 years of Islamic beliefs and thoughts in Afghanistan (land of religion or Mazhabestan) where the fundamentalists have changed such a democratic country into a country of mosques, is symbolic and unique. Such a hero not only defeated religious Fascism but also removed the obstacles on the way of freedom. I sincerely congratulate such a brave compatriot and hope that others won't leave him alone in such a long and dangerous journey.

This morning of April 28, 2006, the first day of my retirement, I'm thinking about the character of Abdul Rahman. Based on his research and continuous efforts he changed from arrogant beliefs to believing in freedom. Such a personal choice is his right and the right of all others. But Mullahs and other fundamentalists who brought mosques and this religion to Afghanistan have led society and its perspective towards religious corruption and bribery.

Based on principles of freedom and democracy which are the criteria of a modern civilization, each and every individual has the right to mental and physical freedom and due to these rights, individuals and groups can form different political parties so that we can have a democratic system. In order to overcome such obstacles and be able to catch up with international principles, the United Nations is required to provide proper education and training for certain illiterate parliament members and other figures who are involved in the policymaking of Afghanistan. These policy makers should participate in modern educational courses in order to gain knowledge about the importance of democracy, freedom, civilization, modernity and civics including history, political science and social research. These people should get political, technological and engineering training so that they know how to respect individual and collective rights. Otherwise, Mullahs and politicians will use religion as a tool for stabilizing their stance which may cause major challenges for the founders of the new world order.

During the social revolution in Afghanistan which some people call it Communism, the aforementioned political education was promoted everywhere. Farmers used to deliver speeches at most of the meetings and young people used to lead the crowd. This fact is supported by the existing evidence.

Freedom is the natural right of every indvidual, a condition to express your vision without any restraints or oppression.

In 313 B.C. during the Roman Empire, Constantine gave everyone the freedom to practice all religions and Christianity became the primary religion. Consequently, conflicts were raised in the church which in turn endangered the unity among the Empire because the Household of God had announced Jesus Christ as both God and human. This conception was in contradiction with Arianism, doctrine of Arius 250-336, a bishop in Eskandariah of Egypt. According to this doctrine, Jesus was not God but a creature. In a general meeting, Constantine called the doctrine of Arius, the Christian Egyptian bishop, a heresy. However, there are still differing opinions about the character of Jesus Christ.

Brother! Such old fashioned thinking is not penicillin to cure Bubonic Plague, or food for the hungry or clothing for the poor. Such imaginary stories of priests, Mullahs and others have deprived people of constructive thinking.

I also remember the freedom enjoyed by women in Afghanistan, democratic freedom. Especially during Spring and New Year (Nowruz) they used to cook Samanak (meal made from wheat) and sing and dance 'till sunrise. During spring, some families used to grow wheat in pots and put the pots on the rooftop. The rain provided water and they sprouted. When the plants were 10 cm high, they mashed the grain, added sugar or sugarcane syrup, and boiled it in large pots. In Nowruz, people cook different foods and arrange everything nicely. It is a great pleasure for everyone.

During Nowruz, women used to gather together and cook meals and swing from the trees. Such Nowruz traditions ended by singing and dancing. Men used to watch women from a distance and I can't even remember one time that the women were denied such festivities. However, today, due to the religious fanaticism, women have been deprived of all that freedom and joy. As a matter of fact, people of the past were considered heroes compared to what they are now.

At springtime people, mostly the younger ones, used to play different games. In one traditional game in which a goat is carried by people who are riding horses, even women used to play with men.

In the Andarab village in the north of Afghanistan where I used to live, we had a good looking young neighbor called Sahebjan. He used to play this game with such bravery. One day I went to the rooftop of the house, I saw him fallen down on his horse and unconscious. He was such a good looking, peaceful and polite man. Due to repeated falls from a horse, he was disabled and finally died at a young age. May his soul rest in peace.

During spring and autumn, different games were played like wrestling, throwing stones, baseball, etc. The elders used to pair up youngsters for wrestling. I had to wrestle with Hakim Mola Hafez, who was one of my friends. Hakim beat me and I bit his ear but he didn't show any reaction. I laugh a lot when I remember that moment.

I could see the tears in the eyes of Professor Jamshid Yazd, when he told me that our people had lost their minds due to listening to legends of beasts and fairies. He said that this chronic illness will not go away, unless replaced by dynamic and innovative measures. He put his bag on the ground, took out a sociology book and showed me a few chapters.

The period between the end of the Roman Empire until the 8th century is called the dark medieval ages until the emergence of Renaissance. The West gained a great deal of knowledge and wisdom from this period which totally changed their primitive way of thinking. Unfortunately, we Khorasanis, are still trapped in this nonsense and immaturity. Fear and anxiety are suggestive states of mind which prevented us from daring to seek civilization and be sociable.

The professor attributed the old fashioned thoughts to the imported culture of Arabs. While wiping away tears from his bony cheeks, he said that there was nobody to explain and describe the importance of life, reading and writing, and teach the differences according to old and modern sociology. He added that we needed interdisciplinary methods based on academic foundations.

The conditional discipline which creates special habits is not accountable to different social requirements of students. But different fields such as Social Sciences, Anthropology, Economy, History, Geography, Political Science, Sociology and Social Anthropology could provide students with insight into certain social distinctions in life. Unfortunately, in our country, religion is preferred over teaching Social Sciences or Sociology and this has become the biggest reason behind the psychological poverty of our young men and women. Cause and effect theories should be taught to students to provide them with the necessary knowledge about nature or social circumstances. For example, what is coldness or warmth and the reason behind it. Why did the 1979 revolution occur? How did Ikhvan Al Muslimin come into power? These issues trigger the curiosity of our youth and form their character. They are the future of Afghanistan. Curiosity and imagination are important characteristics which lead mankind towards exploration and advanced science.

Professor Jamshid continued that wisdom is the basic power of mankind. It has enabled humans to conduct research and discover the earth. Mankind could send animals to space and bring them back alive which provided the grounds for sending human beings to space. We are now living in an era of space and rockets. Physics, matter, energy, heat, gravity, magnets, etc. have given mankind the ability to fly. On the other hand, Biology and the Social Sciences have enhanced these facts and facilitated flying (modern transportation). We have observed all such developments.

In discovering the earth and the whole universe and finding out whether there are any living organisms on other planets, large sums of money have been spent and there were human losses as well but it didn't prevent astronomers and engineers from conducting research on stars and other planets. Scientists, such as Archimedes, who invented mechanics and mathematics, James Watt who invented the steam engine, Galileo who invented the telescope, Newton who discovered the movements of the stars, Albert Einstein who discovered atomic energy, and the others who made the life of human beings a lot easier. Thanks go to these scientists who saved us from absurd beliefs and confirmed that "earth moves around the sun, not the sun around the earth."

The insights of Professor Jamshid and his solutions made me understand why he couldn't become the leader of his country. This great pain was burning me inside. Such knowledgeable individuals have been pushed aside by puppet politicians in a corrupt society.

During my visit to Afghanistan in September and October 2004, I found out that erroneous, rubber-stamp statesmanship and misappropriation of peoples' assets made people concerned. People in Kabul were dissatisfied with the aristocratic regime, feudalism, Islamism and Saudi Arabia's mercenaries (those who through the international charities become millionaires). People will welcome the previous socialist regime because they did not become millionaires, landowners and such. This is the highest privilege people could give them. Piety and purity are the characteristics of the Socialists. Those characteristics give them an advantage over the existing regime of Mullahs. Most of the people, including cab drivers, had complained to their statesmen. The latter's incompetency in running the state have made them so fragile that they will break down with the first storm. Their feudalistic-type rule prevented them from working for the interests of their own people.

Jamshid called the puppet regime in Afghanistan a feudal regime ruled by Mullahs. The common interests of these two will be in contradiction with the interests of the nation in the long run. These rulers have no experience in ruling a country and violate peoples' rights. Sooner or later, those who enjoy the very existence of such a regime will understand that they were wrong.

Professor Jamshid, who had great ideas about the development and success of his country, told me that a few of the best university instructors will have a meeting to discuss the future of Afghanistan. If the meeting turned out to be a success, the decisions made in the meeting would be implemented nationally. I told the professor that I understood his ideas but did not understand what he meant by national implementation. He explained that they wanted to organize people into groups and distribute newspapers widely and hoped that it would have positive results. He believed that solidarity among instructors and students could enhance political victory.

In reply, I told the professor that the political system of Afghanistan was based on democracy and asked him if he wanted to compromise that. His answer was negative. I asked him to elaborate his stance. So he explained that Afghanistan was not a democratic country since the system was based on cheating, gerrymandering, nepotism, sectarian ideas, and not liberalism.

Basically, prior to establishing democracy in a new chaotic society, the ideology and its importance should be conveyed to people through various video and audio means so that they could understand the values of establishing a democracy. However, the government did not successfully implement the system. The news was broadcast on Radio and Television using Arabic in order to create a type of pessimism in peoples' minds. Phrases were written in beautiful Arabic transcripts and were hung everywhere by Mullahs in government offices and a few cowards who worship foreign cultures, rather than their own, were ashamed to show some of the historic scenes of Afghanistan, which not only are considered as fine arts but also indicate the maturity, competence, elegance, dignity and pride of our ancestors.

Professor Jamshid continued, saying that adding Islamic to the name of Afghanistan in the Constitution was proposed by Hamid Karzai. This suggestion was totally in contradiction with the essence of democracy. Such a great betrayal was unique in the history of Afghanistan. He had unwisely denied the high level of understanding of our compatriots.

If Mr. Hamid Karzai would want to explain the above, he should come forward and state that in a magazine, committee, assembly, newspaper, radio, television and other media he had referred to the system (not Islamic system) of his country. We believe that he is not brave enough to make such a statement in an environment of terror and fear.

We are not an Arab country. Arab traditions have been imposed by the force of terror and fascism.

The fascism was a bundle of rods strapped together around an axe, and it represented the unbreakable power of the state.

The Islamic system doesn't exist in any Arab country which has exported Islam to other countries. There is no indication of such a system in Islamic history.

Implementation of democracy in Afghanistan came at a great cost; however, Washington was the loser in developing a democratic political system in Afghanistan not realizing the fact that giving the Islamic title to a country like Afghanistan could only help the fundamentalists in and out of the country. As a matter of fact, such a decision would result in blocking any scientific development in the modern era in all dimensions and aspects and prevent society from having a decent life.

Catherine the Great, 1729-1796, brought intellectual ideas from Europe to Russia. She nationalized church assets, utilized freeloader bishops and closed monasteries. The Russians call Catherine's period of reform a tumultuous era in Russia. As a result of her efforts, Russia was able to gain access to the waterways of the Black Sea through the Caucasians.

Voltaire, 1694-1778, the French philosopher who promoted Catherine in Europe, had stated that, unfortunately, there are insane people who blame Catherine for what she did for the church, whereas this brave woman loved Russia, rebuilt and changed a very backward country into a civilized European one.

I, the author, used to study in Russia. During a visit arranged by the Kiev Agricultural Academy in Ukraine in 1964 or 1965, we went on an air tour of the Republics of Latvia and Estonia and the cities of Leningrad and Moscow. I appreciate their offer of arranging such a tour, because otherwise it was financially impossible for the students to visit all those cities. The instructors took us on a tour of the Leningrad Agricultural Academy. Wonderful students of the Academy gave each and every one of us a flower bouquet. I grabbed the girl who welcomed me and asked her out for dinner. However, she got rid of me with a smile.

We visited Hermitage Palace and the Summer Palace of Peter the Great which was 20 miles from St. Petersburg. We traveled through the Gulf of Finland and the Neva River. Paintings, golden statues, waterfalls and several rooms in the Palace built during the period of Peter the Great and Catherine the Great are amazing. Reactions are similar upon seeing the paintings in the Hermitage Palace. Looking at them you feel that you are in another world. The Russians should feel pride in Catherine's era.

Many ignorant people have limited attitudes and bind themselves to old beliefs, resisting any new ideas. During the 1996 elections in Moscow, a Russian woman told Michael Gorbachev, "get lost (Judas), you sold the country." One professor stated that simply because Gorbachev wanted to change the feudal Russia into a modern, civilized society, many people opposed his reconstruction policies.

Professor Jamshid quoted Auguste Comte, 1798-1857, French philosopher of the 19th century, on the social life issue as saying that "the greatest service is to privilege the progress of mankind and building a rational society." His doctrine was Positivism, which uses science to understand phenomena. His research in other sciences was of great value to human society.

Sociology is a young science, compared to other modern sciences such as Economics, History, Law, Political Science and Ethics which I call competencies; however, they have influence on other fields.

The professor said that there were different races living in our country. Some could easily learn good habits but some not. Scientists have attributed this to Anthropogeography and to factors such as climate change, conditions of the earth and accessibility of natural resources. Willpower, patience, knowledge and techniques used by a ruler are necessary to change the cultures and patterns of peoples' lives to which they have adapted themselves for several years. The professionalism of social workers who could teach people new and decent ways of life shouldn't be ignored.

The professor said that all the above factors are effective in changing people's culture. However, sociologists have considered the use of an iron fist in certain cases in order to introduce new ways. Implementing a new economic and political system in a society whose people are used to the old system is not easy. Therefore, the Ministry of Education and other behavioral institutions are responsible for providing practical education in Sociology and the Social Sciences, Anthropology, Economics, History, Geography,

Political Science, Psychology and Biology for students, grade 6 and up. Government officers should take new courses and be given the opportunity to express their ideas for improving peoples' lives freely and without any fear and if they prove to be competent, they deserve to get a promotion.

In order to expedite this process, academic tours should be arranged and students should be exposed to mass media (radio, television, and news) and other educational materials. This is necessary in order to establish a democratic system.

Technological discoveries which are the result of unending endeavors of mankind, plays an important role in bringing change and development in all social aspects.

Professor Jamshid said that if we were unable to use our physical and mental power for improving the lives of disabled and hopeless people, then we would be held in the lowest esteem by history. Within the framework of education, teachers should be resourceful. Teachers and students should have access to libraries and laboratories in connection with different research projects. For better education and training, students should be sent to Europe and America, as well as to India, China, Turkey and Middle Asia which are not narrow-minded and attach great importance to technology.

An American scholar "Horace Mann" once said that an apple is not an apple in any proper sense until it is ripe, so a human being is not a human being in any proper sense until he is educated.

توانا بود هر که دانا بود   زدانش دل پیر برنا بود
(فردوسی)

زبان خود فروشم هزار گوش خرم   که رفت بر سر منبر خطیب شهد کلام
(مولوی)

111

I was the Director of the Agricultural Department of Badakhshan Province during the period of 1972-1977. It came to my mind to write a few paragraphs about the importance of tourism. I knew that there was a country whose people used to earn their living through tourism. I called the principal of Faizabad school and asked him if there was a Republic called Honduras (in Europe) with tourism attractions? He answered in the positive. A few years later, while abroad, I found out that there were two republics. One was Honduras in northeast Central America and the other was Andorra in the east Pyrenees between France and Spain, which is the only place in the world that earns its income from the tourism industry and has a population of 19,000. I don't want to find fault with the principal of the Faizabad school, since locating these two tiny republics in two different continents was not an easy task in a place like Faizabad in which there was no library, resource books, or atlas at the time. Andorra is located in an area of 191 square miles and its capital is Andorra La Vella. Honduras is located in an area of 43,277 square miles and its capital is Tegucigalpa.

Involving students in discussions about evolution and the beginning of life will not only cause them to gain knowledge and experience but also paves the way for them to express their ideas.

In 1668 the Italian biologist, Francesco Redi, (1626-1697), proved that worms didn't grow spontaneously but came from fly eggs (larvae). For 100 years scientists used to believe that big creatures originated from the old ones. Pasteur, the French scientist, stated that organisms didn't emerge spontaneously but they emerged from the old species. However the question "how did such organisms come to exist on earth? " Maybe from other planets". Other scientists don't much believe in Panspermia (the hypothesis that life on Earth originated from microorganism from outer space) due to probable killing of organisms such as algae, fungi, ferns, moss by radiation before arrival on earth.

The point is that all of these discussions between students and instructors will encourage more discoveries. Furthermore, such artistic and scientific achievements help humans to rationalize better. Such discussions motivate those who have the least spiritual power to think better.

During the 1970's, I was the Director of the Agricultural Department of Badakhshan Province. At that time they were working on a project called Rico Rice and the Agriculture Minister did not give us any information about this project due to certain considerations. So, we didn't know which organization was supervising the project.

Our country is mostly desert and, due to bad climate, there is not much greenery except for a few Rico Rices and even those few plants are cut and destroyed, as the government ignores the fact that forests and greenery are crucial for the environment. It was amazing that a Minister couldn't distinguish between good and bad when it came to the interests of the state.

It was so unfortunate that they cut the plants and left the big holes uncovered. The other day, a farmer came to me and complained that his cow had broken his leg after falling in one of those holes. It was a pity. I had the governor general, Taj Mohammad, write a letter and send it to the Ministry of Agriculture to stop exploitation of Rico Rice in Badakhshan Province. Due to my letter, the project was suspended throughout Afghanistan and the Ministry of Agriculture gave me a bonus in appreciation. Only two weeks later, I received a letter that the project was resumed. I went to the Ministry of Agriculture for some other business when the Head of the Forestry Department and National parkings Engineer, Anam, told me that although they appreciated my efforts, the Minister had changed his mind. While we were talking, Dr. Anwar Afghan, who was standing nearby, called me to say that I was about to destroy a USD 300 million project.

Conservation of Natural Resources

Proper utilization of natural resources (water, soil, wildlife, forests and minerals) and their conservation is very important. Forests and greenery preserve water in the soil and prevent erosion. Whereas those people who don't know anything about agriculture, damage ecology and social life. This is why planting trees and conservation of forests are so important. Preservation of water, accumulated from rain and snow through construction of dams, a technique used in the past and present, will not only prevent flood and erosion but also adds to the source of underground waters. However, it should be noted that soils are always exposed to the "silent thief"; natural storms always wash away the precious top soil. Protecting the environment results in more greenery and water preservation, conservation of wild life and national parks which are so important for our very social and economic existence, as well as for excursions. Rills, which are formed after rain or snow, turn into gullies and wash away top soil and sub soil which contain humus (organic substances).

A piece of land was divided into two parts, on one part they planted grass and on the other, only seeds. The land with grass was washed away by 7 inches in 34,000 years, while the soil in the one with seeds was washed away by 7 inches in only 11 years. Therefore, increasing the amount of greenery and forests could prevent the soil with humus being washed away. I recommend that officials of the Ministry of Agriculture take note of this important fact and form a workshop within the Ministry. I also recommend that Dr. Mohammad Anwar Afghan stop exploiting Rico Rice? since they have deep roots in the ground and prevent erosion. Selling the soil, in this way, and exploiting plants are a kind of robbery and should be stopped.

I was called to Headquarters by telegram. In order to find out why, I went to the office of Mr. Ghofran. He told me that the Minister opposed my remaining in office. After that, one of my connections told me that the Minister had stated that since I am from the northern parts of Uzbek, Tajik or Hezarah, I could not remain in office. Now you can see the judgment of a stupid Minister and how they played with peoples' faith based on discrimination.

Tribalistic sovereignty enables rulers to force their ideas onto inferiors. Such an invidious policy of tribalism and racial discrimination made foreign countries reluctant to carry out projects on Helmand's salty lands and Nangarhar's sandy region.

Hey Minister, during the nationalist movement in 1800 in Europe they tried to distinguish between languages and cultures within a specified political territory but failed. For example, in Belgium there are two equal language groups called Walloons (French) and Flemish (Dutch). As a result of the two World Wars, Turkish was added to the language of West Germany. On the other hand, Europeans speak two languages. Whereas you, as the Minister, preferred a language which is inferior to others. Such an attitude reflects your knowledge, insight and cultural position. Such Ministers who give privilege to meanness, lack of principles and immaturity, are not only doomed in history but are also doomed to the oppressed people of Khorasan.

I should point out that during the years of office of this Minister; I didn't come across him even once. Whereas a Minister at the head of such an important Ministry should be informed about officers in his Ministry. This idea is supported by the fact that in Afghanistan there were not so many activities in manufacturing and production sector which could make a Minister so busy as not to have contacts with his inferiors. This was an indication of his being indifferent towards what was going on in the Ministry.

After a long waiting period, the Minister appointed me to the poorest and most underprivileged province of Bamyan. Within less than a year, the regime was changed and Noor Mohammad Taraki became President. Since another country was added to the Communist Block, the west, the world of Islam, especially Saudi Arabia, became very agitated. On the other hand, the immaturity of the revolutionary youth made me have doubts about the stability of the new regime. Unrest was expanding and people were armed, due to the interference of foreign countries, which, in turn, caused a lot of concern.

The Ministry of Agriculture called all the provincial directors to a one-week seminar in Kabul. All the directors were members of the party except for myself and Doost Mohammad Zarmati. At the end of the seminar, tables were set on the lawn outside the Soil and Water laboratory. The Minister, Saleh Mohammad Ziri, wanted to evaluate the directors. He called every director separately and asked questions. When Doost Mohammad returned, I asked him about the questions. He replied that he was asked about party membership. I asked him what did he reply.

He had responded that he had already applied for the membership. It was my turn. Before asking any questions by the Minister, Deputy Minister, Abdul Ahad Sarsam, told the Minister that Nawaby was my classmate and that we two knew each other very well. He also said that I was a benign person.

The Minister said that Nawaby had remained Director of Agricultural Department of Bamyan for that long because of his characteristics. On the other hand, Hassan Peyman, Director of Plant Conservation recommended me and added that they should look up to me. The Minister asked me if I was a party member. I said that I was amongst the 98%. He asked how? I said that the great leader, Taraki had stated that 98% of people supported him. The Director of the Forestry Department was a recent graduate from the Faculty of Agriculture and I suppose that he was from Harat. He asked me how was it possible that I had studied in the Soviet Union but had not become a party member.

Ziri told him that it was not necessary for everyone studying in the Soviet Union to be a party member.

Brother! If I had a seventh sense at that time and knew that those people could turn into Mujahideen and ransack the peoples' assets, commit so many crimes, force people to migrate, nail peoples' heads, pronounce human flesh and blood as Halal, fill up their saddlebags with the ears of innocent peoples being cut, blow up statues in Bamyan, ruin the beautiful and developed city of Kabul and sell my free country to the imperialists of <u>the Saudi Arabia, for sure I would have became party member, grabbed a gun and fought for my country.</u>

It is quite amazing that the unique statues of Bamyan were totally destroyed and there is no talk about rebuilding them in any book or national and foreign news. And not even talk about the identity of those who committed such a historical crime.

Currently, during the so-called democratic regime which claims social justice, I don't have any official post. In other words, they replaced me without any formal written letter or telegraph. As a result, until after Hafizullah Amin was gone, I didn't hold any official post. In order to find out if they were going to give me any post or not, I went to see Mr. Noorudin, General Director of Administration, who was my classmate in the College of Agriculture. He promised to appoint me to some post but for some reason unknown to me, he did not do so. I thought there must have been some conspiracy involved. The other day I was passing by the room of the Deputy Minister when Abdul Ahad Sarsam came out of his room. He asked me to see him in his office. We entered his office. He joked with me and said that my uncle, Abdul Ghafoor, was the king's general. He was conveying the notion that I belonged to the upper class. I replied that General Abdul Ghafoor was the King's henchman but not me. Sarsam laughed. He brought up another issue and said that I had stated that Russians lived a bad life. I told him a white lie. I said yes, I had said that Russians had a bad life before the October revolution. Anyway, he did not accept my words but told me there was a vacancy at the Agricultural Department of Jalal Abad. I told him that I had to consult my family and let him know afterwards. He added that the party was very powerful there and warned me not to get myself killed.

Later I informed him that I wanted to go to Jalal Abad. I saw that someone was erasing the mottos of the Taraki era and replacing them with the mottos of Amin. I was surprised, since Sarsam had focused a lot on those mottos. I told him that I wanted to discuss something with him later.

The same day I saw Aminullah, former director of Jalal Abad's Agricultural Department. We used to be classmates. He called me and, in a whispering voice, asked me if anything bad had happened at the Presidential palace. I told him what I had seen at Sarsam's office. He said that Taraki had been killed.

At the end of a seminar, Saleh Mohammad (Ziri), Minister of Agriculture, brought the Directors of the Agricultural Departments of Provinces to Hafizullah Amin, the Foreign Minister, who served as the Deputy Prime Minister as well. We were waiting for Amin, Deputy Prime Minister and, after a while, he entered the room. He seemed to be very happy, confident and powerful.

He launched into his revolutionary speech with a smile on his face. He said that our farming in traditional way is counter productive, farmers and landowners need to have access to modern techniques. He told us that we, as educated directors with the technical knowledge, should assist the farmers in developing their skills and increasing agricultural productions. All of us applauded. He asked the Minister of Agriculture if all the directors were party members and the reply was yes, even those who were not members had applauded.

Amin was in a hurry to join President Noor Mohammad Taraki, his loyal instructor, who was suffocated a few months later by him. Amin was an educated, handsome and brave man but he was a cruel person and a dictator. On his way up the power ladder he didn't have mercy on anyone.

Like Denis Diderot, 1713-1787, Amin used to make fun of religion. He was so angry about the religious Romanticism revolution in Europe which put an end to the Transcendentalist movement of intellectualism in the 17th and 18th centuries which was based on Kant's Theory of Intuition. He preferred Marxism to all other ideologies. One of his ministers at the time stated that they had taken the revenge of the Chilean people from the people of Afghanistan - a hollow and irrelevant statement which left me bewildered as to its meaning and purpose.

Other ideologies, in the name of Islam had done much more worse than Marxism. For example, a coward from the Islamic Party in Kuata of Pakistan, killed Ms. Meena, a great hero and founder of Rawa Party, on February 14, 1987; or the Marxist revolution of Salvador Allende in 1970 which was silenced by the bloody coup of General Augusto Pinochet in 1973.

Hafizullah Amin raised the question, "who founded the religion and why?" He believed that during those periods, when there was no state nor statesmen, wild, uncivilized, powerful humans used to act more wildly and more powerfully than modern humans. In order to survive, they killed others and took their possessions. This type of arrogant behavior resulted in weak and powerless humans being killed. He believed that only Marxism could control such savagery and arrogance in society.

As a matter of fact, those people who felt responsible and, in order to avert injustice, unrest, mistreatment, killings and bloodshed which had become a usual practice, formed their own group and took God as their commander. This way they could threaten criminals. Their idea lacked any scientific basis, and, in the course of time, turned into a powerful force. Even nowadays, and in an era of enlightenment, we still suffer the consequences. He added that societies suffered more when the clergy and the Mullahs took over in the name of religion.

The Enlightenment era of the 17th and 18th centuries and the ideas of the modern scholars who claimed the failure of religion, frightened the religionists. Their rivals stabbed them (their minds and thoughts) unknowingly, meaning that they insisted on logic and reason.

As one philosopher, Ralph Waldo Emerson, 1803-1882 stated," In the end, nothing is sacred but the integrity of your mind." He once said God is in every man. He believed that great truths come from intuition.

Religious fundamentalists claim that the Enlightenment era of the 17th and 18th centuries in Europe was not an organized movement. However, their suggestion doesn't seem very reasonable since at the time of the emergence of the Enlightenment, Europe was a religious center and those who supported the Enlightenment were in the minority. One should acknowledge that compared to writing and telling myths, formulating a scientific equation is not an easy task, it requires experimentation, reasoning and logic which are neither easy to understand nor low in value.

There were and still are many religious God seekers who couldn't perceive God through Mysticism and Meditation and finally gave up. As Mowlana Jalaludin Rumi, the greatest Islamic philosopher put it:

از کفر و ز اسلام برون صحرائیست
ما را بمیان آن فضا سودائیست
عارف چو بدان رسید سر را بنهد
نه کفر نه اسلام نه آنجا جائیست

There is a world in which there is neither heresy nor Islam
It is our heartfelt desire to get there
Once a mystic attains it, he'll obey
There is no place for heresy or Islam

Theosophy which is religious philosophy and coordinated with Mysticism, indicates that past all we can see in this world, there is a spiritual reality which could be called God. However, others don't consider this idea to be supported by logic.

Hojatoleslam (Hamid Ghazali), one of the most credible Islamic jurisprudents, one Muslims are very proud of, couldn't perceive God and his poems below attest to what we stated above.

ما جامه نمازی بسر خم کردیم   وز خاک خرابات تیمم کردیم
شاید که در این میکده ها دریابیم   ان عمر که در مدرسه ها گم کردیم
(امام حامد غزالی)

> I throw the praying mat on the jar of wine
> I got ablution with the dirt of tavern
> Maybe we find the truth in the tavern
> For all the life we wasted in the theological schools

Avicenna, Omar Khayyam, Naser Khosrow, Mohammad bin Zakaria Razi, 529-568 who revived the works of Greek physician, Galen Claudius, 130-200, Ferdowsi, Walid bin Yazed, Ommayyad Caliph all ascertained the above statement.

It's so unfortunate that religionists follow Transcendental Meditation after a Hindi Yogi called Maharishi Mahesh, who resides in a temple free of charge, without paying any rent or mortgage! This yogi is very important in marketing and business in the U.S. compared to the Enlightenment era in the 17th and 18th centuries in Europe. Yogo is considered to be an interesting, but not yet proven therapy mode. The fundamentalist Arab and Ajam Imams (Islamic comintern) are leading a hot market in the US not knowing the fact that their invidious propaganda is in the favor of Al Qaida not the US.

It was because of religion that our country, Afghanistan was worn down by the feckless Islamic parties (Arab Corps), led and supported by foreigners to protect imported Islam, not to protect freedom and other achievements.

Marxists believe that religion has failed to be at the service of the economic and social structures of society but have also produced this type of political associations which are a detriment to society. As a matter of fact, they have tried to restrict their influence which resulted in isolating Ikhvan and its leaders during the presidency of Mohammad Davood in Afghanistan.

But the foreign rivals in this big game were thinking of something else, like internal war in Afghanistan. They planned to hire local devotees (Afghans) and foreign Muslims like rabble, bandits, killers and homeless Arabs in order to form a religious movement and achieve their goals. Obviously, they have spent a lot of money purchasing artillery, including different kinds of missiles. Millions of dollars have been spent to pay mercenaries who have been their loyal servants.

By the collapse of the Marxist regime in Afghanistan and the Soviet Union in 1990, the United States was happy to see everything ended up in its favor. The U.S. was certainly unaware of the characteristics of Ikhvan al Muslimin, because if they knew the reality, they wouldn't have provided them with military training in order to overthrow the Marxist regime of Kabul.

Amin was a Marxist, not a democrat. In order to be a leader one should have good background. Amin favored racism and was a triumphant atheist. Some believe that such characteristics of Amin had given him privilege over other dictators of the 20th century, namely (Khomeini, Idi Amin, Golbudin Hekmatyar, Omar, Osama bin Laden, who prefer theocracy over democracy).

Some may think that Atheism is one of the major components of Communism. The communist countries of Europe: Euro communism Italy, Spain, France, along with Japan, Australia and Venezuela had a common procedure, and had established Socialism through legitimate policy making and free elections, but denied Atheism, one of the components of Communism. Atheos is a Greek word, which means without God. It comes from the works of Epicurus, 341-270 B.C., and his followers.

Epicureanism is pure advocacy, which deals with pleasure and tranquility. Being free from mental and physical anxiety and living a pleasant life. They used to call Epicurus the advocate for moral reasoning. His philosophy is more or less similar to Rumi's philosophy of life.

Such an unlikely event among the peoples' democratic party which caused its internal and external opponents to rejoice, was a hard slap in the face of Russian politicians. This means that such a deadly movement would harm the foundations of a political party not in the Russians' favor, the Peoples' Democratic party; and harm the Afghan people, except for the engineers of the big party who had gathered around the big playing table, using the capitals of Saudi Arabia, the best weapon of the Western Imperialists, to sharpen the double-sided blade of Ikhvan Al Muslimin.

Dr. Najib, President of Afghanistan, who was well informed about the ill will of local and foreign opponents, had warned people not to follow those impostors, but, rather, to protect the physical, spiritual and artistic achievements which would otherwise be destroyed by Ikhvan Al Muslimin. He warned that Ikhvan Al Muslimin would torture and kill our women, sisters, daughters and mothers in their damned, dark jails.

He added that many of our people were killed due to the arbitrariness of others, which was totally unnecessary and there shouldn't be any more bloodshed. He called on all the compatriots living in and outside the country to unite against universal regression.

Najib had invested a lot in the people beyond Afghanistan's borders in order to attract their support but failed. Whereas the English agent "Lawrence of Arabia" had learned the Pashto language and played according to the policies of the big game which finally resulted in overthrowing "King Amanullah".

I call upon all university students nationwide to use their knowledge towards the reconstruction of the people's culture, especially near the southeast borders which are the main source of cultural backwardness. Upon completion of studies at the universities, in their thesis, students should discuss the facts on social, economic and political reconstruction and the way to lead a modern life.

I was thinking about the philosophy of Professor Jamshid Yazd. He stated that wars, especially religious wars, were due to satanic ideas. Consider the land of Khorasanis, empty handed and poor Mullahs had betrayed their country in lieu of money.

اگر میبود حفظ او حصار عصمت ادم
نبودي رخنه آمد شدن وسواس شیطان را
(وحشی بافقی)

If God was dominant in everything then Satan could never deceive mankind.

Chapter Four

ISLAM WAS IMPOSED UPON US

The revolutionary Jamshid supported the French Revolution in 1789 when the government nationalized church assets and clergy, who had initially supported the revolution, backed off. It was decided that certain clergies should take oaths. As a result, low ranking ones stopped cooperating with the government. There were only four of them who took oaths in support of the government. One of the famous mottos of the French revolutionaries was elimination of privileges. They were willing to ignore their political freedom in favor of liberation, especially while Napoleon was the leader of the revolution.

Jamshid continued that if the vile clergy didn't want to support freedom and liberalism, the "raison d'être" of the government, then they would have lost the government's support in return.

I was in deep thought about the ideas of Jamshid Yazd, when I heard people yelling that the Mullah regime in Afghanistan had been overthrown and the new leader was called Jamshid. But which Jamshid, I wondered. Within a week, the news came out on TV, radio and newspapers, that the new leader was Jamshid Yazd. I told myself that it must be the same Professor Jamshid who had become the leader of Afghanistan due to his knowledge, competence and insight. When we had taken leave of each other, Jamshid said we'll see, we'll see what will come next.

I went out of the house, sometimes looking up at the sky, sometimes looking down and pressing my forehead with the fingers of my right hand. One of my sons was concerned so he came to me and asked if I was out of my mind? I told him not to worry and that I had to go to Kabul. He interrupted me and asked if it was because of the change of regime there, since I had always been complaining about the incompetence and lack of ability of the latter. He added that maybe the new leader, Jamshid, elected by the people, would be a good choice. My son added that social unrest and disturbances seemed constant. Khorasan was disturbed by evil Mullahs and the followers of Saudi Mullahs, while in other parts of the world, natural disasters incurred so much damage to the inhabitants and their cities.

In Indonesia, the tsunami claimed the lives of thousands of people just like Katrina did in New Orleans or what happened in Arizona in 2005. I cried as I saw the tragic scenes on TV when Arab terrorists exploded the beautiful towers in New York in September, 2001 and those who didn't want to be burned in the fire of (Arabic hell) threw themselves from the 90th story and higher. Unfortunately, there are people who still don't believe such a heinous crime has been committed by terrorists. A typical gesture for some politicians when they can't take it anymore is to hit on the table with their boots or say Satan the great, evil empire, etc.

The hostage crisis in a school in Beslan, September, 2004 in Russia by the Chechen terrorists resulted in the massacre of 331 people, mostly children. It was the most disgraceful event took place in the 21st century. I couldn't lend them even a penny, due to my impoverishment, but only offered my sympathy for their sorrow. I'm a human being and have more sympathy for the misfortunes of people than some coldhearted fundamentalist terrorists.

Jamshid Yazd was shocked by the arrogance of such terrorists. Eric Hoffer, 1902 -1983 called them the plague of society. Jamshid promised that upon his success in the campaign, his first priority would be to enlighten the younger generation who misleadingly have been engaged in the religious fighting. After considering the capabilities of Professor Jamshid, a true compatriot, I was convinced he would be able to make improvements in a backward society, and so decided to pay him a visit. One day before my departure for Kabul, they announced Afghanistan as the Republic of Khorasan.

My kids provided a ticket and helped me board the plane to Kabul. On board, I was thinking about so many things. In a country with a 30-year long imposed war, bringing people back to civilization could be an important commission. The Lufthansa plane landed in Khaje Ravash Airport. Light rain was falling, which I took as auspicious sign of flourishing greenery and productivity of the Khorasan Republic. Families and friends welcomed me at the arrival gate.

The following day, I went to visit President Jamshid Yazd at the Taj Beig Palace. Mujahideen, these predators, had left only a skeleton of the Darulaman and Taj Beig Palace. Anyway, the young guards had discipline. They welcomed me and asked about my business. I showed them my ID and told them that I had a meeting with the President. The guard gave my ID to his superior who greeted me and walked with me, on his peg leg, to the waiting room. He offered me some refreshments.

After about a half hour, someone came and took me to see Professor Yazd. I was surprised why he didn't use the word President and only used Yazd. In any case, I proceeded towards his office. He was standing in front of his office and I recognized him 15 m away. Yes, truly, it was Professor Jamshid Yazd. We hugged and I congratulated him on his victory. I asked him how did he win? He replied that it was a long story and he would talk about it later. But now it was time to name this victory, era of Enlightenment which occurred in 17th and 18th centuries in Europe. I told him that was a good suggestion but the Enlightenment was not really victorious in Europe. Jamshid Yazd interrupted me and said that the churches and skeptics like

David Hume and Immanuel Kant played an important role in the failure of the Enlightenment.

Hume believed that repetition leads us to renew that act without being driven by any reasoning or process of understanding. Reason has no role in willpower, emotions, desires or appetite. Reason cannot describe nor control such behaviors. Reason is the basis or motivation for an action or a decision. Most philosophers then concluded that reason cannot explain the complex nature of humans and historical dilemmas. Notwithstanding, the ideas that founded the Enlightenment failed due to the above considerations.

They tried to explain why religions were created by humans. The only Enlightenment movement which totally changed the European culture is still somewhat alive. Catherine the Great brought the ideas of social revolution to Russia and changed the backward country to one of Europe's most civilized and powerful centers. Voltaire, the French writer, spread her fame all over Europe and worldwide. "This world is only a mass of molecules" wrote Denis Diderot 1713-1784.

Francis Bacon, Rene Descartes, Copernicus, Galileo, Gottfried Leibniz, Spinoza Baruch and Thomas Paine were the revolutionary leaders of the Enlightenment. Most important of all was Isaac Newton who explained the universe and justified the rationality of nature. He denied the empiricism of David Hume, which stated that the senses were at the origin of science. The same way that religionists relate science and spirits to ideas, Newton said that the universe could be understood by active reasoning and discovery of science was possible through the observation of matter. A great example of this could be Galileo's discovery concerning the rotation of the earth around the sun and that the sun is stable, but the clergy didn't believe it.

President Jamshid Yazd added that the Enlightenment occurred in the 17th and 18th centuries, but I'm talking about the 21st century and not the era of Romanticism, the religious revolution against science. There was a time when people died due to simple illness and Mullahs were against any medical care and opposed physicians but scientists never backed off because of stubborn Mullahs and other bishops. It was due to the constant efforts of physicians and scientists that societies were able to find their way towards success. Microbes couldn't be seen by simple microscopes even 10 years ago, but the new and powerful microscopes of today make this task possible. Scientists who denied those ideas lived in an era when it was commonly believed that the sun revolved around the earth.

Jamshid Yazd stated that the Enlightenment failed in Europe because it was composed of totally religious states. Kant, Hume and other skeptics did not consider the ideological power of the two sides. But Catherine the Great used Enlightenment privilege in Europe and applied it in Russia, which, in turn, changed the country into a civilized European one. She dragged the clergy from their churches and employed them at government offices.

Another example is Afghanistan. Secularism failed there because of a religious majority although the former regimes used to be secular. The Great Abdulrahman didn't know about Enlightenment but used to rule the country and did not let religious groups interfere. He cut off the head of one of the famous Mullahs called Moshk Alam with a sword.

However, in the Enlightenment era, in spite of criticism from the religionists, they could develop their scientific realm and introduce new concepts in politics, law, economics and history.

David Quammen has supported Darwin's Theory of Evolution. Quammen states that scientists have provided us with techniques, which were not so popular during Darwin's time. These techniques have helped us learn more about creatures based on the Theory of Evolution.

The Renaissance in 15th century Western Europe influenced western culture in conjunction with the Enlightenment era of the 17th and 18th centuries.

The President had formed different committees upon the request of so many people in order to change the concept of the younger generation who were out of their mind due to constant indoctrination by the Mullahs. I asked Jamshid Yazd why he stayed in such a ruined palace. He replied because it was one of the prides of the Great Amanullah, a hero who granted freedom to women. He admired each and every brick, which he believed retained a smell of "Amani" (referring to King Amanullah).

Jamshid turned to me and said that democracy was a good thing but we had lost it several times due to certain considerations. "Social Development" caused democracy to be implemented for the third time in Afghanistan but, due to incapable statesmen on one hand, and its clash with Western interests, on the other, we lost it.

Trying to protect their interests, foreign enemies resorted to Islam and by pretending that Islam was endangered indirectly, asked for the support of Muslims. By doing this, Islam became more violent. Applying wrong policies and superficiality turned people into enemies. We witnessed such huge losses in life and finances worldwide but the Americans realized this political threat too late; that Islamic fundamentalists, especially Arabs, are the true enemies of civilization and democracy. However, the US is trying to reestablish democracy in Khorasan. President Jamshid pointed out the fact that establishing democracy in backward countries would be a threat for feudalism, tribalism and religion and therefore will be rejected by the squirearchy. Could Hamid Karzai, who was brought up in such a religious environment, be able to establish democracy in his country?

As a matter of fact, we decided to take necessary action before it's too late. If you remember, I once said that we should establish a political campaign and that notion was expedited by the untimely death of my son, Parviz Yazd, who was killed as a result of falling from the roof of a mosque. The president said that the process of undergoing fatalities or injuries in order to gain freedom and keep it is much more valuable than the process of losing freedom and regaining it. Isn't establishing a less violent dictatorship in an era of suppression in order to protect democracy a valuable undertaking?

Jamshid Yazd recalled the five fundamentals (pillars) of Islam as an example of constant dictatorship imposed on the captive individuals and during the past 1400 years no one could merge the five fundamentals (pillars) into one.

The survival of democracy depends on the motivations and spirits of capable, reputable and dedicated instructors and the younger generation (girls and boys) nationwide. Afghanistan requires generosity and heroic scholars in order to flourish. Democracy evolves slowly, affected by constant developments and it's necessary to take informed steps in due course, even to the point of applying some obligatory steps, if required, due to the fact that the politicians may disagree with the process. It is hard to digest this bitter reality due to its economic, social, political and artistic values, especially for those opportunists who would otherwise lose their unlawful privileges.

In order to establish freedom in our country, financial aid and valuable advice from all the compatriots are necessary.

President Yazd designated the political system of the country to be a Republic (of Khorasan). He quoted scholars who said that religion could never make a tribe proud but whats important is knowledge, enlightenment and art. He added that there was no place for religion and religious symbols in the government.

Mr. Yazd accused Nadir Shah, and he red a few sentences from the book of Afghanistan written by Martin Ewans "He annulled all Amanullah's secular legislation and confirmed the Habibullah's enforcement of Islamic law through religious court. He also endorsed the latter's cancellation of all of Amanullah's more liberal social measures, including those governing women's rights. He reintroduced purdah and enforced the wearing of chadari".

In order to get more information and give advice, Jamshid Yazd then referred me to the head of committees "Sohrab Rostami". He was an old but powerful wise man with long white hair and a prominent mustache which looked so amazing. Works of famous philosophers were all over his desk and this indicated his deep knowledge. Photos of Shah Amanullah, Mahatma Gandhi, Dr. Mosadegh, Jamal Abdul Naser, Albert Einstein and Mustafa Kemal Ataturk, Samiteru a Japani, victim who, says "My Burning Back" were hung on his office walls. A small framed photo of Karl Marx was on the left side of his computer. A table of social reforms prepared in nice colors was on the wall behind him. In the first table it was written:

1. Opening Diplomatic Missions between Israel and Khorasan. Rostami said that unfortunately, Non-Arab Muslim countries have become enemies of the nation of the first Prophet, Moses. This was the result of poisonous propaganda of Arab countries and he stated that we should break this taboo. He added that Einstein was a Jew and also a genius. In his relativity theory of mass and energy, he shows that a small particle of matter is the equivalent of an enormous quantity of energy. According to the scientists, television and other inventions are practical applications of Einstein's discoveries.

2. Wartime compensation with regards to the imposed war. I was curious about this phrase. I told Mr. Rostami that the 25-year-old war had caused much physical and mental damage but who can we ask for compensation? He smiled and elaborated that he didn't mean the quarter-century-old wars but he was referring to the wars of 1400 years ago during which Arabs ransacked physical and spiritual achievements, massacred the people and imposed their imaginary ideas on the Khorasani people. He said that we had to confront the Arab Peninsula which is now called Saudi Arabia.

3. Lawful Religious freedom. I asked Rostami, in a country which is full of ignorant people, is it wise to act like that? While covering his head with both hands, he sighed and remained silent. His secretary put a glass of water on his desk. With his eyes full of tears Rostami told me that religion had become dysfunctional in Afghanistan, but Christians had revived it without thinking about the consequences.

4. Feminist Movements: This is the most significant step forward because in the course of history, our women did not have fewer legal rights. In the 20th century, the reverent king Amanullah offered them equal rights but the British imperialism on the grounds of political considerations helped the mullahs to overthrow the kingdom and our women lost their freedom. During the era of the late Mohammad Dawood, the women freedom movement flourished again. But in a sudden and violent political disruption, the whole world (because of their self-interests) backed the Mullahs. Consequently, the Mullahs succeeded and they applied the Sharia Laws which resulted in our women losing their freedom for the second time. Now regardless: "The ideas of muscularity, intellectuality, customary laws or other disturbing attitudes toward women should cause the feminist movement to be revived again" said Rostami.

He continued that "Political wisdom and social knowledge" tell us that we should arrange our time according to the situation and requirements. Religion is something personal, it's not a national property. Constant losses the people suffered during decades have left them exhausted. Rostami continued that with regards to naturalism, philosophers had described religion as "the doctrine that all religious truths are derived from nature and natural causes and not from revelation." Religion is one of the branches of philosophy which is related to metaphysics. When complicated scientific equations could not be solved through metaphysics we pose the questions such as: what is time? What is space? What is an object and how is it different from an idea? Are human beings free to make decisions regarding their faith and destiny? Or is their behavior determined by external situations?

There have always been struggles between materialists and idealists in society. Individuals can move as they wish, unlike objects which must be moved. Science and technology are advancing everyday but the voice of religion doesn't go further than the church, mosque or synagogue.

Scientists say that without their knowledge about physics and their efforts, modern life was impossible. The foundation of all natural sciences is physics because it embraces all major aspects of matter and energy, as well as action and reaction in the whole universe. For example, based on the study of physics we discovered that atoms are comprised of smaller parts and an object is formed by joining millions of molecules. Naturalism explains the natural phenomenon without any religious prejudice.

In relation to this, Rostami said that religion couldn't give any answer to this phenomenon during 1400 years. Religion does not help us construct a bridge over a river. Natural scientists, in the past or in the present, didn't find anything regarding products of religious technology (construction of large bridges, excavation of canals, and construction of tunnels which link different regions or even about heart surgery) in any book or wherever. Show me the difference between Islam and Christian behavior toward scientific knowledge.

Omar, father in law of Mohammed set fire on Alexandria library and Justinian closed the door of Aristotle philosophical schools.

I asked Rostami about the use of the term Jihad in his reforms table. He whispered that it was the first part of No. 2 on the table and that it was an imported word brought about by religious policies. This word had penetrated the culture of Khorasani people with the main purpose of concealing vanities of the Arab religion and it had nothing to do with the Khorasani people who had a totally different religion.

What's Jihad?

Thanks to Shojaeddin Shafa, the famous writer who wrote that after 1400 years, after the demise of Mohammad and especially during Abu Bakar, caliphate, had inserted new words into the Quran. Parallel to 33 verses regarding killing, we can find verses in the civil parts of Quran regarding Jihad. They have tried to attribute a meaning to Jihad similar to the killings verses (offensive Islamic invasions) and there is no guarantee that any of these words really have the attributed meaning because Jihad in the Quran always meant "to attempt" or "to try" without necessarily being related to armed attempts.

The Historian and sociologist Ibn Khaldoun who explained what is Arab, allows Jihad in order to expand Islam.

If the literal meaning of Jihad was the one which "Shafa" stated as being used for the prosperity of individuals in social life, then the Arab historian Ibn Khaldoon Abdulrahman, 732-808, wouldn't have used it for the expansion of Islamic imperialism which embraces violence, slaughter, estrangement and factionalism.

During the crusades, the occupying Arabs who were powerless against the invasion of Christians in the land of Moses, gave Jihad a political attribution. Incorrect usage and interpretation of this word have caused so much bloodshed and it's meaning in the uncompromising culture of fundamentalists has driven analysts and writers crazy. Thomas Walker Arnold, in his research work, *The Preaching of Islam*, published in 1896 in London, wrote that nowhere in the Quran are Muslims asked to attack unless threatened by infidels. The concept of holy war which was invented later on during the Caliphate is attributed to the Quranic phrase of Jihad. Leone Caetani 1869- 1935 attached importance to the work of Arnold, the British Islamist and wrote that this kind of evaluation reveals that what is stated on Jihad in the Quran refers to the wars between Muslims and Quraish and their allies. Verses No. 97 and 101 of Chapter 9 (Repentance) and Verse No. 67 of Chapter 21 (the Prophets) confirm the statements of Caetani. In Mohamed Chapter, Verse No. 1, has been stated that "those who reject Allah and hinder (men) from the Path of Allah,- their deeds will Allah render astray (from their mark)." They belonged to Quraish and were Satans.

From Wikipedia, the free encyclopedia

Caetani concluded that most of the early traditions of Islams could dismissed as fabrications by later generations of authors.He also suggested that the Arab conquests during the formative era of Islam were not driven by religion but by material want and covetousness.

Caetani was not a Moslim and he did not believe in the literal truth of the Quran. Instead his views about its origins were as follows. As long as Muhammad was alive, he could answer any doctrinal questions that arose, so there was little attention paid to written documents. The reign of his successor Abu Bakr was characterized by increasing confusion as multiple written and oral versions of Muhammad's teachings coexisted. To his great credit, Uthman understood the danger of this situation; he had an official version of the Quran developed and ordered the destruction of all unapproved version. To summarize, Caetani thought that the Quran as it exists today did not come word for word from the pen of the Prophet, but was the result of a standardization and clean up effort ("Uthman's recension") undertaken many years after his death.

Caetani was a leftist and Karl Marx was also. God is also because he recommended the heart to the left side of Adam.

It is obvious that the word "Kofar" (infidels) was attributed to the latter. Verses No. 97 and 101 of Chapter 9 (Repentance) and Verse No. 67 of Chapter 21 (the Prophets) confirm to the aforementioned. Due to this fact, upon final surrender of Quraish in Mecca in the 8th year of Hijra, no further verses were revealed regarding holy war against the infidels. In Verse No. 8 of Chapter 29 (The Spider) and Verse No. 15 of Chapter 31 (Luqman) Jihad has been referred to as "strive". In this verse, Mohammad advises the children to strive, not to obey their parents and return to him. This kind of policy will not only break the family ties but increase animosity within society.

Wars, due to their characteristics, are not holy practices. Therefore, how can we call them holy? Wouldn't it be wise if scholars refrain from using this word "Jihad" or at least not recognize it officially Eric Hoffer, 1901-1983, called Jihad "a plague" and said that "to kill and die is easy here when some stupid people are the stage directors of dramatic plays and worship."

To be associated with 72 angels and drink "Antahore", wine in heaven, is some kind of psychological encouragement for people to kill themselves and other innocents.

Jim Hoagland, in his article on the Civil War of Islam, in the *Washington Post*, March 3, 2004, wrote that during the Arab Conference in Tunisia, Arab leaders should deprive killers from such privilege (Jihad). He continued that Jihad will vanish once the world of Islam calls a terrorist, a terrorist not "Mujahideen", otherwise these parasites will earn their livelihood at the expense of their supporters.

Professor Mohammad Abdulsalam, the instructor at the University of Ghaed Azam in Islam Abad, Pakistan and the 1979 Noble Prize winner in Physics who is a Muslim too, in the commentary of his book "Islam and Knowledge" has written that compared to the civilized countries worldwide, the level of knowledge in Islamic countries is at its minimum. He continues that advancements in the sciences requires freedom of expression, freedom in practice of religion and freedom to criticize and none of these conditions can compromise with the institutionalized oppression in Islamic rules and regulations.

Affirming the statements of Professor Abdulsalam, Mr. Rostami said that the Mullahs could deceive people and take advantage of the mentally ill, causing them to fight with each other like wild animals in the name of Jihad. If a nation is invaded by a foreign force, it will fight for its freedom due to patriotism and love the reaction does not stem from Jihad. Jihad is not a civilized language due to the fact that among the nomads it means murder, massacre and ransacking which is attributed to ignorance and dictatorship and has nothing to do with our religion.

Zarnegar Park in Kabul

Rostami was concerned about the park of Zarnegar located in the center of Kabul. The park is on the verge of total destruction, as it is not properly maintained. Everyone should take steps towards reviving the park, which will be named after the Great Abdulrahman and its mosque will be named after Parviz Yazd who died there.

However, I'm still not sure how Jamshid Yazd became president. He said that his friends' clever efforts, on one hand, and untimely death of his young son, Parviz Yazd, and the people's support on the other hand, helped him to get into power. Otherwise, dethroning a puppet government was not an easy task. These were a few of the factors working in his favor but there are other more effective ones which helped him in his victory. I wanted to discuss this with Sohrab Rostami but he interrupted me and started talking about omitting two unnecessary Ministries, the Ministry of Tribes and the Ministry of Haj. He said that certain individuals are using the budget of the Ministry of Tribes, which goes against social justice.

I was struggling to make Mr. Rostami give me a clue about the political victory of the new regime, but he was smarter than I thought. He started talking about the younger generation of his country and the fact that they are the main components of the society possessing knowledge. Rostami looked at one of the thick books sitting on his desk and cited it: "philosophical ideas and social ethics influence the rules and regulations of every country and its government". The existence of a rich and powerful culture will help complete those concepts.

Aristotle, the great Greek philosopher who founded Political Science, used to teach his students the relationships between government and people. His writings were taught in many places until the Middle Ages. Mr. Rostami said that it was first necessary to build the nation's spirit which was damaged because of the fractious theocrats and improving it is one of the hardest parts of the social ethics agenda.

Buddha or the King of Two Swords (Shah-e-do Shamshira), an Arab invader

Rostami was so disturbed by the tragedy that the <u>Buddha statues</u> had been blown up. Such a tragedy happened because of uncultivated, ignorant and jealous people. Looking at the photo of the great statue he asked me to consider what our intelligent and concerned compatriots might think about this historic tragedy based on our great artistic, economic and touristic achievements.

The mercenaries of the southern tribes blew up the statues of Bamyan which were universally popular. On the other hand, they lick and kiss the grave of an Arab invader (Shah-e- do shamshira) who used to behead the defenders of our country using two swords. What happened to the gallant and brave Kabuly men who cut off the heads of the invaders?

Down with you poor Khorasani traitor! Your brain is malfunctioning due to the influence of the Arab culture over the past 1,400 years and even modern science couldn't wipe away the corrosive Arab culture from your mind. The fortunate country of Egypt earns millions and billions of dollars every year because of mummified kings, queens and princesses. The mummified Pharaoh of Tutan Khamun is rented for millions of dollars to be shown in the public in the U.S., Europe and other countries and this way it earns a lot of money for Egypt.

What was the fault of the beautiful statues of Bamyan? Our devoted artists and hieroglyphists had worked hard for decades to create such unique masterpieces, but they were all ruined due to the dauntlessness of the democratic world and to tribal struggles. They were not only an indication of the elegance of our artists but they were also a symbol of our ancestors (cultural heritage of the past); we were proud of their advanced arts, culture and handiwork under difficult conditions. These traitors intentionally damaged the reputation of our tourism industry and Bamyan statues, representing our artists.

Good heavens! The foreign intruders (Arabs, Jenghiz Khan, Timor, British and Russians) didn't damage the statues but the tribal and ignorant mercenaries, followers of Abdul Wahab, destroyed them completely. Such traitors indifferently kiss the grave of the bloodthirsty Arab whom they call the King of two swords.

I asked Rostami about the faith of Buddha which no longer exists. He said that he was awaiting the decision of UNESCO and the Artists' Union. I asked him about his personal idea and he said that he wanted to keep the empty place of the statues to show the world and the future generation that such a crime was committed by people who are obsessed by religion and have actually lost their minds. He added that if possible, other statues of Buddha will be built near the destroyed ones to forever bear the mark of such disgrace in history; a disgrace committed by ignorant and retrogressive tribe.

There were many other questions to be asked of Mr. Rostami, requiring his responses, but he excused himself to attend the burial of Parviz in Zarnegar Park, whose name had already been changed to Amirkabir Park. I reminded him that Parviz has been buried already. He replied yes, but temporarily. He told me that some friends at the Kite flying Union and sympathetic people of Kabul had suggested that the mosque at Zarnegar Park, originally constructed on the basis of bribery and for the personal interest of some businessman, to have its name changed to the shrine of Parviz Yazd. People had suggested that others didn't have the right to destroy or occupy public property for their personal interest.

Rostami asked the protocol department to send me to Amirkabir Park to attend the burial ceremony of Parviz Yazd, son of President Jamshid Yazd. Before burying Parviz, Rostami told people that, due to social reforms, Friday will not be the holy day anymore, but Saturday will be considered the holy day, as pronounced by the prophet Moses. He continued that, for coordination purposes, he would like all other religions to have Saturday as their holy day. However, it was not mandatory because religion was personal. He announced that Friday should be called by its previous name (Shesh Shanbe).

Amirkabir Park was very crowded. Young and old, men and women, all had gathered. Hotels were all full. Young people in clean, white outfits were holding flags bearing some photos of Parviz while flying kites and chanting "Parviz, Parviz" . It was so emotional. People noticed a tank was getting close. In front of it there were motorcycles and at the back the black motors were in the cascade. The coffin of Parviz, the hero, was placed on top of the tank. People rushed towards it but the guards asked them not to disturb the peace of their hero.

The tank stopped in the front of the shrine. Rostami, who was wiping away his tears with a napkin, carried a part of the coffin on his left shoulder until it was laid down in the shrine. Watching such a tragedy was so painful for everyone. All the people including me were weeping for his loss.

There were containers of drinks and glasses on each side of the entrance hall. Rostami was so excited. He sometimes put his hands in his disheveled hair and sometimes touched his mustache. He finally found higher ground and addressed the friends of the late Parviz Yazd, "Dear compatriots, I'm glad that you could participate in the memorial of my dear Parviz. I hope that the existing solidarity and unity could help us achieve our bigger goals for the freedom of the country which the Mullahs have deprived us of over the past few years. We shouldn't let the Mullahs deprive us from the joys of life by telling their mesmerizing myths and because such immoral people don't have a clue to what the joys of life are.

حیف است که پیش کر زنی طنبوری   یا یوسف همخانه کنی با کوری
یا قند نهی در دو لب رنجوری   یا جفت شود مخنثی با حوری
(مولوی)

Alack! Playing tanboor for a deaf
Or Yousuf lives with a blind

> Or put sugar in the mouth of an infirm
> Or an effeminate marry a houri (nymph)

Rostami asked everyone to hold up their glasses in the memory of Parviz, the hero, and pray for the elimination of the enemies. He added that our ancestors (Kushanis) used to serve drinks in memorial ceremonies and it was good to keep up their tradition rather than following the tradition of strangers (Arabs).

He further continued that he wanted to put an end to the dominating Arab culture in order to build a new society. An Iranian writer had once said that during the early years of the Qadesieh massacre, places of worship were destroyed and fires in the fireplaces were extinguished. Barbarous Arabs plundered and leveled cities and villages. Latitudinarians were killed, the women were taken hostages and Zoroastrians were deprived of the mercy of Ahura Mazda.

1400 years later another Iranian writer wrote about the violent culture of Arabs:

یک مشت گدایی عرب از راه رسیدند در میهن جانانۀ ما خانه گزیدند
با روضه و با روزه در این باغ پر از گل چون گاو دویدند و چریدند و خزیدند
با چوب و چماق و قمه و دشنه و چاقو سرها بشکستند و شکمها بدریدند
گفتند که این منطق اسلام عزیز است اینان که سیه کارتر از شمر و یزیدند
انگه به صحن چمن دانش و فرهنگ هر جمعه چو گلّه بزغاله چریدند
در میهن ما منطق اسلام چماق است اکنون همگی پیرو این دین جدیدند

There are a hundred years difference between these two writers and their works. However, the struggle between the Iranian culture and the imported Arab culture continues on. The 1400-year history of Islamic Iran is full of clashes between the two civilizations, cultures and conceptions which never compromised under any condition or by any force.

This is because the real problem of such controversy lies in the rational divergence between the Semitic culture and the Aryan culture. In one culture, human beings have a predetermined faith without the possibility to change, while at the same time they should be responsible for their actions and punished. In another culture, the same human being is free, having the power of decision making and liable for the outcomes. The fundamental difference between these two conceptions has never been digested by Iranian thinkers. As a matter of fact, not only has there always been an unanswered question throughout Persian literature, but also different religious sects such as Mu'tazili, Qadiri and Shu'biah and the Iranian Mysticism movement posed questions in this regard and did not get any answer.

1,100 years ago Zikria Razi, one of the great scientists in history, declared that all human beings are born with equal rights and therefore one can't privilege a prophet by labeling him as having "inherent superiority"; this was stated in both of his books, later labeled as heretic, relating to the same subject of confrontation between liberalism, the foundation of Aryan Iran, and the dogmatic beliefs of the Semites. "Miracles" attributed to the prophets are fabrication, cheating, or fancies. Various teachings of these religions are an indication of their conflict with reality which should logically be the same for all of them.

These religions are only capable of creating wars and causing their followers and others to be killed. When they claim that a certain tribe has been appointed by God to convey the message of reality using force, this is lying to God, people, and reality itself. Because God himself can convey this message without using any force.

As Razi said, the powerful poet, Naser Khosrow had revealed all those lies and hollow expressions, by writing a poem for reality lovers:

خدایا راست گویم فتنه از تست   ولی از ترس نتوانم چغیدن
سخن بسیار اما جرئتم نیست   نفس از بیم نتوانم کشیدن
اگر اصرار ارم ترسم از انکه   که غیظ اری و نتوانم چغیدن
اگر میخواستی کاینها نپرسم   مرا بایست حیوان افریدن
اگر نیکم اگر بد خلقت از تست   خلیق خوب بایست اوریدن
تو در اجرای طاعت وعده دادی   بهشت از مزد طاعت افریدن
ولی این مزد طاعت یا شفاعت   چه منت ها ز تو باید کشیدن
اگر خود داده ای در ملک جایم   نباید بر من از ازارت رسیدن
بکس چیزی که نسپردی چه خواهی   حساب اندر طلب باید کشیدن
همانم باز وقت باز دیدن   اگر صد بار در کوره گدازی
تو گر خلقت نمودی بهر طاعت
چرا باید شیطان افریدن

به ما اصرار داری در رهٔ راست   به او در پیچ و تاب ره بریدن
به ما فرمان دهی اندر عبادت   به شیطان در رگ و جانها دویدن
به ما تقصیر خدمت نیست لازم   بَدیم و بَد نبایست اوریدن
اگر بر نیک و بد قدرت ندادی   چرا بر نیک و بد باید رسیدن
اگر مطلب به دوزخ بردن ماست   تعذر چند بایست اوریدن
بفرما تا سوی دوزخ برندم   چه مصرف دارد این گفت و شنیدن
تو که ریگی به کفش خود نداری   چرا بایست شیطان افریدن

In the 2nd volume of his precious works, after 1,400 years "Discovery of India", Shojauddin Shafa quoted Jawaherlal Nehru (1889-1964) while writing a letter to his daughter Gandhi, Indira (1917-1984) from jail, "Following the military triumphs of Arabs in the Middle East and North Africa, the people in the occupied territories lost their national identities, including their language and nationality, and like Syria, Mesopotamia (Iraq) and Egypt mixed with the Arabic culture. Although they are separate countries with political borders, they are still considered Arab countries. Iran was conquered by the Arabs as well, but the invaders couldn't integrate Iranians like they did in Syria, Iraq and Egypt because the Iranian race has its roots in the historical and powerful Aryan race and has fundamental differences with the Arab race.

In addition, the Iranian language was Aryan, so in both race and language they remained separate from those of the Arabs. Iran didn't change her color for the Arabs and didn't integrate into the Arabic complex due to the fact that the rational and philosophical viewpoints of these two cultures were in contradiction. This contradiction even existed in the type of Islam which was established in Iran." If I'm telling all this to you, my daughter, it's not because I want to put a burden on your memory, but I want you to know how this neighbor of ours for more than 1000 years, has managed to keep her cultural identity in spite of amazing historical developments."

Rostami said that unfortunately a few traitors who were bribed by Saudi Arabia betrayed our homeland Afghanistan. "I'm glad that the death of Parviz, our hero, has expedited our freedom movement. All of you, men and women, old and young, should keep working for the cause of freedom and break free from the influence of Arab culture. I'm so thankful." The entire crowd, gathered on dry land at Amirkabir Park, rose to their feet and applauded Rostami.

Policemen and Peacekeeping forces were monitoring the area, communicating with each other via cell phone. I used the opportunity and asked Mr. Rostami about his opinion on international peacekeeping forces. He replied that he had discussed the issue with President Jamshid Yazd. The President said that if the forces could keep general peace and order while carrying out their mission, they were not only welcome but he would also have extended his full cooperation. Otherwise, in their pursuit of imaginary heavens, the brainwashed terrorists would deprive us from all our freedoms. He added that when peacekeeping forces are carrying out their mission, there is no need for Longbows, Crossbows, or gunpowder.

Mr. Rostami criticized the propaganda of political religions (Christianity and Islam) and said that these two have many things in common since the Quran which is written by Arabs is a copy of the Christian Bible. The two have theoretical and practical similarities. As a matter of fact, religious politicians, when constricted, use one book to support the other.

I'm afraid that upon failure of either of these two religions, the two compromise, in which case our world would become a fundamentalists' heaven.

In 1802, Saudi Army invaded Karbala in Iraq during which pregnant women were slain. In 2005 in the US, Lisa Montgomery, a churchgoing woman, cut open the uterus of Bobbie Jo Stinnette and removed the fetus, killing the mother.

Jerry Falwell, a famous reverend in the US has called the 9/11 tragedy a punishment for infidels, child killers, homosexuals, liberals and advocates of women's rights. The Muslim fundamentalists, especially Arabs, agree with him. They were celebrating on the streets. Rostami added that the God in which Jerry believed not only didn't condemn the massacre of more than 3000 thousand Americans, but approved of the bloody al Qaida terrorist crime due to his own personal interest. He even went further and opposed the rights of political and reactionary groups which had conflicts with his personal ideas. So what is the difference between Ayman Al-Zawahiri and Jerry Falwell? According to someone, if he was a genius then what was Hitler?

Rostami said if religion mentally and physically empowered the political system of a society it becomes a powerful "Titan" and a very destructive force to the constructive ideas of modernization. Look at Afghanistan, Pakistan, Iran, even London and America, Hamas and Hizbullah.

Pat Robertson, yet another reverend and founder of Christian solidarity had declared that in order to prevent growth of Communism and Islamic fundamentalism, Hugo Chavez, President of Venezuela should be murdered. Robertson knows well that not only Communists but all other founders of modern society are more interested in exploring social and economic aspects of life rather than theology. However, theology is the only source of living for clergymen and therefore, they should resort to such conspiracies against the modern movement.

Such religious conspiracies have a dark history. As stated in "After 1400 years" written by "Shafa", different groups started fighting over the succession of Mohammad even before his burial. In Saghineh, Bany Sa'edeh beat Meghdad bin Asvad Kandi, the famous follower of Mohammad, and hit him in the chest. In another event, Sa'd bin Abadeh Ansari, head of the Khazraj Tribe who had opposed the succession of Abu Bakar, was killed on his way to Syria and claimed that he was killed by jinni. Everyone knew that the so-called jinni were Khalid bin Walid and Mohammad Moslemeh Ansari. Upon Mohammad's death many tribes abandoned his religion.

People of Ghatfan, Bahrain, Khatm, Oman, Yemen, Mohreh, Ak, Hazrmot, Bani Salim and others abandoned Islam and lots of them joined Talheh. In many other areas, the agents of Mohammad were killed and the women were ordered to color their hands and play music.

The massacre led by Khalid bin Walid, as mentioned in the Tabari History, was so brutal and violent. Ali and Abu Bakar had ordered him to decapitate and burn those who had abandoned Islam and color their hands. He chopped off their heads and set their bodies ablaze. Khalid bin Walid, a terrible murderer who had shed the blood of many innocent people, was called "Seifullah" (the sword of God) by his commander. Lions and foxes are mistaken for one another in a sick culture and primitive society in which competencies cannot be distinguished from brutality.

It was Khalid bin Walid who broke the famous idol of "Izi" in Ka'ba. If it was not because of this bloodthirsty and brutal Arab, Mohammad and his ideology would never have been established. There were a few others, including a woman who had claimed the prophecy. One of them was "Aswad bin Ka'b Ansi" who conquered San'a and called himself (Rahman Al Yemen), however he didn't last long and was killed in a conspiracy, led by his wife. Another prophet was "Ibn Khalid Al Asadi" known as "Taliheh" who converted from Islam. He exempted people from performing prayers and fasting

(May his soul rest in peace). Even Yazid Ibn Muawiyah, the 6th Emir al Mo'menin didn't believe in Islam. He killed Husayn bin Ali, Mohammad's grandson in Karbala in 680 CE. A dastardly crime committed by a typical Arab.

With regards to the two religious Empires of Europe and Arabs, the great Shafa wrote,

> "Two parallel efforts in two great historical places in the world, Asia and Europe, resulted in an inevitable clash between the two religious Imperialisms that lasted for more than 10 decades. Pages in the history of humanity are full of massacres and ravages which took place in the name of God, without (God, Jesus and Mohammad) playing a role except as being a tool for exploitation."

By the order of Shah Ismail Safavid and Sultan Salim of the Ottoman Empire, and as for keeping the rear safe during war, 20,000 Iranian Sunnis and 40,000 Turkish Shiite were massacred in Iran and Turkey. Those people never participated in any war. Van Hamer,? an Austrian diplomat and literati, in his famous book "the history of Ottoman Rule" which was written during his years of service in Constantine, has called the massacre of 40,000 one of the most violent crimes that occurred in the name of religion and believed that it was the most gruesome event compared to the ferocities of Peter Bartholomew of France, (during the Inquisition era, 1575, ended the killing of 20000 people) During the first crusade, 1096, Peter Barthelemy, another religious man, said that he had seen in his dream three times that the lance which ripped off one side of the body of Jesus, was hidden under the altar of the church and if they could find it, they would have won the crusades. It turned out to be true and they defeated the Ottoman Empire (a dream which led to victory) but it was nothing but a trick.

He wrote that by the order of Sultan Salim, the clergy of Istanbul unanimously declared that the reward for killing one Shiite was more than the reward for killing 70 Christians or Jews. Rostami told me that all the wars, massacres and other adversities that occurred as a result of the Crusades which ended in hundreds of fatalities originated in a religion in which jealousy and rivalry has encouraged separation and disunity among society.

I asked Mr. Rostami that due to having defeated Marxism our people had become fundamentalists for more than a quarter century; and that how was it possible to introduce such people to social and peaceful coexistence? He replied that he wanted to ask those humanitarians who respect freedom and human rights to give assistance with the mass media.

Second, we should try to replace useless religious programs with productive ones. Religious practice and discipline of the God's Corps (Mujahideen) has caused the oppressed Afghan women to become blind and crippled. Violent acts stemmed from Arab culture, which is reminiscent of the practice of Bartholomew in the Inquisition era in France, conducted in the name of God. During the 16th and 17th centuries, for religious stability, due to witch hunts, many innocent women were tortured and sentenced by the clergy.

Artists, writers, dramatists and those whose humanitarian acts are effective and useful for the general well being, development and reconstruction of a society, should be encouraged so that useless cockeyed, adulate practices and methods of the clergy would fade away.

Mr. Rostami swore that he won't spend a dime on religious teachings (neither inside nor outside Afghanistan) from the public treasury of the poor Afghans who had become disabled as a result of religious wars defending Arab dignity. Such religious teachings were only useful for defending Arab culture for 1400 years. Not only did they not promote any agricultural products but also caused our country and the disabled, unemployed, and the ill to be destroyed. The Mujahideen (Arab Corpse) defended Arab-imported culture and killed many of our brave men and women who wanted to defend the freedom, dignity and pride of our country. Their crimes will remain as a black mark in history forever.

I whispered, how dangerous! Rostami, who looks like Mohamad Reza Lotfi - the great Iranian Setarist, continued that it would be dangerous, but such a struggle in the way of development, progress, solidarity and freedom requires dedication and self-sacrifice. He further added that the primitive people who didn't hear anything else other than the Mullahs preaching and the call for prayers from mosques and have only seen head coverings, are suddenly exposed to new things in life and inevitably go through major transformations; this is due to the fact that such discoveries and explorations are considered as humiliating to their culture and to their religion.

They can't digest such new ideas and then comes all the jealousy, Oedipus complexes and anger resulting from ignorance and illiteracy. All such people like Hassan al Bana, Qotb, Osama bin Laden, Al Zawahiri, Zarqavi who are all Arabs, have not only disempowered Islam but also discredited it. They are afraid of research and reform in education and methodology because it reveals their corruption.

Farah Diba, former Queen of Iran, in her memoirs (Kohan Diara), wrote that the Ayatollah had set up certain nights and people went on their rooftops and chanted "Allah Akbar" (God is Great). These words used to be a peaceful prayer for me since childhood, but they turned into horrible words and when I heard them it seemed that my blood froze.

Denis Diderot wrote that the most dangerous, insane people are the religious ones; Those who intend to cause a society to collapse well know how to use such insane people.

Newt Gingrich, professor, politician and Speaker of the Congress (Republican), stated that we have two uncompromising enemies, Islam and the evil dictators who support Muslim fundamentalists. Bernard Lewis, an Islamicist and a Professor wrote, "I think there is an underlying assumption that Muslims are different and incapable of running a democratic society."

Why are the outsiders worried so much, each time there is a democratic movement in Afghanistan?

Thomas Edward Lawrence, 1888-1941, an English spy in the Middle East had two political advantages for the British. He not only divided and separated Arab countries but cut the Ottoman Empire out of the Middle East. He was the one who caused the collapse of the Royal kingdom of Shah Amanullah in Afghanistan in 1929. In 1980 they played another game in which they used the naïve Muslims against the democratic regime of Afghanistan. They claim that they were the ones who dismantled the Berlin wall, put an end to the cold war and caused a superpower to yield. They were pushed towards the complete destruction of Afghanistan and promoted the Islamic atomic bomb in Pakistan. It means that these people were the political lackeys for others. However, none of the international and humanitarian organizations praised their accomplishments! Maybe it's because of this that they are engaged with the Christians now.

We should remember that our world used to be a peaceful place. However, this is not true anymore and unfortunately, one cannot predict whether such religious, nationalistic or logical unrest resulting from political imbalance in the world would ease?

Steven Hawking, the British physicist said, "Life on earth is at the ever increasing risk of being wiped out by a disaster, such as in sudden global warming, nuclear war, a genetically engineered virus or other dangers". In a statement before boarding he said, "I think the human race has no future if it doesn't go into space. I, therefore, want to encourage public interest in outer space."

Or based on the Law of Universal Gravitation of Newton, will the moon fall on the earth?

Religious hypocrites, whose position is endangered, arm youth, poor people and the insane with suicidal bombs. Godfrey from Bouillon in 1099 in Jerusalem trampled and killed the slaves; The Christian pilgrims on their way to Jerusalem were not only robbed but trampled by Arabs.

سوی حج رانی و و در بادیه ام قطع کنی   اشتر و اسب مرا قسمت اعراب کنی
(مولوی)

Wrong policies have turned mosques into a cradle of terrorism and city of mosques and people are desperate for their lost freedom. In Kabul there were rumors that mosques will be displaced. Different groups were talking about these rumors at every corner. Such a change was totally new for everyone and I was confused also. Quickly I went to Mr. Rostami's office but he was too busy and I couldn't meet with him.

The following day I went to visit him and told him about the rumors. He said that I shouldn't be concerned since people had been making complaints for a long time about such noise from the mosques. He continued that due to social reforms and democratic rules, the government needed to take necessary action. President Yazd had promised people to take care of this issue. In this regard, a committee of experts comprised of Zal Toorani, representative of the clergy, Darius Sassani, representative of the kite flying union, Faramarz Kavoss, representative of reciters, and Bahram Kaman representative of craftsmen, was formed in order to investigate the case. By order of the president, Darius had adopted an agenda with regards to the subject and stated that his house was near a mosque and his children were disturbed by the sound of muezzin, five times a day.

Jamshid Yazd sometimes glanced at the photo of his son Parviz who died in youth and the other times looked at the reform committee. When Darius finished his speech, Jamshid Yazd asked the group to submit their comments to the committee. A committee member called "Ghelich Jorjani" suggested dismantling mosques but the representative for the clergy opposed his idea and called it impractical. He suggested instead, to supply every mosque with a bell or shofar. Faramarz Kavoos, representative of the reciters, told the president they were sick and tired of reciting and asked if it was possible for them to get some training to become musicians and singers. His comments made everyone laugh and have some fun. The representative of craftsmen, Bahram Choobineh suggested that the reciter association merge with the craftsmen association.

بحق انک گزیدی دو لب که جام بگیر
بنوش جام و رها کن حدیث پخته و خام
(مولوی)

Linguistic Fundamentalism

Our nation is comprised of different tribes. Religion and language are two aspects which have been used to divide our nation. The people had no say in this but rather, those old-fashioned professors and dissenting politicians who attempted to expand Pashto language with the use of force are responsible for that division.

One good example would be the notes by an old-fashioned professor named Abdulhay Habibi that were used in the worthwhile book written by Abdulhamid Mohtat, The Analytical History of Afghanistan. Professor Habibi is held in high esteem among Afghan historians and scholars. When Hashem Khan, the Prime Minister, was trying to impose the Pashto language in the non-Pashto tribes, in the 1930's, professor Habibi not only supported, but encouraged him to implement the use of force. He presented his poem called "The message of the Martyr" to the young king:

قـــوم من ! ای تودهٔ والا نــژاد
وی نـــیاکان غیورت مرد و راد
بـا تـو دارم گفتگویی محـرمی
تــا ز اسرار حیـات اگـاه شــوی
بشنو ای پشتون بـا صدق و صفا
حــافظ کـــهسار و قـلب اســیا
یـا چو اسلاف غیـورت زندگی
گر بـزرگی خـواهی و ازادگی
اولا پشتو زبـانت زنـده سـاز
هم بـر این شالوده کاخت بر فراز
تــا تـوانی تکیه بـر شمشیر کـن
کـاخ ملت را بـر ان تعمیر کـــن

Wise readers! I'm so ashamed of such poems written by an old-fashioned professor, showing his anxiety over whether the Pashto language (golden language) would remain viable. Mr. Habibi! You who are so concerned about Pashto, why did you write your poems in Farsi? Isn't it true that you are trying to deceive us, Mr. Habibi? Language is not only used for speaking, it has many uses, like for provocation.(1) Tasting (2) Licking, spitting. Secondly, as an author and a cultural figure you're forever doomed (in history) due to the exaggeration used in your poems. Finally, your ideology and your qualifications as a professor are under question now. Mr. Habibi is not alone with his critics.

During the 1950's I went to visit the late Abdulrazaq khan Hamid, a close relative of mine. There was a man talking to him about the Pashto language and how Pashto was being ignored. The visitor was asking Abdulrazaq khan to bring this to the attention of the king. Abdulrazaq khan said that he had tried several times, but the king thought that the people didn't want Pashto. Later on I realized that the man talking to Abdulrazaq khan was the head of the Pashto Association.

Mohammed Daud, the Prime Minister, supported a nationalistic and one-sided reunification of the pashtun people with Afghanistan.

155

However, this would have involved taking a considerable amount of territory from the new nation of Pakistan and was indirect antagonism to an older plan of the 1950s whereby a confederation between the two countries was proposed. The move further worried the non-pashtun population of Afghanistan like the minority Tajilk, Hzara and Uzbek who suspected Daud Khan's intention was to increase the pashtun's disproportionate hold on political power. During that time, the pashtuns (or Afghans) consisted roughly 35-42 percent of Afghanistan's ethnic demographics but they presented over 80 percent of the government and held all impotant ministries, such as the ministries of the Interior, Foreign Affairs, Economic Affair, Defense and even most of the banks. (Wikipedia, the free encyclopedia)

The late Roshandel Roshan, who was imprisoned by rogue revolutionaries in the Polcharkhi prison, emigrated to Pishavar when he was released. While in Pishavar, he wrote several books. One of his sons once asked him why he wrote all those books in Farsi. Laughing, he replied: "because no one reads Pashto books". However, he did write a book in Pashto for his son. The judgment and ideology of this author was far more practical than those of the old-fashioned professors. Mr. Habibi! You wanted to create a "Pashto-Esperanto" language? That type of endeavor has been unsuccessful in the world.

Different languages and dialects may be spoken in a single country. However, depending on the culture, language development is a straightforward process. Pashto, Kurdish, Baluchi and Ordu, are different branches of Persian. Although there are different languages spoken in a single country, there is only one official language. It is the language of communication and it is taught in schools. For example, in France, French is the official language, but not all the French people speak only French. The people of Alsace-Lorraine also speak German. People speak Breton in Brittany, Basque is spoken in the Pyrenees mountains and the dialect spoken in southern France sounds different from the official French. The accent is very different and expressions differ.

In Belgium, both French and Flemish are official languages. In Canada, there are both French and English. In Yugoslavia, Macedonian, Slovenian and Serbo-Croatian languages are spoken. There are 14 standard languages in India but English is the official language, despite the fact that those who speak Hindi are in the majority and have protested several times. In Ghana, there are 50 different languages but English is the official one. There is no first class or second class language there.

Farsi has been the main language for more than one thousand years and has been used in books and for communication purposes - this will remain the same. Otherwise, the country will probably suffer a schism.

Language means using voice and written symbols which form our thoughts and with which we can express our ideas. Afzal Khatak, a famous Pashton historian, has described Pashtons as the successive generations of the Jewish tribes "Asfeh" and "Afghaneh" who were expelled from Syria and immigrated to Iran and Khorasan, residing near the mountains. Ghazi Ataollah khan, a Pishavari historian, and one of the allies of Ghafar khan has written a book called Pashto in History. In this book he wrote that the ancestor of the Afghans is Khalid bin Walid who was Jewish and later converted to Islam. Therefore, can't we call Pashtons Khaledians? According to other documents, Pashtons act very humbly with Arabs and even invite them over to their houses. Khalid is a very common name used among Pashtons, Mr. Habibi! Why so much bloodshed for Islam? Why so much bloodshed in the name of language? I sense that Imperialism has some connection there.

A rich culture is somewhat like a powerful plant. When a plant grows big, it covers the smaller plants underneath. Now, in this case, should the big one be cut back by the sword?

There have been different discoveries in various fields in the modern world. For example, the art of writing requires impartial ethics, because otherwise it will result in some invidious, emotional and baseless piece of work which won't be acceptable for real journalism and will not only discredit the writer but will also reveal the incapability and poor genetic heritage (DNA) of the writer, whose writings lack any scientific base.

On page 102 of his book, "Mohtat" wrote that in the mid 20th century, the Pashton rulers, especially during "Sardar Hashem khan" and "Sardar Davood" tried to impose the Pashto language over the Afghan nation. In an interview in 1937, "Hashem khan" announced that by 1938, Pashto would become the official language and Farsi would vanish. This way, everyone would be exposed to our myths and poems and we would be proud of our rich culture and finally it would unite the nation.

Truly, we used to be students at schools with such cultural prejudice practiced by certain people. Obviously, it was animosity against the modern, contemporary era of reconstruction by King Amanullah. However, being under such spiritual and physical pressure imposed by unknowing and ignorant rulers, taught the Afghan nation during these political, social and cultural campaigns. When Dr. Najib's regime collapsed, Afghanistan was once again taken over by Tajiks, Hezarahs and Uzbeks. In order to gain back their position, Pashtons had no way but to beg Pakistanis. Pakistani military rulers, who were expecting that move, immediately accepted the request made by the Pashtons and Mullahs.

The vice-ruler of Lahor requested "Zahirudin Baber", 1483-1530, the King of Kabul to support him against the invasion of Ibrahim Loudi. In his memories, Baber wrote that he had been waiting to conquer India for 20 years and it was such a great opportunity for me to achieve my goal. The compromise of a few traitor Afghans had opened the victory corridor for the Pakistanis.

Military men, politicians and mercenary Mullahs who serve Saudi Arabia, managed to mobilize the Pashton militia under the name of "Taliban". This 20,000 strong militia group is supported by Arab capitalist countries, the most important of which is Saudi Arabia. Pakistani officials, who provided false information, caused the US to be involved in the tragedy of Afghanistan. In reality, that was the Pashtun's concealed expansionism plot of the 21st century.

Tim McGirk, in an article in the Washington Times on October 5, 1996, wrote: "Maybe Taliban is good for Washington and Pakistan but they are totally unacceptable to the Afghans." He added that while body of Dr. Najib, President of Afghanistan was still hanging on the gallows, Clinton's administration rushed in to provide support for Taliban.

Pashtons don't share anything in common with the other tribes, whether in language or in religion. As a matter of fact, their negative nationalism and liberalism are under doubt. Not only language, but also religion has become a part of their nationalism. A good example of this is the cultural movement of Taliban in southeast Afghanistan which has embraced the culture of terrorist Arabs and Ikhvan al Muslimin.

The traitorous and based on prejudice method of Mohammad Gol Pacha (Muhmand) who had close cooperation with Nader Shah, the puppet of the British, hated Farsi language a dishonest person who cultivated hatred and separatism amongst non pashtons and Habibi was a follower of Mahmand Fascism. Based on such policies, head of tribes started asking for privileges which was totally in favor of Pashtons.

Pashtu Association was established, the issue of Pashtonistan was raised for which millions of Afghani, Russian Rubles and Indian Koldar were spent but all in vain. Special schools were opened in Kabul in order to worship Pashton great figures. Gholam Mohammad (Piaz Khor) who was raised in Germany by Nazis was added to the traitors and established the Afghan Mellat party which is a shame in the history of Afghanistan. Pashton scholars used to make fun of this party. They didn't know that the Farsi language was the literature for playing chess among Turkish and Indian emperors. The conqueror of Constantinople, Mehemed the Second mastered Farsi and used to write poems in this language. About 7% or nearly 4 million people in Turkey speak Farsi (Quran of Mawlana) was matured there.

هم بان قرآن که او را پاره سیست   مثنوی قرآن شعر پارسیست

در این گلشن به این تنگی نباید غنچه گردیدن
چو گل یک چاک دل وا شو به دامن کش گریبان را
(بیدل)

We should be specific about society. In order to carry out research on a group, a sociologist should first determine what the composition of the group is. The group is only together until the end of the game. This kind of temporary unity will be studied since they form human habits. It's so important to discover the forces which keep nations together throughout decades. Sociologists carry out a few experiments to discover these forces.

First, they look into the genetic patterns of human beings and how they are assembled to form a group. The initial impulse is love and affection which forms a family or a group of people living in a city. The second factor, shown by sociologists' studies is sentiment, feelings, and bonds. Religious beliefs are an example of that. Being loyal to a nation is something else. Social habits and politeness are factors defining a group.

The third and most important part is assignment of duties. According to Plato, Greek philosopher, interdependence and the assignment of duties are the foundations of human societies.

We Khorasanis hug each other when we greet each other which is one of the outstanding examples of a rich (Aryan) culture and certainly will last forever since it brings us closer as a family. So, when we have such a rich culture, we shouldn't give way to a few opportunists who try to promote separatism and threaten our national sovereignty and solidarity.

Fourth, exchanging duties within a group is valuable and will bring society closer. In our country, Afghanistan, intermarriage is an important factor which brings nations together without which solidarity and national sovereignty would be impossible. People can't understand how important the role of recreation is in our children's growth. Or how religious sabotage could cause the freedom of our women to vanish?

The first and foremost purpose of exercise is to be refreshed and relaxed. Excess energy and catharsis theory are related. Heat is produced when an individual has physical activity which in turn helps the circle of life. By having physical activities, individuals in every age group can reduce tension and relax. When children play in playgrounds, they discover new things, either physically or mentally, they get to know their environment which helps them to become sociable and kind individuals. It also helps them at the preschool stages.

Jean Piaget, a Swiss psychologist, born in 1896, believed that playing is the best thing for children who want to become familiar with their surroundings. Later on, this will provide them with different methods of discovery. According to Jean Piaget, a child's brain will develop while discovering things and playing helps them to gain experience.

We need parks which play a role in the social, economic, artistic, tourism and other aspects of people and on the other hand are valuable income resources. In 2004, Egypt could have an income of about USD 5 billion from those visiting the pyramids and the mummies. In Afghanistan, we had Buddha statues and museums, which unfortunately were destroyed due to the ignorance of certain tribes in which Arabic culture rules.

Women used to go to parks, gardens and orchards in the past when they enjoyed freedom. Why are our writers silent on these issues? Why don't they write about women's freedom? Mothers who took care of their children in the cold winter nights and stayed awake beside their baby's crib all night long. Unfortunately, on the basis of fancy religious stories, they are locked in jails today.

I wonder what the responsibility of the Omaid weekly newspaper for Afghan people here in the US is? Is the newpaper interested in making money or in ridiculing scientific issues? Remember that a few years ago, I sent Mr. Kooshan a paper regarding Mao (leader of the People's Republic of China). However, I couldn't figure out why Mao's name was omitted from the news and this is a good example of an educated Afghan person in the United States who prefers religion over intellectualism. On the basis of demands and needs, we've got to find out the spirit of the marketings and the quality of commodities.

The great Mr. Rostami who was having a confidential conversation, started laughing suddenly and turned to us saying that the religious groups who couldn't confirm the existence or non-existence of God, have resorted to the idea of ridiculous innovation, an intelligent designer who put everything in place.

Both theories, Cosmological and Intelligent Design have been criticized by philosophers including David Hume. Some wise intellectuals argue that, if in fact there is such an Intelligent Designer, and, if he is worshiped for his goodness, he should be criticized for his deficiencies as well. Hume asks why faults such as evil-doing are not attributed to him. Is this some fault with the Designer or is his power limited? If his power is limited, then such a Designer can't be powerful. Therefore, we are left with no choice but to refer to Physics.

Immanuel Kant, 1724-1804, in his Pure Reason theory argues that thoughts are based on real objects. Pure reasoning without referring to the outside world is impossible. He continues, saying that we believe something only when we realize it through our senses.

Rostami added that religion based on its foundations tries to restrict the freedom of thought of intellectuals who can reveal the deficiencies of religion. A good example of this was the inquisition of the church which ordered Galileo to recant his ideas.

Walid bin Zaid, who was a knowledgeable person and a powerful poet, succeeded as a Caliph and replaced the son of Hesham bin Abdul Malik. He was beheaded because he tore apart Quran. Shams Tabrizi and Mansour Hallaj disappeared in the same way. Salman Rushdi was threatened by Mullahs and had to hide in different places in fear for his life.

Huss John, 1369-1415, the religious reformist who was burned at the stake by religious fundamentalists on July 6, 1415, in Bohemia of Prague (Czechoslovakia), accused of being an infidel.

Mr. Rostami stated that President Jamshid had visited Kabul University. He had given a lecture for the students regarding the character and bravery of the great "Amanullah" stating that he led the movement for political freedom in Afghanistan, during the reign of the then superpower, the British. He was the one who granted freedom to our women. He brought all the students, boys and girls, under one roof which was a valuable move from sociological point of view. He banned polygamy and cut off the support of parasitic tribes. He banned tribalism 90 years ago. It is because all of the above facts that we love "Amanullah" and he is the symbol of freedom, independence and national sovereignty.

He wanted to implement secularism. Mr. Rostami added that certain opportunist groups cause riots for such minor reasons. He said that the dark days of Afghanistan started when Mullahs and the British servants inside the country and the opportunist Shinwaris led by Lawrence of Arabia, who claimed that Islam was endangered, inflicted hard strikes on the qualified, pure intellectuals. Professor Jamshid added that we should revive and renew that golden era.

Mr. Rostami quoted a philosopher as saying that some people could achieve freedom, paying a high price for it, yet lost it so easily. However, others fought for it with their lives and never lost it. Mr. Rostami said that Afghanistan has lost her freedom for good. He quoted some parts from "Afghanistan" a book written by Martin Ewans, the British writer and diplomat, as saying that His Majesty Amanullah was a hardworking and dedicated man. He loved to modernize his country but lacked a globalist approach.

Amanullah was a self-absorbed, impatient and hot-tempered king who was surrounded by incompetent and sycophant individuals. His luxurious living style and lavishness caused dissatisfaction in the nation. As the grandson of Abdulrahman, he should have realized that ruling Afghanistan required an iron fist. Mr. Rostami added that, unfortunately, such a devoted national hero was sorely missed.

An individual by the name of Hazrat Shurbazar caused the constitution to fail. It's surprising that such a sore political event was not mentioned by any writer or journalist. After 90 years, his son, Sebqatollah once was elected as the President. He was the Majlis Speaker and is the Senate Speaker now. Professor Jamshid told the students that impatience in the nation was caused by impudence, ignoring religious corruption, oppressive policies of the rulers (Nader Shah father of Mohammad Zaher Shah and Hashem Khan, the prime minister of Zaher Shah's uncle), fundamentalist clergy and other old fashioned leaders who were opposed to the ideas of our hero (His Majesty Amanullah).

Professor Jamshid Yazd thanked the students for their willpower and decisive action in toppling the protégé regime which favored tribalism. The professor told the students that they paved the way for reconstruction and modernization, which were amongst the wishes of the (hero) but were impeded by the mercenary clergy. In order to carry out the material and spiritual reconstruction plans which were planned about 90 years ago, a central powerful force is required.

With regards to the special conditions of Afghanistan and the possibility that people might lose their religion, their language and their tribe in the process of modernization, the social scientists have even mentioned the necessity of using an iron fist.

The professor added that the assignment of the knowledgeable instructors and students is to replace the hollow curriculum which contained the Arab culture with a high quality curriculum. The former curriculum had poisoned the minds of the younger generation for several centuries in favor of Arab culture and against the free world and the Jews. At this point, all boys and girls cried hurray, stood up and threw their books into the air.

A young guy Jure Baig who represented the students, started to read his essay regarding the impurity of the Aryan culture! "I think that being a Muslim is a punishment. Just have a look at the fundamentalist movement which aims to destroy our civil society. I kindly ask all the sisters and brothers, Christians, Jews, Buddhists, Shintoists, Hindus, Atheists, Communists, and Rumiests followers of the philosopher {Mawlana Jalaludin Mohammad Rumi}, and other peaceful people to unite against the destructive corps." At this time all the students applauded him.

"Jure Baig" continued, saying that most famous Islamic researchers and philosophers have criticized expansion of the Arabic ideology of Islam which caused so much bloodshed over 1400 years. Exercising force and pressure in the name of satisfying God by Imams, fundamentalists and seditious politicians, have nullified Islam.

The Great Abdul Rahman (1825? 1901), who built Afghanistan with an iron fist, believed that Mullahs were the most ignorant and destructive creatures on the earth. He used to insult them by calling one of Afghan Mullahs whose name was Mushki Alam (Perfume of the Universe) the Mushi-i-Alam (Mouse of the Universe).

The Saudi Imams used to preach that individuals couldn't donate their organs since they were only the guardians of the human body which all belong to God. But in Pakistan, Arabs have encouraged people to sell their kidneys. And as a matter of fact, most poor people have sold their kidneys.

As stated in an article of April 2005 in *The Gazette* of Washington D.C., 250,000 individuals have lost their legs in landmines and Afghanistan is one of the top countries in this list. They believe that they have lost their leg, in the way of God and in spite of suffering physical and mental injuries, holding their rifles try to gundown the enlightenment movement.

The Taliban intruders in cooperation with the commanders of the intelligence service of Pakistan, hung Dr. Najib, President of Afghanistan who had sought refuge at the UN in Kabul. Azim Babak in an article in "Charom (Foruth) Mash'al" monthly of 2006 wrote: "Why did Dr. Najibullah, former President of Afghanistan seek refuge at the UN mission? Because he was not a Marxist anymore."

An Arab intruder in the 7th century, used to fight with two swords at a time in order to impose his religion in Kabul. This signifies that he beheaded many people. His shrine in Kabul is now the worship place for many Afghans who call him the King of two swords. People worship his shrine and kiss its walls. I should admit that I used to visit his shrine but for a different cause. This alien intruder was such a cruel person who beheaded many of my compatriots.

It's so unfortunate that there is no mention about my brave compatriot (Kabuli brother) who beheaded the Arab intruder while defending his country, freedom and all the material and spiritual achievements. Dear reader, based on your fair judgment, how do you evaluate a nation who unknowingly worships the oppressor over the oppressed?

Mr. Rostami pointed out an important fact about the religious policies which has not been noticed by the free world. It's about the symbols and characters used in the flags of Saudi Arabia and Afghanistan. The religious symbols indicate that there is no God but Allah and Mohammad, his prophet.

Rostami quoted a paragraph from "Allah Akbar" book by Dr. Roshangar as saying that Al Bara had stated that during "Hodaybieh" they were very thirsty and needed some water but the well in the nearby was dried out. Mohammad spit in the well and the well turned out to be full of water. All of the 1400 men and the camels could drink water from the well. (Hadith No. 777, volume IV, Hadith No. 471 and 272, volume IV)

The above mentioned slogan is the worst insult and humiliation to non-Muslim countries. When Saudi kings or Hamid Karzai, President of Afghanistan are officially invited by France or the US, the religious flags of the former countries are displayed beside the flags of the US and France. The symbols used in the flags of Saudi Arabia and Afghanistan are an indication of denying the prophets of other religions.

The slogans used are not only an insult to the Presidents of the host countries but also to their people. Second, certain democratic countries tolerate Allah Akbar (God is Great) slogan as an appeasement policy. However, they beheaded the Egyptian diplomat in Iraq while chanting Allah Akbar. They slaughtered Theo Van Gogh, the Dutch painter, killed Daniel Pearl and Nick Berg, Engineer Paul Johnson and the Italian Journalist, Fabrizio Quattrocchi while saying Allah Akbar.

Farah Pahlavi (former Queen of Iran) who is a knowledgeable woman, wrote in page 280 of her memoirs, Kohan Diara, that the Ayatollah had set up certain nights and at exactly 8:00 pm people used to go on their rooftops and chanted "Allah Akbar" (God is Great). These words used to be a peaceful prayer for me since childhood, but they turned into horrible words for me and when I hear them it seems that my blood freezes.

Farah added that the Khomeini regime had sentenced the Education Minister, Mrs. Farokh Roo Parsa, to death. Her sentence was carried out in such a way that I'm ashamed to write about it. Ashamed of this fact that how could Iranian behave in such a horrible manner. She was wrapped in a gunny, so that men wouldn't see her body after being shot. Thousands of women were killed in the same way. Girls were raped, because according to religious thoughts, virgins would go to heaven. I want to ask these Mullahs (great Satan) that to which heaven will they go after having raped and killed all those Iranian noble women (daughters of Darius the Great)?

In Koran, in Sura Baqara 224, it says do not make a napkin from the name of Allah.

ولا تجعلوا الله عَرضة

It was Allah Akbar who massacred children of the Beslan school. It was Allah Akbar who leveled New York's twin towers and burned thousands of innocent humans. Islamic fundamentalism has committed numerous horrible crimes. These very same fundamentalists have been living in the generous western countries, slept on king-size beds and use Social Services assistance to perform Haj and visit Saudi Arabia. They chant Allah Akbar right under the nose of the US President, George Bush, leader of a superpower.

Muslims are enjoying blessings in European, Australian and American countries. They could never have such blessings in their own countries, especially religious freedom and building mosques designed with expensive chandeliers. Still there are Muslims in countries who don't have electricity or even a horse to ride on. Whereas in western countries, they drive or ride in the latest model cars.

It's a fact that if they had such blessings in their own countries, they would never have immigrated to America or Europe. Such unfaithful people have been living a high standard life but have violated the principles of democracy and chant Allah Akbar.

A religion which doesn't have any mercy on Muslims, Christians, Hindus or Jews. Such ignorant people who immigrated to the US due to economic poverty, lack of freedom and democracy in their homelands, instead of struggling with such a regressive Islamic culture, start fighting with Jews and Christians. These people don't appreciate the great value of having freedom. They prefer their fundamentalist and regressive culture over those blessings. They cause instability, unrest and insecurity in their heavenly host countries. They have mistreated democracy and should be expelled from Europe, the US, Australia and other North American countries. This is my best prescription for the democratic world. If my suggestion receives approval, then the world will get rid of such evils.

I, who was born in an Islamic country, am completely aware of the intentions of an uncivilized and fundamentalist Muslim. They don't respect or appreciate any other religion other than Islam. For 1400 years they have been praying for the elimination of Christianity, Judaism, Hindu and others at the end of their prayers, five times daily.

Here in America the mosques unlike other faiths are opened every day and imams the white capped those who do not respect the reasons and ethics, on the bases of ineptitudes and hideous discourses infatuate the dumb people, and in the end this mania causes to violence, therefore as a Muslim I ask the congress of America to make Muslims here to pray like others once a week.

If the free world (Europe, America, Canada) and others say nothing to the irrelevant tautology of Islam Paradox, the Sharea law because of such appeasement policy soon or later would be diffused all over the areas.

One of the Islamic slogan here in America is the written symbol of Halal meat (to slash the throat of animals) hanging over on every Islamic shops and cooking areas which plainly it is a discriminating subject.

Muslims apportunists under the Jewesh shield (Judaism dietary law) extending their Islamic slogans every where and this practice must be stopped. Look at the hypocrate Muslims how much they hate Jewesh people but they like the Jewesh laws.

Double tortured:

In Albany New York, a Muslim friend took me to Dominick's farm to buy Halal meat. Dominick grabbed a red one year old calf and took it into slaughter house. Dominick was a christian and he hit the animal on the forehead with a sledge hammer. Then, the Muslim put slashed the throat of the animal.

In this sterner circumstance or others I'm convinced we can disrupt the cohesion of these thugs drastically, and the white capped imams got no another choices except to leave the country or lose the customers. Believe it or not these white capped imams with the unctuous position are very harmful to the American's society.

My dear brothers and sisters: never trust Islam paradox, in Kuran in the Female Cow chapter verse 286 which it is not a verse Muslims begging Allah, Oh Allah succeed us over the infidels and the white capped imams read this verse the end of every pray, but I do not know who are the infidels?

May be I would have not denied any religion if it had not interfered with politic and freedom, but Christianity involves politic and Islam is the follower of Christianity. Because of Christianity Islam has become more organized and more political in Europe, Australia and American, which is not a very good sign for America. Providing this terrorists prisoners with kuran in person is also a sin because through of this sort of appeasement policy you still making your enemies dummy and brutal.

I asked Mr. Rostami if he had any message for the outside world. He welcomed my proposal and told that he has been waiting a long time for this moment. His message for the peace-loving world community regarding the oppressed yet proud people of Afghanistan is that the Arab religion has offered nothing but has imposed some fancy ideas,bloodshed, ransacking, physical and spiritual damage over the past 1400 years.

We, Khorasanis, have seen the horrible crimes of Arab nomads during the 1980 tragic political developments and how Arab and Taliban intruders destroyed our homeland, raped our women and blew up the 2000 year old Bamyan statutes which were our national pride. We have seen that upon downfall of the democratic regime, Afghan troops surrendered to Mujahideen, puppets of Arab criminals but the latter beheaded our troops and cut off their ears and most probably the Arab Zarqawi had a hand in beheading Afghan troops which was the worst insult and disrespect to the brave Afghan nation. Most Afghan Generals (loyal to Pakistan's ISI) and coward Mullahs could never cleanse their hands from the blood of the Afghan nation.

My expectation from those who have faith in a free, peaceful and equal world is to oblige Arabs, especially those in Saudi Arabia, who have imposed their religion on my country (Khorasan currently called Afghanistan) to pay compensation. Because not only millions of our people were killed due to their religious conspiracy, but thousands others have been disabled, widowed and unemployed. They suffer from poverty and illness. Children cannot go to school, sick people don't have money to buy medicine, etc.

کو خدا کیست خدا چیست خدا   بی جهت بحث مکن نیست خدا
(ایرج میرزا)

Rostami called on the Afghan nation, men and women to break their ties with Arabs and wisely judge the crimes committed by the latter during tragic events in the past and present. He said that the more we distance ourselves from such savages, the better and wiser our country will be.

As a matter of fact, and based on the advice of President Jamshid Yazd, Mr. Rostami called on all the jurists including Mr. Afrasiab Boresh, the Ambassador and special envoy of the president to the UN, who holds a Ph.D. in law from India, to gather in a forum to discuss the nation's rehabilitation; a nation whose achievements and glories were suppressed because of the imposed religion by Arabs. As a result, and based on war time rules and regulations, they should oblige Saudi Arabia to pay one hundred forty Billion Dollars compensation through the UN.

This new idea which was unique throughout the history of Afghanistan had surprised everyone especially Mullahs and certain other groups who had sympathy towards Arabs and their imposed religion. One of the wise professors of Kabul University by the name of Kamran told people that World War I, sparked by Germans in 1914, caused European countries to incur lots of losses. The war committee on compensation, obliged Germany to pay USD 31.5 billion to the Allies. World War II, started by Adolph Hitler in 1939 resulted in the massacre of millions, mostly Jews. They asked for compensation from Germany. It's the same with Blacks in the US who asked for compensation from Whites, Koreans from Japanese, Japanese from the US and the rest. As a matter of fact, and based on credible evidence, our country has the right to ask for compensation from the Saudi Kings. People who were surprised by all these facts, agreed with the professor.

After a few months and asking for the assistance and clarification of some foreign jurists, the Afghan jurists finally came to terms, put up a request and submitted to Mr. Rostami. The latter reviewed the request and submitted it to the presidential office. A week later, the president invited all the jurists to a dinner at the presidential palace and appreciated their efforts in drawing up such a reasonable and logical letter. He then gave the letter to Ambassador Afrasiab who was off to the UN, along with two special and confidential notes to the Secretary General of the UN and Head of the Security Council. The president promised the jurists that if they succeed, their sincere services rendered to the long suffered nation wouldn't be wasted.

Ambassador Afrasiab, who was so happy, in replying to a question asked by a journalist at Khajeh Ravash Airport in Kabul, said that: "Yes, the people of the world are all well aware of the violation of Afghan's human rights and their long-time suffering and I'm sure that they will raise their voice in support of Afghanistan's nation".

The plane carrying Ambassador Afrasiab landed at JFK airport in New York. He was warmly welcomed by the Afghan delegation at the UN. The delegation was proud of the initiations of the Republic government, especially Mr. Sohrab Rostami, a hardworking and knowledgeable man. The following day, Ambassador Afrasiab submitted the confidential notes and the request during his meeting with the Secretary General. After a few months, the Secretary General who was a law professor called in Ambassador Afrasiab to a meeting and jokingly told him that even a big fish couldn't escape from a small net. He meant that the proposal and initiation of the new government in Kabul were not in contradiction with the law and could be presented to the Security Council.

The Head of the Security Council, an experienced diplomat, didn't oppose the proposal of the Republic of Khorasan and sent it to the Council's secretariat to be dispatched to the International Tribunal of Hague. Ambassador Afrasiab was waiting to hear good news about the proposal. Journalists, who were informed about the event, prepared themselves to write reports about it. A few months passed and people were waiting for the result. Finally Ambassador Afrasiab was informed that he should take part in the hearings. The Ambassador who was so concerned about the outcome told his colleagues that if luck was with the long suffering nation of Afghanistan, they could win, after taking such a risk.

Ambassador Afrasiab went to the hearing. Since it was the first time in the history of the tribunal that such a proposal was submitted, the news was rather disappointing. Did the tribunal have the authority to enforce the judgment? In answer to the question of one of the jurists, Ambassador Afrasiab said that it was clear that Saudi Arabia had indirectly supported Taliban and there was a time when the Saudi kings and other capitalist sheikhs used to call Taliban, the heroes. The Ambassador added that he was surprised why the world ignored all these violations. He wanted to mention the cruelty of Taliban but he burst into tears. Members of the tribunal were so impressed. However, the Ambassador quoted the following phrases from a book written in English, "The Saudi paymasters provided the enormous quantity of $15 million worth of high-tech weapons, rifles with telescopic sights, transmission equipment, and infrared night vision goggles."

Outside the tribunal, the Afghan refugees in Europe, while flying beautiful flags of their country, chanted slogans indicting Saudi Arabia and other Arab capitalist sheikhs for spending billions of dollars every year in support of universal Islamization and sabotage. They should pay compensation. International terrorism led by Osama bin Laden under the name Al Qaida has its roots in Saudi Arabia. The court announced recess for two hours after which the judgment was issued. Saudi Arabia has to pay $ 140 billion to the Republic of Khorasan within 25 years. Hearing the good news, the Ambassador fainted.

In the Republic of Khorasan there was a big celebration. Children were running on the streets barefooted, while the women watched them from the rooftops. Sohrab Rostami, Head of the Reform Committee announced a three-day national celebration. Girls and boys were dancing together on the roads, photographers snapped shots everywhere and people chanted slogans including "Long live

Jamshid Yazd". A young girl by the name of Tahmina jumped out from the crowd fissed her left hand in to the air and said to young Saudi generations we are with you please rise up against the dictator.

Sara Yazd, the only daughter of Jamshid Yazd and a few other girls were flying a new flag with Yellow, Pink and Blue colors, bearing symbols of wheat, rice, and the Red star on top. Sara, who was weeping from time to time, told the other girls that she wished her brother (Parviz Yazd) was with them in their celebration.

Chapter Five

RELIGIOUS DIVISIVE PROPAGANDA

Brothers and Sisters! It is not only the Khorasani people who complain about Islamic fundamentalism and Arab terrorism. Here in the US, professor and former diplomat, the Senate Speaker from the Republican Party, Newt Gingrich wrote in his book, <u>Winning the Future</u>, that the future of the US in endangered by five factors. "The Islamic terrorists and rogue dictatorships will acquire and launch nuclear or biological weapons."

I should tell Mr. Gingrich that when the Soviet Union collapsed, the capitalist Arabs (Saudi Arabia) thought of replacing it with an Islamic power. They believed that they could defeat the Roman Empire and the Atheist Empire). Destroying the US is simple. As Osama bin Laden put it, "the US is afraid of war" so you can hit and run.

On the Afghanistan issue, Newt Gingrich wrote that in 2004, the opium growers could earn a huge sum of foreign currency. They can now acquire modern technology easily. A lack of proper analysis of efforts for constructing a modern and free Afghanistan could increase the threat for the US. He wrote that another danger is that Pakistan might suffer an Islamist military coup and that Pakistan's nuclear weapons could be given to or taken by terrorists. He quoted

Iman al Zawahiri, an Arab terrorist, that we haven't yet as much as the Americans. We have the right to kill 4 million Americans including 2 million children and exile the rest. We have the right to disable thousands of others. Moreover, it is our right to fight them using biological and chemical weapons and so on.

Seyed Iman Al Zawahiri! Are you really a man of war? Because real soldiers fight unmasked and eye to eye. Those who are afraid would cover their faces in black masks and take refuge in caves like bats, or hide under the chador of a Pakistani woman and baggy trousers of Taliban. Based on regressive sermons by clergy, you are capable of killing innocent people with bombs, closing your eyes to all human morals and values. You should know that you are nothing but a few chicken-hearted, cowardly, disappointed and defeated guys.

Note: I kindly ask those countries who assist in reconstruction, liberation and establishment of civil society in Afghanistan either financially or technically, to warn Hamid Karzai's regime not to dispatch students to Arab countries for religious education, by using such financial aids, or use the money in Ministry of Haj who are involved in religious activities. It was because of these religionists that Afghanistan's freedom and sovereignty were violated, economic poverty was boosted and thousands were disabled and killed in the name of God. Millions of Dollars of aides were used by Mullahs for dethroning of the democratic regime, which is fact should have been used for the disabled. These Mullahs have now become businessmen.

Not only millions of families became homeless and refugees due to religious wars between different sects, but developed cities have been totally destroyed as well.

Religion is a method of understanding and reaction between people and the environment. It is an acquisition transferred from one generation to another. It's culture which can develop due to demands, needs and requirements when faced with the constructive ideas of the modern era. If not so, valuable historical developments could have never occurred in the social life. Religion is based on confabulations of some nomads, told by dogmatic and narrow-minded clergies. Why should our world burn in their hell? Those who like vultures are awaiting the death of Rostam Pahlavan (democracy).

As stated by Emile Durkheim, 1858-1917 the French Sociologist, religion seems to be for purification of human beings. It was the individual's way of becoming recognizable within an established society and helping them to surrender to spiritual failures and give away economic demands. Believers would come to solidarity and that's when religionists claim that they are privileged.

In addition, organized religious societies donate money and time and help the above societies to gain power over those who appreciate family and friendship values. In fact, if religion is such an amazing phenomena then there would be no need to learn natural sciences, engineering, technology, etc. Durkheim stated that religion cannot perform it's role as it used to in the past and it should go through major changes before it vanishes. Certain churches in the US have already begun the process.

After 1400 years, there has been no major social development in Islam. Since the bloody political developments in my country (Ariana), religion has become more fanatical than in the era of Caliphate of Umayyad, Abbasids and Fatemis. By the end of 2002, polio was diagnosed in three Asian and three African countries.

In 2004, 602 cases were registered worldwide, of which 476 cases were in Nigeria's northern states, mainly in the Muslim community of Kano. There were rumors that the polio vaccine caused infertility in women, therefore Muslims banned the vaccine.

David Brown had an article in the *Washington Post* of August 27, 2004 which was quoted in Children's Manners by the revered writer Shakiba Naurau as saying that maybe it is a game between Muslim leaders in the North and Christians in the South. After 16 months, Muslims finally accepted the vaccination conditionally.

First, the purity of the vaccine must be tested. Second, vaccines should be manufactured in Indonesia, which is an Islamic state.

Interesting to note that polio does not exist in southern Nigeria, which is a Christian community. If Imams have prohibited using Polio and Vatican prohibits using Condoms then what's the difference between Christianity and Islam based on theology? Edward Jenner used Cowpox vaccine against Smallpox in 1796 and rescued the mankind of such a fatal disease.

Also Dr. Zabdiel Boylston and his wife Lady Mary Worthley Montagu contributed a lot towards fighting Smallpox but the Chancellor of Yale University, Timothy Dewight opposed using the vaccine against Smallpox claiming that it was interfering with God's creation.

People and their neighbors insulted them and threw dirt and spoiled egg and fruits to such considerate human beings and called them bad names such as raw head and bloody bones, illiterate, negligent, ignorant and mischievous.

However, the two compassionate and dedicated human beings not only rescued millions of lives but also prevented them from becoming blind or deaf.

(The initiatives of the world of Christianity) will provide the opportunity for other religions to follow Vatican and include whatever trash about futility in their religious vocabulary and Mulsims who are following Vatican and copy the same trash. According to Christopher Hitchens, "There were those who said that the fossils had been placed in the rock by god, in order to test our faith."

The outstanding Afghan scholar, Gholam Ali Ayen, had an article in the Omaid Weekly, published in Virginia. He wrote that Islam does have some benefits in theory, but as far as practice is concerned, contemporary Muslims have tragically proven to be ignorant, incompetent, regressive and narrow-minded. The professor believes that such delinquency exists within themselves and as long as it's not detected, practice is impossible due to the fact that the theory is defined as the practically organized knowledge which is adjustable in almost all conditions especially the hypothesis system of accepted principles of thoughts and ideas. "Theories can analyze, predict and explain the nature of phenomenon."

I'd like to share a funny story with the readers. I met a fundamentalist Afghan in the US. We had a controversial conversation. He asked me if I was a Muslim or an Afghan. Upon hearing that, I felt as if a bomb was planted in my heart. I felt as if all my hair stood on end when I heard his disrespectful and shameful question. The fundamentalist man was not only hurt but confused by my reaction, since I told him that I was an Afghan.

This traitor fundamentalist is like a sheep who has turned into a dog due to indoctrination of a few fraudulent in a way that he has put religion above his nation whereas the nation is the mother of culture. Rodney Stark, a sociologist with Washington University believes that social ties are greater than faith. This means that social ties stem from culture. Religion is one of the components of culture, but not a necessary one. Some even believe that it's extra to culture.

We can bring an example of one of the disciplinary components of religious stability (Witch Hunts) which played an important role in the violence and cruelty occurred in the 17th and 18th centuries in Europe. This communicable disease was spread once again in 2001 in the world of Islam. The religious seditious politics of Imperialism brought about Taliban to which we were the witness of the worst historical crimes. Iranians, Afghans, Uzbeks, Indians, Indonesians, British, Spanish, Americans, Russians, Iraqis, Arabs and even Theo Van Gogh all have been burned in the fire of such disciplinary factor of religious stability.

The atrocities by a culture which has not only prevented any development during the past 1500 years but have turned more violent in the course of time and Quran reciters with their nice voices especially with their twisted veins while reciting which of course is some kind of a deceit have intoxicated the naïve people. If religious reforms don't take place, Islam and it's component factors such as religious discipline will be united and we will die in the prison of inquisitors.

As a result of Renaissance, European philosophers turned from super natural to natural or rational explanation of external world. The idealist philosopher, Berkeley is one of them.

George Berkeley 1685-1753 argued that things not perceived did not exist.

Those who can't differentiate between wisdom and indoctrination should call religion the ruling wisdom. It's amazing that wisdom commands humans to accept a hollow and unbelievable idea, which is indoctrination, with no criticism or reaction.

Indoctrination is a special way of thinking free from any authority or control, jurisdiction, criticism and evaluation; A dictatorship-type method which does not conform to wisdom. By wisdom you can differentiate good from bad, but you can't do this with indoctrination. Religion is like a bomb and indoctrination is like gunpowder which even increases it's destroying power.

Fundamentalists call it the spiritual section of the religion. To indoctrinate is to instruct in a body of doctrine, teaching the acceptance of a system of thought without criticism; Indoctrinating the workers with an incessant stream of propaganda.

There are various religions in India which are in conflict with each other, making religious unity impossible but in emergenceies they are a united nation.They are united as a nation but not in their religion. Arabic countries share the same language and pray in the same mosque but have differeces regardidng political and religious issues.They can't be united as a single nation because of religious differences.

I want to ask sociologists and social science scholars whether an impose religion is the integral part of national identity of a nation? A religion which does not represent the tradition of our ancestors and is an imported and imposed one which blocks the process of development in social life except for religious aspects.

I wonder if the politicians at the White House and others would be succesful in establishing democracy in the fundamentalist and regressive Afghan society who even here in the US work in the favor of Ikhvan Almuslimin and are against their master, the US.

Dear friends, I'd like to draw your attention to this fact that the imposed religion Islam (Ishlam) brought nothing to my country but poverty, distruction, illiteracy, war,and superstitious.

It was due to Saudi money that the Afghan nation and Mullahs supported the leadership of Arabs and refused to defend freedom and independence of Afghanistan. An Afghan professor at Al Azhar University who was bribed by Saudi Dinars and US Dollars, once stated that all of Afghanistan is not even worth as much as two units of prayer. I have never seen or heard of such a traitor and lowlife human being in the history of any country.

A group of British once traveled to an African country in order to sign a contract. Upon return they saw that their shoes were polished and cleaned. When they asked for an explanation, they were told that the host didn't want them to take home even one gram of the soil of their country.

It would have been nice if Afghan politicians could have taught Mullahs and other traitors that mothers and the motherland are the most sacred things in life and as a matter of fact our freedom is closely related to our country's freedom and is more important than any imaginary, fancy heaven or angel.

The abundant money of the Christian world enabled Afghans to perform Haj several times and throw stones at Satan, worship

Ka'bah, pray Allah to eliminate the Great Satan (US) since the latter supports Jews. These Muslims are so poor in their own countries and are unable to visit even one of the cities of their homeland. The tragic events in Afghanistan not only made them millionaires and Haji, Hajia but more fundamentalist treason, corrupt, and fond of Arabs.

Those bearded Muslims, women under chadors, and other fundamentalists who abuse the generosity of the liberal countries and waste millions of dollars in the Arabic peninsula while their sisters, brothers, parents, neighbors or compatriots live in poverty and don't have money to pay for medicine, food and school.

Some blind and deaf Muslims weep and cry at the end of Ramadhan because they've lost a very dear guest, whereas other Muslim intellectuals complain about this stubborn guest of 1400 years.

Here in the US, either due to business or making fundamentalist Muslims glad, at the time of Eid, they post cards bearing "Eid Mubarak" which is a religious symbol. Dr. Michael Newdow calls these symbols illegal and has launched a campaign against them.

In July 2006, Muslim terrorists trained in Pakistan, planted bombs in trains in Bombay and killed and injured hundreds.

On Nov 29, 2008 Pakistany's terrorists attacked the Taj Mahal Hotel in Bombai to kill 5000 people.

If you look at the feature of these terrorists, all are indigenous Indians who converted to Islam. During the 62 hour siege of the Taj hotel, 3 terrorists, 18 foreigners and 16 security personnel (including two NSG men) were killed.

Newt Gingrich, former Republican Speaker of the House, in his book, Winning the Future, wrote about an atomic Pakistan that another danger is that Pakistan might suffer an Islamist military coup and that Pakistan's nuclear weapons could be given to or taken by terrorists.

The new Pakistani dictatorship even announced that a weapon had been "stolen" and argues that it would not be to blame if a bomb went off in the United States, Israel, India or Europe.

Predictions of Mr. Gingrich raised concerns due to the characteristics of the religious fundamentalist society of Pakistan and the geopolitical situation of the region. Due to political tensions in Pakistan, if terrorists take over the nuclear reactors, I think that the first missile will hit Hamid Karzai, President of Afghanistan who is protecting the interests of the US. Considering all these facts, would the existence of a nuclear-powered Pakistan still be necessary in such a critical region?

In his book, Allah Akbar, Dr. Roshangar wrote in the February 1983, in a Shiite village in north Pakistan, a village girl claimed that she had a dream in which Husayn bin Ali, the third Shiite Imam told her that he had called the inhabitants of the village to go for his pilgrimage and that if they throw themselves in the sea, he will take them to Karbala safe and sound.

As soon as the villagers heard about this dream, thousands of them threw themselves into waters near the Karachi shore. Soon after, dead bodies of more than 30 people were floating on the waters. Dear readers, if modern Muslims don't take action in putting and end to such superstitions, I believe that religious fundamentalists, either Hezbullah or Hezbulmohammad will cause constant turmoil. The intellectual youth and instructors of Saudi Arabia are waiting for the time when they can enforce social, political, economic and religious reforms and establish a secular regime, which will put an end to all such superstitions.

In the index on page 237, the second paragraph of Winning the Future written by Newt Gingrich, Hamid Karzai was misspelled as Kharzai Hamid (Khar in Persian means donkey) but it must be corrected to Karzai.

On April 2, 2009, Roman Deutsch was on CNN's Jack Cafferty show and he stated: "Hey Jack. As a father of two beautiful daughters I think Karzai along with the idiot from Japan who made a video on how to rape a woman, need to exit this planet. Whether it be by their own hands or by the people. Which it seems as though in both cases the people are just as they are. What a world we live in! Nuclear talks from countries who want attention to these Karzai legalizing raping of woman. Sometimes, I think there is no hope for mankind. Maybe by the grace of God, a real earth shaking event would be in order for Karzai. So ignorant he is and he likes to think of himself as a leader. Cow Dung is better than him. At least dung fertilizes the ground. Karzai poisons the ground he walks on".

When ministers and representatives were sworn into office, Karzai put the Koran in front of them in order to take an oath not to commit any sin. Never before in Afghanistan has such a childish measure been taken. However, I started thinking why can't we take our oath on mothers, the homeland or the sun. It would be better than those books, which do nothing but separate people in the world.

Mother, the most sacred creature who nurtured me for nine months giving me the utmost care, breast fed me in the cold winter nights, took care of me and taught me how to speak, how to walk and finally sent me to school.

John Bachofen, a Swiss scholar, in his book in 1861 has written about the role of mothers called Earth Goddess, Mother Goddess and the Great mother in the Cretan society of Greece. He wrote that people used to worship them in the past.

In Egypt, Hatshepsut, 1503-1482 BC, took political power and her monument still exists near the Nile river. It means that women used to hold power and political positions in the past. We can mention those women who have been active in the feminist movements and have offered great services. Florence Nightangale, Elizabeth Cady Stanton, Margaret Thatcher, Catherine the Great, Golda Meir, Olympe De Gouge and Indera Gandhi could be named as a few. Queen Soraya, wife of King Amanullah of Afghanistan, Queen Farah Diba Pahlavi of Iran and a revolutionary woman, Nancy Pelosi, the democratic speaker of the house.

One day, my daughter "Suraya" called me on phone and asked why I have ignored Hillary R. Clinton. To respect her reminder, I want to write down a reminiscence of mine about Hillary.

On January 29, 2008, I had an appointment at the office of Dr.Yusuf in Laurel, MD. I knew a woman who was working as a receptionist in the emergency department at "Laurel Regional Hospital", asked me what I thought about the Presidential candidacy of Obama and Hillary. At first, I asked her opinion and she said that she prefers Obama because she is black.

In response, I told her that certainly Mr. Obama to me is a very intellectual person but my choice is Hillary because men have always been a dominant force throughout the course of history. In 250 years, in a democratic country like America, a woman has been not elected as a President. Why?

Look at Asia, Europe, Latin America, and Africa. Regarding this aspect, they are a head of America and I added that Obama is a man. I told the nurse that she should defend her own gender and then on my way out, she put a sticker of Hillary on my jacket.

Really, Hillary is a wonderful, outstanding and very hard working woman. I want her to win and I wish her the best.

However, I should mention that it was a man who deprived women from such authorities by force. Women give birth to heroes, poets, writers, politicians, artists and others who will then make the society proud of them.

After the 1789 revolution in France, the government ruled over the churches. Some of the clergy, who supported the revolution, stopped their support and the government obliged the clergy to take oaths but many of them didn't bow except for four big heads.

What are oaths?

Oaths are solemn, formal declarations or promises to fulfill a pledge. Often, oaths call upon God as witness.

There is a story about a young guy who loved a girl but the beautiful girl ignored him. One day he came face to face with her, begging. He told the girl whatever she wanted he would prepare and asked her to stop torturing him. In a moment of sudden madness, the girl asked him to bring his mother's heart. He headed home in a deathly rush, went to the kitchen, took the knife and attacked his mother. On his way to bring the bloody heart to the girl, he stumbled and hit the ground, the heart was thrown away but it was saying Ah! My son got hurt!

The purpose of mentioning the above story is that taking oaths on some outdated books which provoke separation isn't right. I personally believe that if we take oaths on sacred things for their decency and competence, there is nothing more sacred in the world than a mother. In memory of mothers, the poem says:

پس هستی من ز هستی اوست   تا هستم و هست دارمش دوست

My being is from her being, till I'm alive I love her.

One of my cousins, Abdulghani, who was 8 or 9 years old had dysuria. Since there was no physician in the area at that time, his poor mother wept and tried to help her son by sucking his urethra but the poor kid died of that disease. So, isn't it wiser that all of the academicians in the world come together and prepare a universal affidavit in the name of all mothers.

Some people are not very fond of Afghanistan's flag. Out of 206 other flags in the world, this flag is one of the most religious. It even dominates the flag of Saudi Arabia. The only difference is the size of the swords on the flags. During the presidency of Mohammad Davood and the new democratic regime the flag was somehow moderated but was transformed to a more religious theme during Mullahcracy!

I kindly call upon the young generation, men and women, intellectual instructors, as well as other understanding groups who share the same thoughts as myself, to change the flag and national anthem, which both lack any national characteristics.

Such flags bearing the names of Allah and Mohammad should be burned, ground and desecrated. Our artists, writers and modernists are bound by the boundaries of these superstitions, created by religious beliefs. The spells and myths of religious heritage in the past centuries have prevented people from enjoying their lives.

The narrow-minded religious groups try to prevent disclosure of realities. They label others as heretic, atheist and apostate and issue death sentence for the reformists. The professional unions of artists and writers, the Human Rights Commission and others have the mission to defend the aforementioned groups who try to enlighten peoples' minds in writings and artwork and reveal the true face of the reactionaries, enemies of civil society and reconstruction.

Such reactionaries as Abdul Aziz bin Baz who claimed that the sun moves around the earth. Saint Augustine from Canterbury, who died in 605 A.D. said the same thing before Islam was born.

For a thousand years, myths and stories have been passed from one generation to another. Islam is one of those collections of myths. Muslims are encouraged by Allah Akbar to kill the Jews, Christians, Hindus and Buddhists.

If they do so, Allah will send them directly to heaven where beautiful virgin angels are waiting for them and servants will serve them steak and kabab with wine. Such a hypothesis will certainly encourage them to burn or behead me and you. So what's the point in welcoming such killers into the US or provide them with the Allah Akbar book in Guantanamo which denies the existence of and desires the elimination of all other religions but Islam. What's the point in providing them with such a book in their mosques?

With due consideration to all of the above facts, before it's too late, the free world Europ, America, Australia, Canada, especially Great Britain, should deport all Fundamentalists Muslim and This is my best advice for you.

Mustafa Kamal Ataturk, 1881, the Turkish hero who slapped Islam hard, in the face, Deported 1,300,000 Greeks from Asia Minor. Greece deported 353,000 Muslims from Macedonia while neither of these two races were terrorists or fascists.

Muslims can perform their prayers at home and there is no need for Imams and Mullahs who deliver invidious speeches to our youth in order to provoke them against Jews, Christians and others.

Islamic fundamentalists plant bombs in Quran and put them in airplanes, ships and trains or make their followers swallow bombs or make fundamentalist woman carry a bomb between her legs. Even if physical and financial losses would be small, the mental ones would assuredly be great.

All of these terrors that now exist in the free and democratic world of old are due to such fundamentalists who overthrew the democratic regime of Afghanistan and the Monarchy of that of Mohammad Reza Shah Pahlavi (1925-1979) in Iran who was replaced by the Ayatollah Khomeini.

Mohammad Reza Shah stood against fundamentalists like the Great Emir Abdulrahman. Fundamentalists and their followers don't believe in anything else but their dear Islam! They have no respect for their own wives and children, freedom, democracy or even their country. Like that Afghan Mullah who said that his country was not worth as much as two prayers. Mr. George Bush, the US President during his visit to Kabul in 2006, praised Islam and by this gesture approved the regime of Mullah Karzai.

One of the outstanding scholars of Afghanistan, Gholam Ali Ayen, in one of his articles in the US media, posed the question, "Islam and Democracy"? - there is no place for democracy in Islam. This is especially true with Afghanistan since by establishing democracy, tribes will lose their religion and language and there would be no room for tribalism anymore. I suggest that in order to establish democracy in Afghanistan and Islamic countries, we should use the philosophy of Jalaludin Mohammad Rumi, based on secularism.

In The Children's Manners by the revered writer, Shakiba Naurau, there is a nice story quoted by France De Wall about the Dutch zoo regarding the feelings of two chimpanzees called Nikkie and Luit.

Nikkie got angry with Luit, screaming and yelling at him. Luit who is also a male chimpanzee was afraid and jumped on the Oak tree which could barely tolerate his weight. De Waal said that after ten minutes Nikkie offered Luit his hand for reconciliation and coexistence. When both of them got down from the tree, they hugged and kissed each other.

This reconciliation story reminded me of the 1400 years of war between Arabs and Jews. There are 250 million Arabs and only 15 million Jews in the world. Is it possible for angry Arabs to bring peace between Arabs, Ajams and universally; to reach out for friendship with their Jewish brothers, sons of Abraham, who are related to Arabs instead of all these killings and bombings which result in the loss of lives of dear Palestinian and Jewish youth, which has been going on for over a decade. How is it that animals in custody think more wisely than free humans? Long live civilized chimpanzees whose feelings of reconciliation are very powerful than the feelings of some dumb people.

Genetics is a science about the origin of creation and discovery of genes. Why do sons resemble fathers? Biologists have claimed that, based on heredity, such similarities are transferred from one generation to another. They claim that similarities are carried by genes in the cell units which cannot even be seen by microscopes. The part of biology that deals with genes is called Genetics. However, Mullahs cannot make it clear why mutations occur in RNA or DNA nucleus, that marriage or birth rules don't matter, and, in the end, humans (Jews) are changed into monkeys, jumping from one tree to another.

The chivalrous, Abdul Rahman Yahud

Around 1960's a few Jewish families used to live in Kabul and people especially the merchants used to have close ties with them.

Another Abdul Rahman Piaman, from the law faculty in Afghanistan, now lives in Arlington (Virginia), He told me that his friend wanted to marry a young girl but he couldn't afford to do so. So, both friends went to Abdul Rahman Yahud (Jewish) to ask him for help, Abdul Rahman Yahud the generous man lent him the money.

I believe that the problem of both fundamentalist groups (Jews and Arabs) regarding Jerusalem,Temple Mount will never be solved unless neither parties gain power over it or it'll be divided into two equal parts. We all know that even God was incapable of securing justice and equality. Satan, the fallen angel and Adam both disobeyed God. How is it possible one became malicious and the other benevolent?

Azzam, an Israeli Arab tourist who was imprisoned in Egypt for eight years, said "I suffered because I am Israeli. But, I am proud to be Israeli and Israel is the best country in the world. See how Jews, Muslims, Christians and Druze show support for each other. I'm proud of you for coming and I'm proud of myself. God bless the state of Israel."

Someone has written a book here in the US and tried to overt the opinions of Afghans living here, in a civil and free society. People who bought the book have written notes on the pages of this book which is full of curse and blasphemy and returned the book to its resource center. The book has created too much fear in the minds of readers and has made them believe that the writer was a Jew.

The poor fundamentalist, who was born in a mosque, wasn't aware that most scientists and inventors in the world were Jews. Moses the only prophet is a Jew. The Arabic opium has made him so dizzy and he cannot realize that those Americans who are protecting women and children in Afghanistan are mostly Jews. From quality point of view, if we put a few Arab and Ajams in one side of the balance and put a few Jews on the other side, certainly the Jews side will go down. We haven't heard any Jew blow himself because of the love of God and entering the imaginary heaven.

The Greek and Roman empires created valuable civilizations. There was a Renaissance in Italy from the14th to 16th centuries which then spread all over Europe. The Enlightenment era in the 17th and 18th centuries changed the viewpoints of Europeans totally and resulted in the enjoyable works by scholars (such as the story about humans being changed to monkeys, the fanciful tales which have stunned everybody).

Arabs not only hate Jews but they also hate women. Mrs. Jean Sasson in her book, Princess Sultana's Circle quoted one of the Saudis Princesses (Sultana) as saying, Arabs like their camels better than their wives. They sit their camels near themselves beside the air conditioner and sit their wives behind a non-covered area. In other parts of the book, she complains about (Prince Ali) and his son who went off to Thailand, Philippines, Pakistan and India for sex and prostitution. They buy women to have sex with them and bring them to Saudi Arabia. In a trip to Cairo, Sultana unfolds a rather bitter reality!

"Most disturbing of all, Ali had joined Hadi in his perverse behavior! While in Cairo, Sara and I had inadvertently come upon Hadi and Ali sexually assaulting a girl who was no more than eight years old! The scene had been one of horror and violence, and neither Sara nor I had ever overcome the haunting images of what we saw that day."

Sultana is so afraid of the horrible acts of the butcher of Ministry of Interior (Seyyed al Siayaf) who beheads people with the sword of Prince Ahmad bin Abdul Aziz Al Saud. She wrote, "Our family will eventually lose its control. I greatly fear that Saudi Arabia will tread the same path taken by Iran and Afghanistan. The Islamic fundamentalist ripple is growing in to a tidal wave that will engulf every Muslim country."

Prince Kareem, Sultana's husband has a more bitter voice! "Besides, the only reason we're still in power today is because the United States needs Saudi oil. One day, that need will be filled by some other fuel sources. Already scientists are starting to find substitutes for the fuel needs of the West. When that day comes, Saudi Arabia – and our family – will be expendable to the Americans. "

"The idea of Saudi Arabia going the way of Afghanistan causes my heart to pound with fear. The sad story of Afaaf, Sara's maid, made one thing quite clear. Should Saudi Arabia ever be ruled by fundamentalists, the lives of Saudi women would become more oppressed. Our fathers do not listen to their sons. A few concessions here and there would do no harm. It would make our position stronger but, "No". Our fathers are deaf. They can hear nothing but the ghost of their own father, a man who thought of himself as the hammer, and his subjects as the nails." Tears of sadness began to roll down my face. Kareem searched his pocket for a handkerchief. He pleaded, "Sultana, please do not cry."

Political changes in my homeland, Afghanistan, in the late 1980's, when her destiny was in the hands of Marxists, serving as a bridge between the Soviet Union and the Indian Ocean, was the most explosive situation which caused a lot of fear in the West.

Defeating the Marxist regime that had been strongly supported by the Russians was not an easy task. The West, who won the big prize, reached out for their enemy, "Ikhvan Al Muslimin" who were supported by the Saudis and they even strengthened the idea that Islam was endangered.

Mel Goodman, one CIA expert, disagreed with providing the Muslims with modern and high tech weapons. He argued that the Muslims called the West their enemies and it was possible that they use weapons against the West. Dupree Louis, an expert on Afghanistan, told me in an assembly in Pishavar in 1984 or 1985 that the US should provide the Afghans with Stinger Missiles which would have caused lots of damage to the Russians, leaving them no other choice than to leave Afghanistan. He added that if one or two fighter jets crashed in Qandahar, they should wait for a while and target a few more in the Eastern parts.

Zbigniew Berzezinski, the National Security Advisor during Jimmy Carter's presidency, had visited Khaibir Valley on the border of Afghanistan and Pakistan. He told the Afghan refugees that their religion was endangered and that they should have fought for their homeland to be able to return. Pakistanis hung a wreath of yellow flowers on him. It was obvious that due to the imposed treaty of "Duran Sir Mortimer" in 1893 where the border between Afghanistan on the Northeast with the Great Britain were set up, the Afghans would have wiped Islam out in Pakistan, meaning there would have been no more Pakistan.

However, this was one of the mistakes of the United States. In the post-Vietnam war, they were indirectly interfering with the internal affairs of another country and it could have had unwanted effects for them in the future, since they hurried into toppling the Marxist

Regime of Afghanistan by using "Ikhvan Al Muslimin" without studying their philosophy thoroughly. The United States with the cooperation of the Saudi and Pakistani governments and other Muslim fundamentalists in the world, especially Arabs, and by assembling them in Pakistan created such a monster which resulted in the total destruction of Afghanistan, financially and spiritually.

"The Americans wanted Afghanistan to become Russia's Vietnam. But I say to you, continuing such genocide to kill Afghan people will result in Afghanistan becoming America's second Vietnam" said Dr. Najib (the late President of Afghanistan).

Brzezinski, in his book "America And The World," on page 77 writes:

> An attack on Iran would create a situation the United State is involved in a war that spans Iraq, Iran, Afghanistan, and increasingly Pakistan, and certainly spills over into the Persian Gulf.I wish he would have said such a scientific political literature three decades ago about Afghanistan.

After two decades, the Americans wanted to remedy their mistakes and in order to restore peace in Afghanistan are using groups consisting of Jews. In their anti-terrorism war in Afghanistan, they are killed or disabled and in order to appreciate the sacrifice of these American Jews, Mr. Hamid Karzai's regime or his successor should recognize Israel, due to the fact that the Israeli government has political representatives in all Islamic countries of Middle Asia, some Arabic countries and in India.

"Ikhvan Al Muslimin" who wanted to destroy the empire of the so called non-believers, through chanting slogans of "Allah Akbar" (God is Great), the westerners equipped them with bazookas and provided them with dollars and dinars, the only effective strategy which not only toppled the Marxist regime of Afghanistan but also the Soviet Empire.

Since then, Muslims have gained prestige in the West, optimism and leniency of Europeans and Americans towards Muslims have provided the fundamentalists with such an opportunity to escape to the West bringing their destructive ideas and implement their political goals which were promoting the uncompromised religion of Islam and destroying other religions throughout the host countries, since the latter are not aware of their secret or even if they are informed, do not attach great importance to it.

Maybe fundamentalists have forgotten something. They had lost what they had in common with the West. The fundamentalists are not assimilating into the western culture. The only thing they have in common is their places of worship and religious gatherings. A few Imams who are given money, give speeches for youth in which they preach prejudice, pessimistic ideas and hate towards other religions and deny any other religion other than Islam and cause the darling young Palestinian and Israeli people to die.

What is their motivation? Why do fundamentalists do this?

1. Exaggeration of feelings, anger, meanness, disappointment, defeat, being a minority, and the most important of all, rivalry which makes victory impossible and leads the individual or the group to suicide attacks.

2. The fundamentalists are afraid that Western culture, advanced technology, movies, etc, would make Islam, an imposed religion, unacceptable and unsubstantial.

3. Changes in the balance of power will result in migrations and easy border crossing. Considering the importance of the situation at the time, the Westerners decided to renew the power of Ikhvan Al Muslimin, already in power, by bringing Ayatollah Khomeini to power. He was an illiterate Mullah who forced fashionable Iranian women to wear the chador (the black veil). Then, the habit of wearing the chador was transmitted to other Islamic countries. Young girls in

Turkey defended the chador, actually a product of nomadic Arabs, despite the fact that Mustapha Kamal Ataturk had previously prohibited wearing the chador. In the 1960's when I was studying at the American University of Lebanon, the only fashionable girl there was an Iranian girl named Homa Pezeshki, a student of pharmaceutics.

In his book The American Era, in the chapter "Globalization, Culture and Conflict", Robert J. Lieber writes, "The idea that modernization can be disruptive to traditional societies and that this can cause revolutionary turmoil is not new. In the mid 19th century, Alexis de Tocqueville concluded that rage and political upheaval stemmed not only from poverty and deprivation and/or the exercise of power itself but also from other causes including rising expectations, feelings of humiliation, and reactions against a ruler considered "illegitimate… and oppressive."

The American social scientist Seymour Martin Lipset, identified "relative deprivation" as a source of upheaval and found that disruptions caused by economic and social modernization could radicalize sections of the middle and professional classes and, thereby, cause them to be attracted to extremist movements.

Should the Arab Empire, formed by shedding the blood of innocent people, be eternal? Can this Empire be revived by taking revenge on Buddhists statutes in Bamiyan (in the East) or the twin towers of New York (in the West) or by blasting innocent Palestinian, Israeli and Iraqi people (in the Middle East) or others worldwide?

Islam was in a dissolute stage even though the prophet was still alive. Many had converted and a few (including a lady) claimed prophecy. She was killed by the agents of Muhammad. Verse 101 of the Repentance Chapter of the Koran states that, "Certain of the desert Arabs round about you are hypocrites, as well as (desert Arabs) among the Medina folk". Or in verse 97 of the same chapter, "The Arabs of the desert are the worst in non-belief and hypocrisy". Verse 29 of the Repentance chapter says, "Fight those who believe not in

Allah or the Last Day". Verse 33 of the Light Chapter states, "But force not your maids to prostitution when you desire chastity, in order that ye may make a gain in the goods of this life. But if anyone compels them, yet, after such compulsion, is Allah, Oft-Forgiving, Most Merciful (to them)"

There are many statements in the Koran which are worthy of being taken into careful consideration. In the following paragraph I'll provide you with some cases where a little means a lot.

In verses 39 and 49 of the Stoneland Chapter, Satan asks God to for permission to be able to freely toy with Muslims according to his own desires. Consequently, he (Satan) appears in the form of Gabriel and reveals verse No. 51 of The Clans Chapter to Muhammad, stating that all the women belong to him. People were provoked by the contents of this particular verse. Muhammad became upset and, in order to mollify him, God revealed verse No. 52 through Gabriel himself. It reads, "It is not lawful for thee (to marry more) women after this, nor to exchange them for (other) wives, even though their beauty attract thee". The question is why Allah himself did not recognize the Satan and he Muhammad did?

In verses 25 and 53 of the Pilgrimage Chapter, God tells Muhammad not to get upset since his predecessors were actually Satan's unwitting victims and, therefore, those verses were canceled. One of those verses is verse 51 of the Clans Chapter which we read in the Koran everyday.

In verse 223 of the Cow Chapter has been stated that, "your wives are as a tilth unto you."

In the Jalalin interpretation (which was the first Arabic interpretation), this verse has frequently been interpreted as giving total freedom to men in their sexual behavior. As stated in article 435 of his book, Ayatollah Khomeini (the leader of an Islamic movement) permitted such freedoms based upon certain considerations.

Verse No. 37 of the Clans Chapter (the case of Zainab, wife of Zaid bin Hareth) is another subject to which no satisfactory answer is given by Islamic jurists.

Hey wise men! If people didn't show such a harsh reaction to verse 51 of the Clans Chapter do you think that verse 52 would have been revealed?

Zaid bin Hareth was a slave given as a gift to Muhammad by his wife Khadijeh. But Muhammad released him. Zaid showed bravery during the battles of Badr, Ohod and Khandagh and consequently the prophet adopted him. The prophet ordered one of his relatives, a beautiful woman called Zainab, to marry Zaid. Once the Prophet paid a visit to the Zaid's house without prior notice he found Zainab very attractive and he fell in love with her at once. At this time verse No. 37 of the Clans Chapter was revealed to Muhammad. It reads, "Then when Zaid had dissolved his marriage with her, with the necessary formalities, We joined her in marriage to thee: in order that in the future there may be no difficulty for Believers in the matter of marriage with the wives of their adopted sons, when the latter have dissolved their marriages with the necessary formalities".

Christopher Hitchens writes:

> Augustine also fabricated the mad and cruel idea that the souls of unbaptized children were sent to "Limbo." Who can guess the load of misery that diseased "theory" has placed on millions of Catholic parents down the years, until its shamefaced and only partial revision by church in our own time? Luther was terrified of demons and believed that the mentally afflicted were the devil's work. Muhammad is claimed by his own followers to have thought, as did Jesus, that the desert was pullulating with djinns, or evil spirits.

When something bad is happening to somebody and he is in a cul-de-sac situation, he has to blame God, Satan, the Demon, Evil, Devil and others as adversary sources persistently tormenting people.

ای گفته که مردم این چه مردیست   کابلیس تــرا چـــنین بــگایـد

مولوی

In Islam, it is believed that all events are predetermined by fate and therefore cannot be changed by human beings.

We know revelation or Satan does not have a foreign form and everything comes from your own imaginations and your own actions. Revelation is a dramatic disclosure of something not previously known or realized.

Due to these many stupefying acts, the Islamic religion is experiencing the ramifications of those acts and the Arabs will soon lose all of their achievements that have been acquired through the use of force and pressure. It should be noted that Islam is based upon two main factors: Fear and Deceit. Islamic and non-Islamic researchers are revealing a whole new set of facts about those secrets and the forbidden stories. The fundamentalists are trying to prolong its life with the use of terror; so, before its death they should spend their honeymoon in Saudi Arabia and Afghans should invite Arab entertainers to their weddings.

While visiting my son Arash in Orange County, California in 2006 I heard that an Afghan family had invited an Arab entertainer to their wedding. It really broke my heart. It would have been better if that fundamentalist Afghan had invited a Koran reciter and a drummer to pray for the long life of the bride and the groom.

There is no "Allah" here in the US nor in Europe, Australia or Canada. There are no loud voices of Mullahs. So, to busy ourselves we should destroy the World Trade Center in New York and have our honeymoon in the deserts of Saudi Arabia. My compatriots who are now here in the US and Europe didn't wear a chador in Kabul but now they dress like Arab nomads and their young people grow long beards, signs of fundamentalism and desperation.

On April, 2009 the opportunistic government of Egypt obliterated three hundred thousand healthy pigs belonging to poor Christians. This was based on Jewish traditions regardless of who created the pig as the ugly animal?

What is glycerin and where does glycerin come from? It comes from fats and most commonly from pork. Some uses for glycerin include: conserving preserved fruit, a base for lotions, to prevent freezing hydraulic jaks, to lubricate molds (in some printing inks), in cake and candy making and sometimes to preserve scientific specimens. Because of their glycerin content, the soaps are very moisturizing to the skin.

Dear Friends!

Fundamentalism is a modern phenomenon which politicians and religionists cultivated in the land of Afghanistan according to their own wishes and desires. Saudi Arabia has established religious institutes all over the world to introduce Islam and, in addition, it has bought many heads of state, diplomats and scientists to work in its interest. I have given some examples in the earlier sections of this book and have tried to show that such a policy indicates their philosophy of promoting and expanding fundamentalism.

Douglas Murray, the author of "Neo-Conservatism: Why we need it" has stated that many want to build a religious Europe. I don't agree with that because the more religious Europe and the United States become, the more powerful Islamic fundamentalism will become; this will cause people to flee towards the West because they can't implement such a devastating idea in their own country if their own people don't welcome it.

Dear Douglas: a famous proverb says that "He who has been bitten by a snake fears a piece of striped rope". Its scientific counterpart is "conditioned reflexes influence habits". I think that we have deeply sensed the problems arising from religious fundamentalism and have sustained losses from the hollow ideology of Hassan Al Bana (Al Qaida), Mowdudi (Hassan Al Bana's pupil), Seyed Qotb, Bin Laden, Al Zawahiri and the like. When we hear their names, we become agitated. Some one says when you unknowingly bite into a wormy apple and discover the truth later, one acquires a conditioned reflex; whenever you want to bite into an apple you remember the worm and feel sick about it. I swear to God (Khuda) that whenever I see a fundamentalist with a turban and a beard, I feel like choking, just as if I were standing in front of a huge, angry gorilla.

One should take note that fundamentalists show no mercy. They have always washed blood with blood. One of these fundamentalists belonging to the Egyptian Ikhvan al Muslimin is Al Zawahiri (the physician of hatred and violent animosity) who lives in the caves of Pakistan and Afghanistan with Osama bin Laden. He says that they (Al Qaida) have not yet equaled the US in terms of the number of people killed and, therefore, they should kill 4 million more people, 2 million of which should be children.

In Hafizullah Emadi's book, Culture and Custom of Afghanistan, Hanchao Lu (from the Georgia Institute of Technology) wrote, "However, readers should be aware that culture is fluid and does not always respect boundaries." Oh brother! Religion is an important part of the Afghani culture. Neither Marxism nor capitalism nor any "democratic regime" could ever make such a hard, "stony" culture, "fluid". The prevailing religious culture currently dominates all of the economic, political and social aspects of life.

Emile Durkheim says religion is an association, more effective than other associations since all of them are correlated. There was a time when people went to their places of worship to relax, because there were no other choices. They used to listen to the fanciful stories of bishops and mullahs and told these myths to their families.

I believe that such places of worship often served as a means for the people to exchange their thoughts and ideas and, in this sense, they were of high social value. However, because of the subsequent emergence of academies, universities and other educational institutions (along with clubs, parks, exhibitions, bars and other social places where cultural exchange takes place), there is no longer any need for such associations. So, we shouldn't blame Sultana if she's afraid that religious fundamentalists will rise to power in Saudi Arabia and in the world.

Kareem whispered, "Sultana, darling, please stop crying." Much to Kareem's relief, I finally managed to control my tears, but nothing could relieve my fear of what our future might hold. Sultana is a knowledgeable lady who wants to change the culture of her primitive compatriots but doesn't know how.

In their essay, found in Chapter 14 of Sociological Footprints, under the title of "Social movements and change" Leonne H. Ballantine and Leonard Cargan stated that, "Social change is the alteration, over time, of a basic pattern of social organization and it involves two related types of changes: in folkways, mores, and other cultural elements of the society and in changes in the social structure and social relations of the society. These cultural and structural changes affect all aspects of society, from international relations to our individual lifestyles. An example of a change in cultural elements is women increasingly entering the labor force.

An example of structural change is the rise of secondary group relationships with a corresponding increase in formal organization. Social change happens through the triple impact of diffusion (defined as "the speed with which ideas spread across / through culture"), discovery (defined as "unpremeditated finding"); and invention (defined as "purposeful new arrangements"); and each of these actions occur at geometrically expanding rates- that is to say, the period of time over which an initial invention evolves may require centuries, but once it is established, further changes related to that invention are relatively rapid. For example, it took less than fifty years to advance from the Wright brothers' twelve-second flight to supersonic travel to trips to the moon. Similarly, the rates of diffusion and discovery are now even greater because of recent advances in communication and travel.

Pressures for change affect every corner of the globe because of the modern interdependence of nations. In the same book, Barry D. Adam wrote that change occurs in many ways. Stresses from outside the country or organization can bring about change, just as strains from within the country or the organization can. Change can be rapid or slow, planned or unplanned. Social movements, usually groups of individuals deliberately organized to resist change in some part of society, are one means of putting pressure on society.

If you want to introduce the impotance of democracy in the Islamic states, you need to include a powerful and influencial position for political development and enlightening of society within the government.

One of the main aspects of development is "social development". It includes two kinds of change. One is a change in the way in which people think about the customs and traditions of their ancestors and their society (cultural change). Another kind of change is change in the structure of society and social relations (structural change). Such cultural and structural changes predominate over other actions of society, such as international relations and individual ways of life.

One good example of cultural change is women coming into the workforce. Another example would be the increasing number of news organizations. As I've said, social changes are fueled by three different factors, "diffusion", "discovery" and "invention". Each of these factors then expands geometrically. It often takes centuries for a useful invention to occur but it frequently brings major consequential and secondary changes to society. For example, the famous twelve-second flight of the Wright brothers indirectly paved the way for the flights to the moon.

Organized single groups (like social movements) often resist social change and, therefore, it is necessary to apply pressure "from the top" (of society) in order to change the system.

The main goal here is to find out which element, invention or force can change the culture of the Afghan people whose destiny is currently in the hands of the fundamentalists. Or, better yet, change the culture of an Arab youth who is actually a European, American or Australian citizen but goes to Iraq and joins the enemy to fight against his master.

The people of Afghanistan are used to their traditional way of living and their level of knowledge and information is very low. Due to the continuous indoctrination of bishops and mullahs they don't believe in any cultural changes based upon foreign sources. They only believe in change in their own traditional way and this is the reason why they ask for their medicine to be produced in Indonesia.

It is, therefore, necessary for technical men to intervene and explain that medicine produced in Indonesia is no different (with regard to ingredients) than medicine produced in France, Europe or the US. Maybe this would be a "slap in the face" to the fundamentalists. Or maybe someone should explain that drawing a caricature of some bishop or mullah is neither a sin nor a crime. Such hypocrisy is the most destructive weapon in the hands of the mullahs who are the enemies of modernity and humanity. In this way, and for the sake of political reasons (and not religious ones), they could prevent those naïve Muslims from using medicine produced by infidels.

However, superstitious beliefs exist all over the world. Here in the US, they believe in Halloween and in Santa Claus. In India, there are those who believe that the cow is sacred and slaughtering or eating it is a sin despite the fact that many people die due to hunger and poverty.

One time, an American killed a cow in a car accident in Nepal. He was jailed but the government interfered and the problem was solved by saying that the cow had committed suicide because he didn't want to live more! I believe that if a mullah or bishop preaches in a church or mosque, a social scientist should also be available to explain social changes. Not only that, but heads of state should also be required to provide sociologists, biologists, psychologists with opportunities to describe and explain their successful experiments in the areas of social, economic, political reforms for their students at universities and during regular public gatherings.

The government is responsible for expanding such movements against social regression and should warn the corrupted ones not to put obstacles in front of constructive social and democratic movements.

Arthur Miller said that in 1986 Genghis Otomatov, (the Kyrgyz novelist) called him and asked him to go to Moscow (as there were no more party inquisitions) and that Peter Ustinov, Claude Simon and James Valdin were also going there. I went to Moscow and there were Americans, British, French, Italians, Ethiopians and other nationalities in the room. Gorbachev entered and greeted everyone.

He stated that inherent changes had started within the Soviet Union. He also said that Soviet foreign relations had to undergo changes. He continued by saying that Marx had never foreseen such a modern era and, consequently knew nothing about nuclear power, electronics or any of the other inventions which occurred in the post-World War II era, dramatically changing society. Gorbachev said that this was the biggest lesson for the Soviet Union and that using old-fashioned political methods and formulas would no longer do any good.

He said that we should move according to the current facts rather than what is written in school books or the accepted "dogma". These facts (changes that had taken place in society) were unknown to thinkers in the 19th century, including the genius Marx, and Marx was certainly not a prophet.

Gorbachev used the term "Moribund Dogma" a few times and appeared to disapprove of the standards set by Marx. Miller says that he wanted to ask Gorbachev whether he was still a Marxist. He replied that he is a "Marxist / Leninist" but not a "Stalinist". I talked about those stories with Harrison Salisbury, the New York Times reporter, who had spent 10 years in Moscow. He thought that I made up all of those stories and asked me to send them over immediately.

But the *New York Times* didn't publish them because they didn't believe that the news was true. Salisbury was very surprised. I also sent the documents to the *Washington Times* but they didn't publish them either. Many years of indoctrination had obviously made it difficult for the Americans to believe that instantaneous changes could occur within the Soviet Union. I believe that even Gorbachev himself couldn't really believe what had happened in the USSR.

Needy compatriots! Men or women should be aware that the modern world has undergone substantial changes due to various discoveries. You live in ignorance. You should stand up to fundamentalism, narrow-mindedness, ignorance and poverty. You should help to create a whole new world for your compatriots.

Al Qaida and its devotees (along with the cooperation of their narrow-minded masters) have destroyed our country. Our country's deep and painful wounds can never be wiped from the memory of my brave compatriots. Al Qaida occupied our land and the plot to destroy our country was carried out, from without and within, most especially from Qandahar. One of the great examples is the assassination of Ahmad Shah Masoud, leader of the Northern union. Another example is the destruction of the twin towers in New York. Finally, the anger of the Americans "clipped their wings".

In total disappointment, they claimed that not only Al Qaida, but Islam itself was in danger and they wanted to hide behind brave Muslims. They asked for help but really they wanted to deceive some kind and compassionate Muslims - in order to form an army. I call on all the Muslims in the world (especially the brave people of Khorasan) to not put themselves and their families in danger because of the outdated preaching of the Al Qaida "conjurers".

Compatriots! General Ahmad Shah Masoud, the leader of the Northern union, was not a religious man but an open-minded and civilized man. But some companions, who were deceived by Al Qaida, buried the hopes and dreams of such a brave man. He was assassinated by Arabs and, even more strangely than that, his mausoleum is decorated with Arabic script, an act that only makes the offense worse.

I advise the brave and good-natured men and women who believe in building their lives in a civil society to support the coalition forces (US allies) who are trying to establish peace and order while reconstructing the country.

Moreover, you should take full advantage of this new opportunity for growth and development which has been denied to you in the past. I hereby call on all the organizations who are involved in reconstruction, I ask them not to lose this chance and to make the most of the support of the people who warmly welcome their projects for reconstruction and renovation.

Mr. Hamid Karzai! You cannot help the country wearing the turban of Mirwais Hotak and cloak of Tamerlane. Moreover, your religious nature and methods of supporting regression invoke 1400 years of backwardness. You renewed the Taliban religious organization, which is a great failure for you and a great victory for the Taliban and Al Qaida. Soon we will see religious police, disturbing people everywhere.

The mullahs that surround Karzai have taken advantage of his inability, his lack of insight and his lack of self reliance. People are concerned; they are now questioning the non-democratic methods of Hamid Karzai, which have endangered their freedom and independence. Thousands of troops were deployed in Afghanistan in order to establish peace and order and millions of dollars have been spent, but neither of these could give more power to Hamid Karzai.

Is there anyone on top who can make Mr. Karzai understand that religion is not science, shelter, food or something vital? Religion can't be used to make laws for the people nor can religion serve as the key to solving economic, social and political problems. If Mr. Karzai has bound himself to the imposed religion, traditions and aristocratic culture, all of which clearly belong to the past, he should also be led to understand that these are characteristics of regression which, in turn, will help prevent the peacekeeping forces from suppressing the Taliban terrorist.

Senator Chuck Hagel from Nabraska threatened Karzai in his office in Kabul and said to him: "sit down and shut up". But Karzai is still the President of Kabul?

It bothers me when an American lady visits an Islamic fundamentalist country and automatically covers her head. This attitude is a very disappointing policy because you break up the heart of civilized ladies there and pump more blood into the heart of a fundamentalist government.

These practices conjure up the negative face of your culture. Look at the muslim people here, do they respect your culture? Thanks to the British for abolishing the Suttee culture in India. However, America, the world and Karzai could not change the Afghanistani people?

I don't know why foreigners in Afghanistan are leaning too much toward Mosquei people and continue to marginalize its hold over educated people. Therefore, I ask the American government to work together with the Russian government to form a democratic system in Afghanistan or Afghanistan will never become a state!.

If I hate mujahidden, Taliban, Alqaeda, I also dislike the creator who provided the ground for stupidity and self interest in my country call her Afghanistan.

The Karzai indulgences to the thuggish people (Taliban) the Patan children nationally and internationally is absurd. Merging these criminals back to the corrupt government makes the regime not merely more corrupt but induces the stagnation of socioeconomic and sociocultural development and unrest. Furthermore, this action is very disgraceful to the other ethnic groups except the Patan tribes.

The malegnants Taliban a mercenary power followers of Alqaeda the Islam social disease the mother of all miseries and their adherents because of so many considerations are already have been defeated and it is not necessary to cry out in vain.

Salute to the reverent Generals and soldiers in Afghanistan. I personally appreciate your struggle against impostors and those who disturb peace and order. The triumph is very close so be firm in your convention and please don't pull out ahead of time. Defeat the Taliban and bring back democracy, dignity as well as peace to the Afghanistanis. Thanks.

The continuous failure of the peacekeeping forces to break the ties between the Taliban and Al Qaida, which resulted from the mistaken policies adopted by Karzai, have caused dissatisfaction among both the Afghan people and the world.

If the family, social characteristics and physical surroundings of Mr. Karzai have caused Mr. Karzai not be successful in achieving reconstruction and establishing general peace and order, he should respectfully step down and let someone else with a democratic spirit and ideology take over. But I think being in power is his great desire. The Marxist Dr. Najib, former president of Afghanistan, became a Koran reciter but even his new religion didn't grant him protection.

Free girls and women of our country, wearing the Burka or chador was punished 80 years ago by His Majesty Amanullah, the patron of learning. This unattractively colored and shameful commodity, called "Cocoon" by the British and "Lettuce" by the Germans, has now been turned into a weapon in the hands of Taliban and Al Qaida terrorists. The defeated Al Qaida has now mingled these feminine practices with the Taliban cowards. We, (the Afghans) have fought the enemies in our traditional dress, pants and turban. It is disgrace for a brave Afghan to dress up like an Arab nomad.

The possibility of using the Burka as a disguise, under which explosive materials may be carried, for the purposes of terrorism is increasing every day, thus raising profound concerns about those who wear the Burka. I would be glad to see women's organizations that support imprisoned Afghan women (who are not the only ones forced to wear the burka) put pressure on Karzai's regime to prohibit wearing the burka in Afghanistan. The Taliban and their followers (Arab agents), the clergy regime in Iran and the region, the reinforcement of tribal dogmatism inside Afghanistan, Pakistani intervention outside the country and the engagement of the US in Iraq have all caused the Taliban to regain their strength. The aforementioned will serve as a great motivation for the allied forces to remain in Afghanistan for a long time.

I'm afraid that the existing situation, which is rather "loose", has helped to create and sustain a "Mafia" (groups of organized criminals) along with political assassinations in the country. We have already witnessed an example of such a cowardly assassination in the north (in Baghlan) in which a few MPs, including Mustapha Kazemi, were killed in a mysterious way.

Immanuel Kant (1724-1804), was a philosopher of the 1700s who ranks with Aristotle and Plato of ancient times. He set forth a chain of explosive ideas that humanity continues to ponder ever since.

He created a link between the idealists- those who thought that all reality was in the mind-and the materialists-those who thought that the only reality lay in the material world. He said that things that exist in the world are real but the human mind is needed in order to give them order and form and to see the relationships between them.

His ideas regarding matter and the mind was the subject of many books written by 20th century philosophers. His ideological revolution with regards to matter and the mind has attracted our way of thinking for years. According to him, we should use our mind to discover the reality of life.

If Afghans cannot actually create the possible reality set in front of them by Kant, the complex system of racial and religious privileges and, most importantly, the tribal organization of Afghanistan, will lead the country towards separation.

If the results of scientific questions posed by scientists will not help to change our lives for the better, then the scientists would never have bothered to ask them in the first place. Moreover, but they wouldn't have endangered their own lives by doing so.

Chapter Six

AJAMS: THE INFANTRY OF ARABS

Miss Taslimeh Nasrin, a British-Bangladeshi claims that the Koran should be rewritten since it didn't give any rights to women. In Verse no. 223 of the Baqara Chapter of the Koran it says that "Your wives are as a tilth unto you". God mentioned women as farms. Your wives are like your farms, you can approach them anyway you want from behind. Ayatollah Imam Khomeini, the onetime leader of an Islamic country, has legally confirmed this. However, this is the worst insult to women in Islam. On pages 270-273 and 275 of his book Nasihat Al Molook, Imam Hamid Ghazali has described women as "pigs", "monkeys", "dogs", "snakes", "foxes", "scorpions", "mice", etc.

Fundamentalists have a small heart but plenty of blood. For example, Ikhvan Al Muslimin of Egypt and its representative, Al Qaida (the inventor of suicide bombs) comes to mind. Most moderate Muslims, who are truly human, not only condemn such terror but also fight against it. So, wouldn't it be better to build two separate worlds of

Islam - Arabist Islam and Ajami Islam

The fatal events of 2001 were the innovation of Arab fundamentalists, which disgraced the Islam of non-Arabs. The Arabs have made all non-Arab Muslims a puppet in their hands and have taken advantage of us. If this hypothesis gains strength, then the fundamentalist movement will be suppressed. Therefore, all non-Arab Muslims are asked to unite in order to establish universal peace and stability and prevent Arabist Islam from committing suicide attacks.

Ottoman Sultan Salim destroyed the last Arab base in Egypt in 1517 A.D. According to Shafa, the Arabs never considered the Ottoman Emperor to be the representative of "their" Islam because the Turks were not Arabs and the Arabs could never imagine a non-Arab as being equal to an Arab. They also thought that no non-Arab could be a "perfect" Muslim and this kind of belief has always dominated their minds. Arabs enjoy having others serve as their servants and because of this they always use other people to keep their cities clean.

During the past 1400 years of war and invasion, in the name of religion, violence and war was the best course of action for the Arab and Turkish Caliphs. The fear and deceit, which prepared the base for their fights, have put Ajams, Arab's servants, in ecstasy. I believe that someday soon the gunpowder of Pan-Arabist religious politics will explode their world.

Some believe that there is a direct relation between poverty, lack of education and supporting terrorism. Maybe they are right, but one should remember that those who provoke such terrorist acts have money and wisely use good reciters to recite the verses from the holy book and, in this way, provoke religious and sentimental people (in spite of their level of education) and use them to achieve their own political goals. Do you remember the terror plot of British Muslim physicians? Such Arabic expansionism, started 1400 years ago, has taken different forms until now, was used to create chaos by taking advantage of the feelings of their followers against their rivals. They even surpassed the largest intelligence service in the world. One Iraqi said that Americans wear dark glasses in order to be able to see women's private parts underneath their clothes. Why shouldn't we non-Arabs refer to the philosophy of Mawlana, whose rich philosophy is based on logic and reasoning? This reality is reflected in his rubaiyat.

Show me just what Muhammad brought that was new, therein you will find things only evil and inhuman, such as his command to spread the faith he preached by the sword." Byzantine Emperor Manuel Paleologus II.

Why should Pope Benedict the 16th have to remind us of the historical realities of 700 years ago as stated by Manuel Paleologus II, the Byzantine Emperor? These statements have been mentioned in millions of books in many different languages. Why should he apologize? Sultana Wafa, in an academic dialogue during her interview with CNN in 2006, supported Pope Benedict and stated that all that the Pope said was true and that he shouldn't have to apologize for it. She was successful in her debate with Imam Hasan Qazvini, who lacked any knowledge of the debate subject. I really appreciate the ideology of this democratic woman and I applaud such a brave woman scientist. The hollow logic of causing disunion and violence (by massacre and ransacking), not only destroyed the Persian, Greek, Khorasani and other civilizations but also brought about the Crusade-like wars in the Middle East.

I went to Kabul in October 2004, (the year in which Hamid Karzai was elected as the president, even though he was selected prior to elections)! I never heard anybody talking about democracy and its importance on TV or the radio. On the contrary, on Radio Azadi Mr. Abdul Latif Jalali, who spent his lifetime in the media, called Friday (which I call "Adina") the sacred day and called killer Khalid bin Walid the commander of Muslim army, whereas Islam was confined to the Arab Peninsula at the time.

Before the invasion of Arab we call this day **"Adina"** but not Juma, the Arab praying day which is imposed on us, therefore I respectfully asked all the intellicts people of central Asian countries including Iran and Kabul Zamin then on to call Juma the arab imposing praying day by its historic name **"Adina."**

Islamic Character

Shakiba Naurau, in his book <u>Children's Manners</u>, quoted Stephen Schwartz (an expert on Islamic terrorism) regarding the philosophy of Tahrir Group. This group was created by Al Qaida in Uzbekistan and was quoted as saying that: "A Muslim should practice all methods of war against infidels. There is no difference between having a gun and fighting the enemy one-on-one or exploding an airplane over an "infidel" population". The author continues by saying that: "If the enemy uses a weapon of mass destruction, as in Palestine, we should use the same against them. It doesn't matter if innocent people get killed in the cities or in the villages. If the elderly help the enemy by revealing our secrets or our plans for attack, they should also be killed".

In 1880, a French research team studied the possibility of constructing a railway in Sudan. They came across an Arab brigade in North Africa called the Kel Ahgar Tuareg. Those robbers carried a gun in their left hand, a gun in their right hand and swords in their belts. They engaged in a fight with the French in the 9,000 ft. tall volcanic mountain range, but were heavily defeated.

Tuaregs of Berber origin surrounded the French for a long time. This caused the French to eat the bodies of their casualties, due to hunger and thirst. They also ate their camels and some lizards. Finally, the Tuareg had mercy on them and gave the French some dates poisoned with Ifa lez lez. It caused the poor French to speak deliriously and run around like crazy, some even committed suicide.

The killing of Ali's sons, Hasan and Hussain, (the grandsons of Muhammad) in Karbala (due to differences with Yazid) is one of the most shameful incidents in the history of Arab Imperialism (which is not Ajami but Arabic). Othman the Khalifa was killed while he was reading his own Kuran.

In April, 2004, on Saudi TV, one of the Saudi pioneer Imams, Abdullah Al Motlaq called the terrorist actions "inhumane". He said that the terrorists were guilty, did not deserve to be pardoned and it was their (the Saudis) mistake to have trained some fanatics. He added that those criminals had connections with Al Qaida and came from Afghanistan. Schwartz called those who attacked the twin towers with airplanes full of people the most destructive terrorist group on earth. It's funny to hear that Britain gave political asylum to the leader of Tahrir Group with the hope of using him sometime in the future in order to establish an Islamic caliphate in Uzbekistan. They've committed crimes worst than Bartholomew. Islamic terrorists want to re-establish "Islamic Imperialism" founded on force and the massacre of millions of innocent people.

If bloody invasions were not useful in spreading the political traditions of Islam, then Muhammad would have never called Khaled bin Walid "Seifullah". In the first volume of this book, the great Shujaeedin Shafa wrote that the mission to kill people was given to Khalid bin Walid, Muhammad's favorite commander and a rich man of Quraish. He was well known for his cruelty. Previously, he had fought Muhammad in Ohod (in the battle against Muslims) but afterwards he converted to Islam and rendered many great services to the prophet. That's why he was then called Seifullah (God's Sword). It was he who broke the famous idol of Izzi during the conquest of Mecca in the 9th Hijira. Referring to this incident, Tabari wrote that after the conquest of Mecca, the Prophet sent Khalid to the village of Bani Hozaimah to invite them to Islam. When the people of Bani Hozaimah saw Khalid, they armed themselves. Khalid warned them they would be defeated, kept in captivity and beheaded afterwards, but some of them replied that they had been converted to Islam and, therefore, there shouldn't be any war and people should be pardoned. All of the Bani Hozaimeh surrendered, but Khalid ordered that their hands be tied and then beheaded all of them. He massacred many people that day.

When the Prophet heard about it he prayed to God and said that he hated what Khalid had done. Khalid told him that he didn't do that willfully, but Abdullah bin Hazaqah had told him that the prophet had ordered to kill them, since they refused to convert to Islam.

In another narrative about Khalid, it has been stated that he was assigned by Abu Bakar to suppress the uprising of the Bani Tamim tribe. He fought with Malik Bin Noveireh, (the leader of the tribe) but Malik surrendered, and to show him his goodwill he invited Khalid to his house. However, he killed Malik because Khalid wanted to sleep with Malik's beautiful wife and set his head on fire. However, Abu Bakar didn't dismiss Khalid because he believed that such a commander was still useful.

Suppressions against blasphemy led by Khalid bin Walid were especially cruel. In Tabari History it has been stated that Abu Bakar and Ali ordered him to behead (and set on fire) anyone who converted from Islam, capture their wives and children and convert all of them to Islam, no less.

If a scientist reveals a shameful, bitter and bloody historical event which results in some violent reactions, including demonstrations, should the broadcasting service hide that out of fear that democratic values would be insulted or because this would give the opportunist radicals the chance to violate democratic rules? I believe that if Arabs provided their children with pens and paper instead of guns and swords, it would be better for them. In his book "Allah Akbar" Dr. Roshanger is quoted as saying "I don't know why Arabs don't respect science and scientists". Also, Taha Hossein, an Egyptian scientist, wrote that Ibn Khaldoon was a selfish and nasty critic who pretended to be a Muslim. Brother! The sociologist Ibn Khaldoon or Pope Benedict the 16th are both guilty since they both revealed a historical truth. In his speech for the Iraqi paramilitary in 1933, Sami Shokat said that the remains of Ibn Khaldoon should be destroyed in his shrine and his books should be burnt throughout the entire Arab world. One should ask these retrogressive people if they knew Ibn Khaldoon and his origin. The translation of verse No. 5 of the Repentance Chapter of the Koran reads that "But when the forbidden months are past, then fight and slay the Pagans wherever ye find them, and seize them, beleaguer them". Words like" seize", "beleaguer" and "slay" all indicate violence which clearly reveals the culture of violence. The verse No. 61 of the Clans Chapter of Koran states "whenever they (hypocrites) are found, they shall be seized and slain (without mercy)".

Consider the egalitarian philosophy of Mawlana Jalaluddin Mohammad Rumi 1207-1273 and compare it to the above-mentioned.

باز آ باز آ هر آنچه هستی باز آ   گر کافر و گبر و بت پرستی بازآ
این درگه ی ما درگه ی نومیدی نیست   صد بار اگر توبه شکستی باز آ

Come! Come again!

Whoever, whatever you may be, come!
Heathen, idolatrous or fire worshipper come

Even if you deny your oaths a hundred times, come!
Our door is the door of hope, come! Come as you are.

The purity, philosophy, ideology and morality of the Great Mawlana Jalaluddin Mohammad Rumi requires Iranian, Khorasani and all other scientists to assemble and make a wise decision in accordance with the new world order and to move the focal point of Muslims from Mecca, Saudi Arabia to Konya. Mawlana (the great philosopher in the sphere of humanity) didn't believe in hypotheses or the Arabic language. He says:

چند چون زاغ بود نول تو در هر سرگین خبر جان چو طوطی ء شکرخا برگو

I now return to the phenomenon of Ajami Islam, the non-Arab Muslim population which is over 1 billion strong. Wouldn't it be wiser for them to become the leader of Muslims in the world and free themselves of Arabist Islam? They can also warn Arabs against using suicide attack and unsophisticated bombs which isolate them politically and give Muslim a bad-reputation ------------------------- --

In 1983, 17 Islamic countries assembled in Kuwait for a conference centered around the theme of using technology in people's lives. The Saudi Arabian representative was against the agenda, stating that the development of technology and its Arabization will weaken the religion. However, it was the use of technology which turned oil (the only product that Saudi Arabia has to offer) into a world product.

The Saudis try to prevent the import of technology to the Ajam countries and believe that such technology will weaken the Arabic religion. One example of this is preventing the importation of polio vaccine from non-Islamic countries. Saudi Arabia should establish profitable economic projects in the Islamic countries, but rather they build mosques and religious schools. Ajams should take this opportunity to stand against the baseless rationalizations of the Arab politicians and their clergy and put an end to their leadership. With the exception of the Arab Peninsula countries like Egypt, Syria, Iraq, Sudan and North Africa were not originally Arab, but were forced into Islam. The Egyptian civilization was totally ruined by the Arab oppression.

Herodotus (484-425 BC), the Greek historian, also known as the "Father of History", appreciated the Egyptian civilization before the arrival of Islam and stated that the civilizations of China and India were not comparable to that of Egypt's. Egyptian youth! The cultural achievements and great civilization of Egypt were ruined by the invasion of Attila (Arab army). How would you react to this? They were not Arabs and their language was not Arabic.

Shojaeddin Shafa, in his book <u>After 1400 years</u>, writes that during the Umayyad Caliphate the idea was promoted that God had chosen the Arabs (over the other nations of the world) to be the leaders of the world and that others are their subordinates who should leave governing to the Arabs. Arabs, during the Umayyad Caliphate, treated people as slaves and they the master. The masters held the rights of the slaves since they believed that it was their doing that saved their slaves from infidelity. Abu Bahayr (an Arab poet) once asked the leaders of the Abdul Qais tribe how such proud Arabs could marry Ajam women and let the Fars, Daylam, Turk and Hindu slaves enter the Arab tribes.

It should be noted that Arabic language has strokes, i.e. adding a dot to a letter will change the meaning. In "The History of Islamic Civilization" by Georgi Zidan he writes that the Caliph Motevakel sent a message to one of his governors asking him to report the number of non-Muslim people in his province. The Arabic version reads:

ان احص من قبلک من الذميين و عرفنا بمبلغ عددهم

The writer of the message has mistakenly added a dot to one of the letters (صخا: صحا) thus changing the meaning and the message now reads, "Castrate all non-Muslims". Therefore, the governor castrated all of the non-Muslims in his region, all of which (except for two) died. Abu Muslim was the first Khorasani who led the first liberal movement against the Umayyad dynasty in 750. The Khorasani and Arab armies confronted each other and the Arabs were defeated in this battle, later called the Battle of Zab. In the history of Islam, this was the only defeat faced by the Arabs and as a result, the Umayyad Dynasty came to a halt.

Abu Muslim ruled a vast territory including Bokhara, Samarkand, Taleqan, Balkh, Harat, Sistan and Neyshapour. However, his victory led to his murder. Abu Jafar Mansur (who replaced Saffah, the first Abbasid Caliph) led a conspiracy against Abu Muslim. He convoked Abu Muslim to Baghdad to see him and signaled for five of his guards hiding behind a portico to kill him.

As I've written earlier, if Ajamis do not distance themselves from the jealous, backbiting and ill-natured Mullahs of Arabist Islam and

Al Qaida (created by Al Bana), they will soon become the slaves of Arabist Islam.

Friends, I proudly advised my kids not to give Arabic names to their kids. It is the patriotic obligation of every intelligent Irani and khorasani to do the same.

My dear friend Taha Hossein: God not only created Adam and Eve but in the Tobeh chapter, verse 36 calendar also.

اِنَ عِدَةَ الشهور عِندالله اثنا عشر شهرا" فى كِتبِ الله

History is telling us that the Sumerians of Babylonia and the Egyptians were probably the first people to create a calendar. Mr. Taha, I ask you, what was the fault of Mr. Zalmai Gouth, a Kabuly academician who translated the Turkey (Meleagris Gallopavo) language in to Farsi why did the Karzai government put him in jail? Mr. Taha in verse No. 3 of the Alail Chapter of the Koran, God swears to one who created male and female, so who is the Creator?

(و ما خلق الذكر و الانثى)

Mr. Karzai!

Long prayers and Koran recitation will neither develop my country nor feed a hungry man. These are kinds of duplicity and an adherence to old-fashioned beliefs. Due to long-lived myths (like the promises of Arabic heaven) and practices like going to the graveyards and praying for the deceased, our peoples' minds, as well as their bodies, have been occupied so today the Afghan community seems cursed and its rulers are afraid to ask for help. Because of this, and the advice given by some traitors, will not only inflict a strike upon our national unit, it will bring the country one step closer to instability and separation.

The incidents taking place "behind the scenes" in the citadel of Kabul are based upon sectarianism, linguistic fundamentalism and the unjust allocation of resources. The so-called "outsiders" have been denied participation in such profit-scheming meetings. This book isn't intended to offend any culture or language but to reveal the true history of literature and art over the the past 1000 years in a country which used to be called Khorasan and Shahnameh of Ferdowsi (which is the center point of Farsi language) and was written by candle light, and in difficult situations, over a period of 35 years.

The late General Abdul Ghafoor, father of the late Abdul Rahim Ghafoorzai, once told a story about His Majesty Muhammad Zaher Shah at an assembly in his house. One day, on his way to Golbahar, His Majesty was accompanied by Foreign Minister Muhammad Nai'm and Minister of Education Feiz Muhammad. They were talking in Pashto. Feiz Muhammad told Sardar Nai'm that Abdul Ghafoor was not cooperating. General Abdul Ghafoor wrote a few sentences in Farsi and gave them to the two Ministers to translate into Pashto. They stopped the car and the two ministers got out and tried to translate the sentences while sitting near some thorny bushes. But after a few minutes, unsuccessfully went back to the car. His Majesty laughed loudly at them. The General said that demand and supply are two different things: I buy what and you sell what, where is the market and who are the customers?

The late Roshandel (Roshan), who served the government all of his life, was aware of many secrets due to his close ties with the rulers. One day we were sitting together in a house in Peshawar, Pakistan. He said that we Pashtons had done injustice to the people of Afghanistan. In fact, for more than one century we used the money of millions of Afghans including poor widows and orphans and spent it in the name of Pashtons, Pashtonistan, the Pashton tribes and the establishment of Pashton organizations. For nearly one century, this chronically sick policy of addicted freeloaders consumed a lot of money. Instead, we could have used the money to complete a portion of Kabul city's canalization project.

It is a shame that the same sick policies of Pashtonism uttered by the first leader of the Pashtons in Kabul have now given a chance to regressive opportunists and the bogus groups that surround Karzai to build Pashtonistan. The same Pashtonistan where, in 1838, Shah Shoja, Ranjit Singh, the Governor of Peshawar, and a British envoy conspired to claim that Afghanistan could not have any claim over Peshawar in the future. According to this treaty, 55 years ago the border line of Duran Sir Mortimer was legitimized in 1893 because the lands on the other southeast side were included in Peshawar territories. However, based on the fact that there are common interests between the territories beyond the southeastern borders of Afghanistan, then Herat should conjoin with Iran, Balkh with Uzbekistan, Hezara with Mongolia, Nourestan and Panjshir with Greece and the rest. I'm afraid that the integrity of Afghanistan would be endangered by some separatist opportunists and the country would be splintered, much like what happened in the former Yugoslavia.

Naturally, scientists, intellectuals and analysts do not approve of such a separation, but when the people's demands are unheard, how can national integrity and unity be secured? The language is not just what's written. The written language is different from the verbal one. Children learn a spoken language without any special education, but reading and writing requires special training. Written language has its own character. Most importantly of all, writing is a formal method. Languages gain in importance based on requirements and the market. Pashto can flourish if it corrects its etymology by borrowing words from other languages or coining its own. I'm not offending any institutions but the reality is that the Pashto language needs to be developed from infancy, in the field of literature.

At the beginning of 1700 A.D. a tribe from Khorasan (which is now called Afghanistan) had invaded a part of the Persian Empire.

A guerilla called Nadir Qoli Beig Turk, also known as Nader Shah Afshar was successful in forcing them out of Iran in 1730. Nader Shah was killed in 1747, near Fath Abad of Quchan, by Uzbeks and Afghanis. Ahmad Khan then came into power. Guerilla Afshar, peace be upon him, we the Duranis could then establish an oppressive regime in the region for more than two centuries. Nader Afshar was similar to Tamerlane in his efforts to gain political power. Ahmad Khan, raised in the same family, also possessed such characteristics. As written by Abdul Hamid Mohtat in The Uprising of Turkistan people in Qunduz, 1754, Ahmad Khan's army made pillars of human heads.

I, as the author of this book, would like to apologize for all the shameful incidents caused by my Durani tribe.

My dear compatriots!

It has been 6 years since Imam Karzai came into power in Kabul. During these years the country has become home to the Taliban and millions of dollars have been spent, but the minds of our younger generation (who are the infrastructure of political, social, economic or creative bodies) didn't undergo any change. Those who commit themselves to major tasks shouldn't jeopardize the historical achievements and national interests of the country which is one of the main national and international responsibilities of a leader. There is an old proverb which says "Wheat grows in the field, not in a mosque".

Unfortunately, Imam Karzai listens to the advice given him by the fundamentalists sitting at the top and ignores his own viewpoints due to certain considerations. Therefore, he hasn't been able to carry out a mental regeneration which is really what our people and the world wants. Certain groups of pessimistic compatriots support the inherited disease of tribal sectarianism and feudalism and they also adore Arabs. They are totally ignorant about democracy and liberalism. Liberalism is a political point of view opposed to any system that threatens the freedom of the individual and prevents him from realizing his full human potential.

Until now, we have never heard or read that an anti-Taliban or anti-Al Qaida movement has been organized in our country. Al Qaida disturbs the peace of our people everyday and fundamentalists prevent any development in freedom of thought and speech. It has never occurred to the minds of those who are responsible, that there are certain deficiencies regarding the regeneration of people's minds. If these deficiencies were taken care of, then such an enlightenment will not only boost the mentality of our knowledgeable people (including the youth) but would also be a big strike against the Taliban, the fundamentalists and their supporters. Any effort in reconstruction and development of the regressive society of Afghanistan, which is ruled by Mullahs, requires the emergence of secular reformist movements and leftist anti fundamentalist religious rulers.

Imam Karzai is a politician with no politics who cheered when, during the Islamic Conference of October, 2003 the Malaysian Prime Minister called the Jews "the US representatives in the world". However, those who protect Kabul's citadel so that President Karzai can have a good night's sleep are Jewish-American soldiers. A journalist asked a question from Hamid Karzai about the Islamic Conference which not only does not support the development of ideas in the modern era but has never realized women's rights or freedom. Karzai approved of the conference. If I were Karzai and had been given such an opportunity by the Americans, I would have never participated in the Islamic Conference and the Non-Aligned Movement which supports the political interests of Arabs along with their morality. These conferences are anti-democratic and anti-Israel.

Aren't you Ajamis the direct representatives of Saudi Arabia? Whenever a Jewish soldier hits an Arab chicken, Arabs become violent and relentless. You Ajamis, defend them in London and Pakistan unreasonably and even without a basic evaluation. You start dancing and jumping up and down like the clowns in Aaron's court, the Umayyad Caliph.

Mawlana Mirza Abdul Ghader (Bidel) describes you fools as:

مانع فیض حلاوت میشود چین جبین   نیشکر در هر کجا دارد گره، کم شکر است

It is clear that you backwards fools will never taste freedom and co-existence in your social life. The creation of Islamic conferences, Islamic banks and Islamic bombs are indicative of your physical and mental inability. It is a backward idea resulting from the culture of certain incapable countries who want to own the whole universe. In the past six years, our people have really suffered from the political philosophy of Imam Karzai created by the opportunistic fascists in his own government. People have been geared up to pay attention to the democratic values of their next leader. That's when the rulers who really believe in the role of science and technology in social life will tell the Mullahs that they can't preach war in their mosques and the government will draw a guideline for the religious preachers. In exchange, the spiritual worthiness of Mullahs in reconstructing public spiritedness should be appreciated.

Why Can't We Afghanis Become More Tame?

In 1783, George Forster passed Kashmir, Afghanistan, Iran, the Caspian Sea, Baku and Estrakhan (on his way to Bengal) and arrived in Moscow. In his notes, he described the Afghanis as "rude, unlettered people whose chiefs had little propensity for the refinements of life and that their country was ill-qualified for supply". In addtion, he considered that they were: "Generally addicted to a state of predatory warfare, their v manners largely partook of barbarous insolence and had a fierce contempt for the occupations of civil life".

Ann Heinrich, in her recently published book A True Book, has claimed that the population of[Afghanistan is 25 million and that two Pashtons out of every five live in Kandahar and the southeast of Afghanistan.

Miriam Greenblatt, in her book <u>Afghanistan Enchantment of the World</u>, quoted a Russian soldier named Hakim Tilaev (who was in Afghanistan from 1984 to 1987), about the fearful and cowardly characteristics of the Jihadists. "I saw a woman with her hands and legs cut off and her eyes pulled out, because her two sons had helped the Soviets. They killed the rest of her family. But they left her alive to suffer, so that everyone else could see what would happen to anyone who worked with us."

Such brutality, violence, physical and mental regression, including the massacre of innocent people, robbery and other immorality which took place and are still taking place in Afghanistan under the name of "Jihad", are simply repeating the same imported Islamic culture of the 7th century which has not only caused our people to become more violent but also created animosity and pessimism among other religions. Verse No. 28 of the Al Omran Chapter of the Koran, which indicates that Muslims should not mingle with infidels (non-Muslims) is the best example. Then why do hungry Muslims, especially Arabs, escape to the countries of the infidels and ignore the teachings of the Koran?

I hope that the fascist Jihadists who performed the worst savagery, while serving Arab tradition, and betrayed their motherland and the cause of freedom and belittled others' achievements, will be recognized as criminals and hanged.Those who are paid by the foreigners and have done such brutality to innocent women. If this case could be referred to an Islamic court, what would be the punishment for such an inhumane crime? Or would the outcome be according to the judgment of the Human Rights Commission of the United Nations?

To Ajami (Non-Arab) Scientists:

If the Emperor Paleologus II, Pope Benedict the 16th, Abdul Rahman Ibn Khaldun Tunisi, Mawlana Jallaludin Muhammad Rumi, Abolghasem Ferdowsi, Omar Khayyam, Nasser Khosrwo, Guilbert de Nogent (1053-1124), Avicenna or any other person criticizes a person or a nation using reasoning based upon historical truth, it shouldn't hurt anyone. Maybe they intend to remind us of an incident which caused confusion. The morality of the modern era won't let us play around and reverse the truth. Such shameful acts won't do people any good and will ultimately be self-destructive for those who establish such fake organizations. Such fake acts provide an opportunity for the artists and writers of the world to take revelations based on historical evidence and embellish the stories. If Arab fundamentalists could stop the cartoonists and other artists by resorting to such shameful acts such as beheading Theo Van Gogh, then the Danish cartoonists wouldn't have drawn such renditions.

The animosity of fundamentalists toward enlightened people is not a new phenomenon. For example, the 50th Muslim Amir Al Momenin wanted to declare Avicenna's works a blasphemy and almost threw them into the sea.

Sultan Muhammad II invaded Constantinople and killed Emperor Constantine XI. The Turks ransacked the city for three days. Muhammad converted the beautiful church of Sofia into a mosque and replaced the Cross with the Crescent. The invading Turks totally destroyed the birthplace of civilization, the Byzantine Empire. Given these facts, doesn't the Emperor Emanuel have the right to express his ideas with regards to public massacre, terror and invasion? If it were you (instead of the Emperor) what would your reaction be? Especially,if someone converted your mosque into a church or a temple?

With the support of the Moors, the Arabs occupied southern Spain in 761 AD and remained there for 800 years. After the marriage of Ferdinand II of Aragon to Isabella I of Castile the Arabs surrendered.

They called Muslims infidels. The last ruler of the Moors was Abu 'abd-Allah Muhammad. On Alpujarras Mountain he looked back and cried because he lost the best palace and the only mosque in Cordoba (which was later converted to a Cathedral).

Reasonable and logical criticism cannot only shed some light on the complex issues of our society but can also strengthen kindness and friendship among us. We should try to eliminate double-dealing Imams and corrupt politicians who try to promote their own agenda by taking advantage of Muslim feelings and shedding blood or, at least, not to listen to their provocative preaching.

What I've expressed under the democratic values of freedom of thought and speech is not so special. I hope that somehow my bitter language hasn't hurt anyone. If I've hurt anyone, by any means, I apologize. It should be remembered that any knowledgeable and thoughtful person should criticize mistakes and prevent the reoccurrence of such painful events in the future.

In Virginia, there is a Namaz Khana (mosque) named Mustafa (which is another name of Muhammed and I do not know who invented this name?). A bunch of ignorant Afghans brown nosers, Muhammed lovers that hate themselves and love strangers named the mosque after this Arab person.

The original name of Muhammed is M. Ameen. Why don't the Muslims use the complete name of this man in their dialogues? In spring 2012, I went to this mosque to pay respect for an Afghan that had passed away. A young reciter would read passages from the Quran every 2-3 minutes and then he would pray for the deceased. At the end, he asked the congregation to pray for god to save Islam from the viciousness of the infidels. To me, this was very startling. On my way out, I approached this young reciter and shook hands with him. As we shook hands, I told him that he made a big mistake. He politely replied: "what was the mistake?". I asked him what he meant by that? Because he used the word "infidels", I asked him where does he live now (America)? Suddenly, he got the message and promised me that he would never make this mistake again. Sure, I'm the only person among one billion muslims that audaciously corrected the wrong perception of a person. Or may be he was right when he remembering how his country Afghanistan was destroyed. His father, brothers, sisters, relatives, friends, and his countryman soaked with blood for the second time by the swords of the street Arabs, mujahidin and Pushtoon ignorant Taliban inebriants of Arabs inner perfume. The mercenaries who were bought, assembled, trained, skilled in martial arts, radicalised by the Saudis, the CIA, Pakistani ISI and other enemies of the Afghan people. The ISI is the most brutal and the most distracted organization in the world.

There are Afghan children from poor, ignorant families in religious schools all over the world (especially in Pakistan) that are being thought to bravely use words like infidel, heresy, apostasy, god is great (کافر ، ملحد ، مرتد ، لعنت) stoning or alike them, nonsense religious terminology (the food spices of the Islamic fundamentalists). Recruiting and training like Sheik Azzam the founder of Hamas, Osama bin Laden and thousands of other Afghan's traitors who are still on the CIA payroll.

Bribing Abolqassem Kashani against Dr. Mossadegh in Iran, the muslim brotherhood against Nasser in Egypt just to kill the national secularism movements, the leftists, and suppressing the freedom of women in the Islamic countries?

"Praying for the time" by George Michael for a good cause (physical and emotional hunger, poverty, hypocricy, and hatred) is not so bad. Generally, your praying whether it is collective or individually cannot be answered by god because you are talking to the air? Or praying may have consequences because god is not <u>clement</u> (بخشاینده) all the time. Most of the time, he is very angry, revengeful (المنتقیم), a deceiver (الماکر) and also very tired. He is the intelligent designer and is still working on his designing map?

A Saint has only one follower and the follower has one testical. One day, he asked his saint to pray for him so that he could get another testical. The saint said that god is very busy and that he does not have enough time for answering simple questions or requests.

The man was very persistent so finally, the saint prayed for him and the man got the testes all over his body. He could not leave his house and the saint got concerned so he went to his house to find out what happened to him. The man started crying and asked the saint please pray for me so that the testes covering my body will disappear. This time, god removed the testes and even removed his original one testical. Today, muslims in general and Afghans in particular through the wrong guidance of their Islamic Pope (**the Saudi Kings**), face the same dilemma.

__Heartbreaking news for Kabul's children, those who's wounds are still bleeding from the unclean conspiracy bullets of the Saudi Kingdom and other enemies of the Afghan people. When I read this unholy statement below on the web I thought somebody planted a bomb inside me because it has been almost three decades that I've been fighting against the hollowlogy known as "religion."__

Saudi Arabia to build $100 – million Islamic center in Kabul?

Kabul: Saudi Arabia will build a massive Islamic center complete with a university and a mosque in Afghanistan, an afghan minister said Monday, describing the project as "grand and unique".

Thank you very much America for smoothening the way for diffusion of superstitions by corrupt people like Hamid Kazai and corrupt organizations like the Saudis, who for his own regional political influences building nonproductive and hollow establishments in Kabul.

Decades ago, these institutions were repudiated by our gallant President Muhammad. Dawood. Therefore, I will never forgive Karzai for the treason and for his dirty government for their fanaticisim propensities attributed to the establishments of religious institutions by a foreign country which is a very disgracing historical crime. I hope the Saudi

234

Kingdom, before the completion of these seventh century establishments, will disappear from the face of the earth.

<u>**Concerning this, I ask the young Afghan generation of girls and boys, the intellects and the outsanding responsible society (especially leftists) to go on strike and say no to the domain expansionism and exerting policy of the Saudi totalitarian regime in our country Afghanistan.**</u>

We know that these Arabising political institutions without economic values, hollow in subject matters, repressing ideology are against Shiaesim and leftists globally. Believe it or not, the Iran government sooner or later collapses. The next day, the Afghan misogynistic government (the Arabs night soil cleaners), then we will see these Arabic institutions be occupied by bats or be blown up by bombs.

Exertion of domination of political religion Islam by despotic Saudi in Afghanistan is not a good sign for the region because such of dissociating institutions as a mental destitution taking the country toward the seventh century and these projects have to be stopped. We have to find out who was or is behind the political assassination generally in the world of Islam and particularly in Afghanistan?

میان گریه میخندم که چون شمع اندرین مجلس   زبان اتشینم هست لیکن در نمیگیرد
" حافظ "

I'm laughing between the weeping like candle in this convention, I have a firey tongue but it does not burn up.

1 – Hamid Karzai sold out our motherland as a prostitute to everybody and there is nothing more left there to sell but his wife.

I'm not sure that what the Turkish Emperors committed during their expansion of religious policies and imperialism was meritorious or sin? Such an expansion promoted the Pan-Arabist philosophy (an imaginary heaven) and shed the blood of free human beings on the earth. If such a culture was noble and not tyrannical, then the Umayyad Caliph Walid bin Zaid wouldn't have detached. Koran and Abu Moslem Khorasani wouldn't have put an end to 150 years of Arabic tyranny and Mostapha Kamal Ataturk (1881-1938) wouldn't have replaced the Arabic alphabet with the Latin Alphabet in Turkey.

Mostapha Kamal was born in Greece. Because he was the top student in his class in Mathematics his father called him Kamal. Such a man who participated in great battles including the Battle of the Dardanelles, in 1915, where he defeated 500,000 British Naval Forces under the command of Winston Churchill or said goodbye to the 400 years of the Ottoman Empire. He introduced "secularism" and announced that Islamic Law, along with the religious schools and institutes, were illegal. He is worthy of being called a hero by the Turkish people because he replaced theology with secularism. I believe that Ergun Mehmet Caner (a Turkish Sunni Muslim who has converted to Christianity) and is the Dean of Liberty Religious University (Jerry Falwell) in Virginia, USA is one of the true followers of Kamal Ataturk. Kamal was the prophet of democracy in Islam and I'm proud of him.

The Koran is all written in poetry. Non-Arab poets and writers can easily write it in their own language in poetry. For example, someone has written the Al Takvir Chapter of the Koran in Persian poetry so that people can understand the meaning and think about it. Why can't our reciters recite the Koran in the same manner? I'm quite sure that if we can succeed in doing this, then we can stop the Mullahs and the reciters who cause people to weep.

هـــر گاهيکه افتاب و ستاره ها تيره ميشوند	ايـن وقتيست کـه کـوه ها هم روندي ميشوند
ماده اشتران بار دار معطل وحوش گرد ايند	دريا ها تبديل به اتش و نامه ها گشاده ميشوند
هنگاميکه تن و جان مـــردگان يـکي شدند	دختران زنده در گور بکدام گناه کشته ميشوند
انگه شود نگاه به عمل نامه هايـي کـسان	پـوست از اسمانها هـم زمـان کـنده ميشوند
وقـتـا کـه اتـش دوزخ شـعـلـه ور شـــود	نيـکو رود بـه بهشت و بـد اتـش بـسر شــود

The author of this book would like to add that he has never understood the meaning of the above verses.

In Koran chapter's Al-Nisa verse 56 reads:

> Those who have denied our words are infidels and we will throw them into the hell fire untill their skin is burned up, then bring them out of the hell fire and grow on them a fresh skin. This is a test for them to find out what hell fire is.

Look 1400 years ago how plastic surgery was very advanced in Arabian Peninsula?

In Sura Al Nisa verse 56 reads:

كلما نَضِيجت جُلُوُدُهُم بدلنا هم جُلُودا" غَيرَ هاليِدُو قُوا العذاب

Terusumi Taniguchi

Terusumi Taniguchi, a Japanese victim of the hydrogen bomb in Hiroshima, was put on a hospital bed for more ten years on his chest. However, his skin did not grow back and he is still receiving medical treatment. Regardless of the role and importance of biology, biophysics, biochemistry, plastic surgery and others the organisms cannot be shaped. A person inside such hell fire is already turned into ashes and he or she neither needs fresh skin or a coffin.

What is worshipping?

The fervent love and allegiance accord a deity, idol, sacred object or other religious forms by which this love is expressed.

Religious adulators and reverent believers through flattering, lies, and exaggerations want to uplift the greatness of their lovers from implosion. Look at the Muslims as the religious ties among them is usually stronger than their national sentiment. For example, Jihad a non-productive pray on the basis of Arabic propaganda, millions of Muslims have been killed all over the world in vain.

In my country Afghanistan, Afghanistanis have ruined completly their own country for the love of Allah. I wish they would have known that the play was a part of the old great game in central Asia, but in different political version (stabilization through instabilization).

If Hindus worship the cow, that is a productive pray because the animal provides them with every physical necessities especially in the fields of agriculture and dairy products.

When I was a kid, a group of soldiers were dragging a young farmer to court because he was shouting and cursing at Allah. The farmer who had a milking cow and it was being burst up because she had been eating fresh clover. He was very enraged, yelling and shouting. He said that he prays every day and starves every year in the month of Ramadan, pays tithes and taxes. Therefore, he is fed up with the oppressive and repressive policy of negligent Allah. "Why did he not save the life of my milking cow?" the only family income he had.

Chapter Seven
TO AJAM SCHOLARS

Chatting with one of my friends, he told me that he has attended the assembly of Sham Erfan (Mysticism dinner) which is held once a month in Virginia and since Afghan assemblies always open with Koran recitation, unlike the Arabs, and everyone should be silent, a few people went to the podium and welcomed Ramadan, even though this unwanted guest will come back again next year. The meeting was too "Arabic", despite the fact that there was not even one Arab in the audience. How long would we be chewing the gritty mucous of Arabs, and how long would we be swinging from the sacred silky hairs of Arab testes?

This love of Arabs and their culture, which I mentioned earlier, has divided people. They didn't say anything about the actual Afghan people or their homeland which was destroyed by the Arabs or their puppets or poor Mullahs who have become millionaires because of tax money from whorehouses worldwide.

No one talked about those who became disabled in their fight to promote Arab culture and tradition or about the total destruction of the Buddhist statues of Bamiyan or the cultural achievements of our people, terrorism or anything else. No one even said "Long Live America who freed us from Islam, brutality, poverty and disease and provided us with all kinds of food, jobs and education". Our people in Afghanistan fast while hungry, just to keep up "Arab's dignity".

Good luck to A. Rahman who converted from Islam. Muslims here can go to church to worship God whereas in Afghanistan, Saudi Arabia and other Islamic countries, they don't even have permission to open a church. The servile behavior of some Afghanis (with regards to Arabs), reminds me of the statements of Ali Dashti who said that Iranians became more "Arab" than the Arabs themselves and even belittled their own traditions and habits. They also tried to promote Arab traditions. They described Arabs as being "prestigious and noble".

The person holding the assembly told us that the reason for such an assembly was to honor the night on which the Koran was revealed and that, except for religious matters, the exchange of thoughts and ideas would not be allowed. However, religion is political in nature and its very existence is based on politics and government.

Students were taught in the schools that the Koran had come down from heaven. Tonight is one of those nights, which reminds me of the past. I'm reading a book that says, "as mentioned in the Koran, this book was kept in a guarded safe from eternity as the mother of all books and at the beginning of Muhammad's prophecy was sent as a whole in the Night of Decree (Shab-e-Qadr)". However, the history of Islam is based on the fact that the 6,236 verses of the Koran were revealed over a period of 23 years, first in Mecca and then in Medina. These verses were revealed to Muhammad gradually by Gabriel. Such a contradiction (between the gradual revelation of the Koran over time and its onetime revelation on the Night of Decree (Shab-e-Qadr) has always been an issue throughout the history of Islamic arguments to which there has never been a good, convincing answer by the jurists. Almost all researchers agree on the fact that the final edition or final version of the Koran was accomplished under the supervision of the Ottoman Caliph, during the Ottoman Caliphate. But it is certain that the Ottoman's Koran, in spite of all the support by the ruling system (Caliphs) wasn't popularly accepted and Qaris continued reciting Koran for a long period since then, based on what they learned verbally which was different from the official Ottoman Koran.

There were also other versions of the Koran, in different centers, which were accepted as the real one, like Ibn Masoud's Koran in Kufi, Abi Ibn Ka'b's Koran in Damascus and Abu Musa's Koran in Basra. There were other versions of Koran, which according to the order of Anas Ibn Malik, the founder of the Maliki Sect (one of the four main sects of Sunni Islam), the bizarre words were replaced by familiar ones. He believed that the spirit and the concepts of the verses were more important than their appearance and this served as the turning point for the emergence of different recitations. In the 4th century (Hijrah), Ibn Mojahed, one of the great philosophers of Baghdad, stated that, based upon the prophet's hadith, Koran was revealed in 7 readings and anything else was manipulated. I have encountered a few Korans which made me concerned. I said to myself, if there were Korans on the earth, what was the reason for the revelation of another one on the Night of Decree?

I was totally confused; however I tried to call someone to get more information. I grabbed the phone, but hesitated for a moment, I was afraid that maybe one of those religious fundamentalists might denounce me as an infidel.

Nevertheless, I was impatient and tried to put an end to these thoughts, but I failed. I said to myself, that I was living in a democratic world in the west, especially in the US, whereas the great Abdul Rahman, the follower of Mowlana Rumi, had caused a great hue and cry a few months ago in Afghanistan, the city of mosques and argued with the bishop, his holiness and other reactionaries.

Anyhow, I picked up the phone and called. The person on the other side asked my name first, we chatted for a while and then I asked him about the number of Korans. He replied that there were quite a few, which had raised arguments and differences of opinion at times, but during the time of the Ottoman they had put an end to it.

But I was not convinced, because if they had solved their differences, then why was the Ottoman Caliph killed while reading his own Koran? At the beginning, our discussion was quite smooth and peaceful, but gradually he became uneasy, especially when I told him that, if the Koran was revealed to Muhammad by Gabriel before, then what was the need to reveal another one on the Night of Decree during Ramadhan? Was there any secret? He replied that, God knows and added that there were many concepts in Koran which we don't know about and only God knows.

This was the only way, which Mullahs, Imams and Islamic bishops could get away with the questions like this, during the past 1400 years. Then what's the usefulness of Hieroglyphic, Pictographic writing, Lexicography and Decipherment for decoding antique writings.

Just take a look at the irrelevant interpretations of broken letters (Alif-Lam-Mim), which appear in the Al-Baqara, Al-Rum and Al-Omran chapters that have been translated differently. The meaning of (Alif-Lam-Mim) is انا الله اعلم and the meaning is said to be "I'm the more knowledgeable God". If there is no one knowledgeable about the concepts of divine verses, then how can some cheat selfishly? They not only bring up the conflict among verses but also create doubt among people. Especially when it has been mentioned that, "I'm the most knowledgeable God", meaning that others were not allowed to add anything, since others may not understand the concept.

I asked the master about the earth's atmosphere and stated that not only there are lots of poisonous gases, but that it also contains harsh cold and hot weather extremes, which may freeze or burn living creatures. And most important of all, there is no oxygen in the atmosphere and may cause living creatures to die in seconds. How come Gabriel travels high and low in such a situation? Master replied that Gabriel used to appear in the form of light. But I would respond that, dear master, light is energy, and when there is no energy, nothing can be seen. However, a more important reason is that many scientists believe that a million years ago, the sun's energy (light) caused chemical reactions which led to the emergence of life on the earth. Sunlight shone on the plants which converted the energy to chemicals, which was then turned into organic matter, with the addition of water and carbon dioxide. This phenomenon in plants physiology is called photosynthesis.

Life on earth, both plant and animal, is made possible by the light-sensitive green pigment in plants called chlorophyll. Sunlight shining on the chlorophyll in plants converts water and carbon dioxide into organic matter, such as sugars and starch. At the same time, oxygen is set free into the air. Thus, plants produce food and oxygen, without which man and other animals could not live.

Light doesn't have a mouth or lips to talk, nor hands to grab or feet to jump.

اي شب که هر دم جانب ما نگري   بي روشني سحر نبيني ما را (مولوی)

The Sun is a star that is the center of the solar system. It sustains life on earth as its main source of heat and light. It has a mean distance from Earth of about 150 million kilometers, a diameter of approximately 1,390,000 kilometers and a mass about 330,000 times that of Earth.

It takes about 18 minutes and 19 seconds for sunlight to reach the Earth but my master didn't explain how an angel can appear in the form of light and can travel so fast. Where was this energy derived? I asked the master which one came first, Khuda or Allah. He said Allah. However, we used to say Khuda before Allah was even there. Allah was unknown in the Ajami world until Muhammad emerged. My compatriots say that "God is One", but may be called by different names such as Yahweh, God and Allah. This statement is totally different from saying "there is no other God but Allah and

Muhammad is the only prophet." According to Al Kandi Abu Yousuf bin Ishaq, Islam and its God (Allah) are totally different from the God described in the Torah and the Bible. However, I've given up writing about this subject. At the end of our discussion, the master threatened me and told me not to ask him any more questions. When I asked why, he said because when I said Muhammad's name I didn't say صلى الله عليه و سلم (May God send greetings to him). Certainly, this greeting is neither verse nor tradition?

This Mullah should have known that white light (spirit) is a natural color.

According to science, when light strikes an object, it may be transmitted, absorbed, and reflected. Light is what makes it possible to see things. The consumed light does not go back to its origin to re-energize the sun.

I wish Sir Isaac Newton and Albert Einstein were alive to address the mysterious flight of Gabriel (archangel acting as the messenger of God) to Earth and back to heaven. When Yuri Alekseevich Gagarin (1934-1968) returned to the Earth, Nikita Khruschev, Premier of the Soviet Union from 1894-1971, asked him if he had seen the god. But when Americans landed on the moon, they suddenly found the god.

As discussed by Plato, these people are like prisoners in a dark cave. Because they are used to darkness, they dislike the light. If they leave the cave, their eyes are hurt by the light, so when they return to the cave and tell the other prisoners their story they are not believed. In his book "Allah Akbar" Dr. Roshanger refers to the above philosophers and writes: "How well did Plato explain the role of education with respect to the nature of mankind."

Plato, in his book The Republic, writes about reality, with regard to the trial of Socrates:

> "Only by studying philosophy for many years can we
> can learn how to perceive and understand the true
> ideal forms existing outside our world. *"The Western
> Experience, 7th Edition, Volume I.*

Plato opposed democracy as a political system dominated by emotion, rather than logic.

The Italian politician Niccolo Machiavelli (1496-1525) denied the existence of any morality in politics and rationalized that political maneuvers are used to retain political power.

Mr. Tony Benn an outspoken English politician says: Moses, Jesus, Muhammed, Marx, Darwin, were the Great teachers. He said there are two things that control people- fear and killing the spirit of the people.

I'm not sure whether Mr. Tony knew that Muhammed the Great teacher imposed Islam religion on the people of the Arabian Peninsula through creation of fear and killing the spirit of the people.

There are so many verses in Koran that say Islam religion is only for Arabs not for Ajam (non Arab) but after the death of Muhammed his followers in disrespect to the Koranic verses invaded others outside of the Arabian Peninsula and applied the same harsh tactics Muhammed used.

The legacy of wrong teaching of these Great teachers in the past 1400 years has not only been uncorrected but worsening year after year. We are witnessed the rewarding teaching of the Great illiterated teacher until recently in Mumbai India 11.26.08.

A group of well-armed Muhammedan's terrorists occupied the Taj hotel, and near by areas and inflicted terrible losses.

When an individual is taught "Allah Akbar" (God is Great) by the family who are in the deep darkness of illiteracy and ignorance, and this teaching is hammered into his brain and faith with sensitivity and vigor, then getting rid of it wouldn't be easy. An individual who hammers such a phrase into his faith, which is not based on wisdom and reveals the idolatry of 1400 years ago, will remain a prisoner to such a superstitious idea. Also, if someone wants to open his eyes towards reality, he will proudly destroy the "Knowledgeable Man".

They will cut off my hands and legs, knock out my tooth, put out my eye or sentence me to death, because it is the order of God, whereas such punishments are rooted in the Hammurabi King's code, (1792-1750 B.C.) of which I'll quote some notes from The Western Experience:

1. If a man accuses another man of murder but cannot prove it, the accuser shall be put to death.

2. If a man bears false witness in a life or death case, or can't prove his testimony, he shall be put to death.

22. If a man commits robbery and is captured, he shall be put to death.

23. If the robber isn't captured in the presence of God, make a list of what was taken, the city, and the governor of the province where the robbery was committed, shall compensate for his loss.

138. If a man wants to divorce a wife who hasn't borne him children, he shall give her money to equal the price he paid for her and shall repay the dowry she brought from her father; and then he may divorce her.

142. If a woman hates her husband and says, "You may not possess me," the city council shall inquire into her case and if he has been going about and belittling her, she is not to blame. She may take her dowry and return to her father's house.

195. If a son strikes his father, they shall cut off his hand.

196. If a man destroys the eye of another man, they shall destroy his eye.

197. If he breaks another man's bones, they shall break his bones.

200. If a man knocks out a tooth of a man of own his rank, they shall knock out his tooth.

Now, I'll return to my comment on the Night Circle of Mysticism, which I had not finished in order to write the above note. I'm thankful for the generosity and courage of the United States of America, whose democracy has provided everyone with freedom and equal rights. However, some people are using it improperly, due to their lack of understanding and lack of ideology.

We, who have sought refuge in America, from the prison of such fundamentalist Mullahs and Imams, are not safe here. We cannot express ourselves freely, write books or circulate news about reforms and the fight against such ridiculous ideas.

I was shocked and asked myself why Americans look for fundamentalist terrorists in other parts of the world when the latter are living such a safe life (which they could never have enjoyed in their homeland) right here in the US, right under the nose of George W. Bush. The fundamentalists never openly criticize fundamentalism in the media but these bastards openly praise Arabs and slander America. That is why the US government should closely supervise their moves and thoughts because such people are not your friends. As stated in the Al-Omran chapter of the Koran, verse No. 28: "Let not the unbelievers be taken for friends".

Muhammad of the second Ottoman Empire, ruled from 1451-1481, occupied Byzantine and converted the most beautiful church of Sofia into a chapel. He destroyed the church's paintings and replaced them with Arabic words such as صلي والله وعليه و سلم (May God send greetings to him). Fortunately, the chapel has now been converted to a museum. Another example is Tatar's chapel in Leningrad, on the other side of the river, against Armitage Palace, or a chapel near Bombay sea in India, which is almost on the water. The largest and most beautiful chapel in the Islamic world was located in Cordoba, Spain. It had 850 pillars and 19 hallways leading to a Cathedral. Other examples are Al Hamara Palace in Granada and Alcazar in Seville.

I asked my friend if there were other questions. He was positive about a few unanswered questions, the most important of which regarded the Koran revealed on the Night of Decree in Ramadan. Stories about idols and satanic verses. And where is that Koran?

بت ستودن بهر دام عامه را   همچنان دان کالغرانیق العلي (مولوي)

Israfel's blow flattened the earth so that the egg is visible at the end of the earth, with 75% of the earth made of water and the first person to sink in the water is Israfel, himself.

In verses No. 23 and 36 of the Al Zomar chapter of the Koran, the verse reads: "He guides therewith whom he pleases, but such as Allah leaves to stray, can have none to guide." Also in verse No. 80 of Al Safat chapter "Thus do we certainly punish the Doers of Good".

A novelist and religious fundamentalist wrote in an article in 2005 in Omaid Weekly, published in the US, that some of our compatriots deny Islam because the prophet appeared in a land different than their own. However, religions and ideologies should not be treated differently. As stated in verse No. 36 of the Al Nahl chapter, "For We assuredly sent amongst every People an apostle", verse No. 4 of the chapter of Abraham's.

A large number of the contemporary Islamic Studies' research inquired into the wars which occurred in the name of Islam, in Iran and other lands, and if they really occurred because of Islam itself; A religion which its founders had claimed was a religion for the Arab pagans, and Muhammad was the Arab's prophet with a book written in Arabic (Shafa).

My dear novelist brother! In the above-mentioned verses, there is no compatibility for a prophet to be capable of being the one for countries such as Iran, Khorasan, Kazakhstan, etc. Please refer to the lecture given by Muhammad during his Farewell Pilgrimage, in which he announced the end of his mission (by the end of Islam) in that Peninsula.

As mentioned in verses 97 to 101 of the Al Tobeh Chapter, one can understand that even those people in the Arab Peninsula, were not very agreeable with the new religion of Muhammad, and because of this, he used to call them Munafiq (hypocrite). As stated in verse No. 67 of the Al Anbia chapter, Muhammad spat on his own people, because they didn't believe in his Allah. He was so disappointed and defeated that he decided to leave Mecca for Medina.

He warned people by referring to verse No. 7 of the Al Shura chapter which reads," Thus have we sent by inspiration to thee an Arabic Qur'an: that thou mayest warn the Mother of Cities (Mecca) and all around her and warn (them) of the Day of Assembly". Why warning? Muhammad Abubakr bin Zikria Razi (865-925), one of the greatest physicians of his era comparable to Galen Claudius (130-200), the Greek physician, said that God can warn people since He is a universal power.

Obviously, when one is not able to reach his goals due to his own weaknesses, he resorts to conspiracies and maneuvers so that ignorant people become submissive and cede their rights and freedom.

What is understood from the above is that Muhammad wanted his religion only for the people of Medina. Even Mecca was not included, not to mention Egypt, Iran, Khorasan, North Africa and other places.

Mr. Novelist then continues by asking whether Buddhism could become our national religion or not? I think that he is either confused or a fundamentalist. It's impossible to call religion a "national idea", especially imposed religion. Religion is a part of culture that varies in different situations. It is the people, not the religion, who are called "the nation". Such a phenomenon is the innovation of religious fundamentalists and this idea has attracted many psychologists and other scientists. A "nation" is a group of people who share the same "profit and loss". However, there is more than one religion, language and race in our country and, as a result, the Afghan nation could not be united as one. Therefore, for 1400 years, we neither called this country "Afghanistan" nor "Islamistan". From the time of the Arab invasion to the end of the Abdali dynasty no one called this land an "Islamic State". Remember the brave soldier Abu Muslim Khorasany who lost his life in order to get rid of Islam. It is clear that the Saudi Kingdom (and the Bob Burns bazookas) made this country an Islamic State and that is a great shame in the 21st century.

National = A group of people identifying under a common entity.

Nation = People who share common customs, origins, history and, frequently, language; nationality.

In the above definition religion is not one of the components identified with being a nation or it hasn't been found valuable to be mentioned here. However, origin, history and language are considered to be important in defining a people as a nation.

Nationality = the status of belonging to a particular nation by origin, birth or naturalization.

Since I belong to a certain nation due to my origin and this nation doesn't share anything in common with Arabs, I therefore do not belong to either the Arab nation or the Arab religion. As Mawlana says!

من از کجا پند از کجا باده بگردان ساقیا   این جام جان افزای را بر ریز بر جان ساقیا
"مولوی"

However, there was a time when the ancestors of Khorasanis used to be in the same army with Arabs and conquered cities, maybe this relation was due to the imposed religion and, forcibly, we integrated into the Arab nation but Arab imperialism was destroyed and we are now proud of being an independent nation. Mr. Novelist not only denies the very existence of Buddhism but also portrays it as an object whereas this religion is the most peaceful and polite one in the world of humanity. Bow, sword, gunpowder, force and chain haven't been used to impose it. In Islam there are Arabs and Ajamis (non-Arabs), which indicates the separation of nations. If Islam relates itself to the nation of Abraham (which includes Jews and Christians), then why is it mocking them? Mr. Novelist not only insults Buddhism, but also uses discrimination and prejudice in his writing, originating from his religious beliefs.

Mr. Novelist writes that: "Samuel Huntington says Islam is a very good religion". If that is so, why does he not convert to Islam? This could be his suggestion prior to 9/11.

Islamic traditions with the help of Bob Burns Bazzoka brought down the Marxist regime in Afghanistan.

In his theory, "The Clash of Civilization", Huntington writes: That, whilst in the Cold War, conflicts likely occurred between the Capitalist West and the Communist Bloc East, it now was most likely to occur between the world's major civilizations-identifying seven, and a possible eight: (1) Western,(11) Latin American,(111) Islamic, (1V) Sinic (Chinese), Hindu, (V1) Orthodox, (V11) Japanese and (V111) the African. This cultural organization contrasts the contemporary world with the classical notion of sovereign states.

Now, I have a question to be answered by fellow Americans: "if America didn't help the Islamic merceneries to topple the Democratic regime in Afghanistan, would we have have the worse political situation of today?

On 27.10.10, in an interwiev with the BBC, Mikhail Gorbachev, former Soviet leader, said America had itself to blame for the rise of Islamic extremist in Afghanistan because it had trained militants in breach of an agreement that the country should become a neutral democracy. He warned America and Britian that a military victory in Afghanistan is impossible." The Americans always said they support this but at the same time, they were training militants- the same who today are terrorising Afghanistan and more and more of Pakistan.

"Joe Murphy Political Editor"

Lyndon H. Larouch, Jr in EIR (Executive Intelligence Review) March 17. 2006 Vol. 33 No 11 writes: "British Arab Bureau Veteran Bernard Lewis revived the global anti-Islam strategy which was taken up by Zbigniew Brzezinski, Samuel Huntington, and other U.S. "Crusaders".

I revert to the philosophy of the nation of Abraham which includes Judaism, Christianity and Islam, whereas none of these religions have been gathered as a nation under one roof. It provides a pretext that nation and religion not only could not mix, but have always been in conflict. We want religion to be separated from government, why not religion to be separated from nationality as well?

This Mr. Novelist, not only insults Buddhism and Zoroastrianism, in spite of valid documents available from museums and findings elsewhere which confirms their existence, but also he denies other religions and those Buddhas in Bamian, which they destroyed, because of some verses and hadith. I not only grieved for them, but shed tears. However, you fundamentalists never did say anything about it.

George Sarton, n his book Hellenistic Science And Culture In The Last Three Centuries B.C., writes (on page 8): "The most famous of the Yavana (Greek) Kings in India was Menandros. He is not well known to us and in the little that we do know, it is not easy to separate fact from fiction. He was king of Kabul and the Panjab and finally, ruled the whole of Greek India down Kathiawar (western Gujrat, west coast, c.lat. 220 N) until his death in c.150-143. He was so well known, however, to his Indian subjects under the name Milinda that he became the hero of a Buddhist treatise, the Milindapanha (the "Question of Milinda").

I think he was a Buddhist himself but in the fashion of Hellenistc kings, he was friendly to the religion of the people around him.

Exploration by Russians in 1979 in Jovzjan in the north in an area called "Tala Tipeh" (Gold Hill), is one of the most valid ones in our country and confirmed the existence of Zoroastrianism.

Such wastes of society support a religion which has shed so much blood, all the achievements and honors of our country were sold to the Arabs, in order to endure the religion of the grandfather of that novelist.

Verse No. 192 of Al Omran chapter reads," Our Lord! Any whom Thou dost admit to the Fire, Truly Thou covers with shame, and never will wrong-doers find any helpers"

I ask the novelist whether this phrase is a verse or a call. I want to ask Mr. Novelist and his colleagues to explain the logic justifying this verse using science and laboratory instruments.

Servants who attacked the Koreyshite convoy, were fighting on how to divide the spoils. Immediately some verses were revealed to Muhammad to his benefit. The first verse of Al Enfal chapter says, "They ask thee concerning (things taken as) spoils of war. Say: "(such) spoils are at the disposal of Allah and the Messenger."

One should ask Mr. Novelist, is this Divine Justice? Is there a necessity for a God who requres spoils?

The dramatist, humorist and epigrammatist Alexander Pushkin (1799-1837),whose mother was of Ethiopian descent, found the Koran to be a very interesting book.

A creature called Satan is called the best angel in certain verses including verse No. 11 of Al A'raf (The Heights), verse No. 61 of Bani Israel, verse No. 34 of Al Baqara (The Cow) and verse No. 31 of Al Hujurat (The Private Apartments) but in verse No. 50 of Al Kahf (The Cave) he was called a Jinn, why is that?

بگفتم منكه از تفسير قرآن شر م ميايد   تكامل كرده از بوزينه و امروز انسان است
(بيدل)

> Because monkeys gradually become human, not vice versa. I'm ashamed of interpreting the Koran which says humans have become monkeys.
>
> (Bidel)

Fatalism based on verses and hadith (tradition) has guided humans towards implacable fundamentalism.

Muhammad bin Ismail bin Almughaerah Al Bukhari was born in 194 AD in Khorasan. He spent his entire life collecting 300,000 traditions of which 7275 have been registered as authentic ones in 9 volumes. Bukhari is highly honored in the Islamic world and Muslim scholars call his books the "second most valid after the Koran". In a way, it's called Imam Bokhari's Koran. In tradition No. 779 of the 4th volume it has been stated that food in the mouth of the prophet chanted the "Allah Akbar" slogan.

In order to identify ions of elements, indicators are used in laboratories. The question is which procedure (ionization /chemical reaction) Imam Bukhari used in order to identify those traditions directly given by the prophet (Nabawi) and those traditions directly given by God (Elahi). If amongst thousands of Elahi traditions only one turns out not to be Elahi, then all the other traditions will become invalid. For exampel, if we add one drop of blood or milk in a glass of water, considerable changes will occur in its chemical and physical properties, even the quantity will change. It couldn't be figured out amongst thousands of traditions, which ones are Elahi and which ones are Nabawi.

The question is this: Why have the Arabs themselves not paid attention to the translation, compiled, to the completion of the authenticity of hundreds of thousands of hadith (traditions)? When it was an Ajami from Khorasan (Imam Bokhari) that did it 200 years later after the death of the Prophet?

Christopher Hitchens asked why the Arabic words written on the outside of the Dome of the Rock in Jerusalem are different from any version that appears in the Koran?

Is there anybody out there who can shed light on these puzzling issues?

بحق انک گزیدی دو لب که جام بگیر   بنوش جام و رها کن حدیث پخته و خام
(مولوی جلال الدین محمد رومی)

Mawlana, one of the great philosophers who mastered the Turkish, Farsi, Arabic and Greek languages, has challenged the credibility and accuracy of the previously mentioned subject.

Religion has been defined by early sociologist Emile Durkheim as a more or less coherent system of beliefs (monotheism, polytheism) and practices (fasts, feasts) that concerns a supernatural order of beings (gods, goddesses, angels), places (heaven, hell,

purgatory), and forces (mana). This rather simplistic definition explains what religion is but does not explain why it is a universal phenomenon.

Muslims believe that the Prophet has said the ink is more precious than the blood of the martyred. No! The blood of a human being is more precious than the ink or color.

We make the ink but we cannot make the blood or human beings.

The color of chemistry is not a new phenomenon. Pigment has to be applied to pottery and carving in a form that would adhere to surfaces.

If my blood is cheaper than the ink, why should I be martyred and turn my wife in to prostitution and my kids into orphans?

Whole blood and its components can be stored in blood banks. Without them, it would be impossible to have blood ready for transfusion to people who have serious accidents. It would also be impossible to plan heart surgery or to have plasma clotting components available for bleeders who lack them.

The former Sociologist, Emile Durkheim defines religion as a kind of relationship between beliefs (believing in a single God or multiple gods) and religious practices (fasting). He believes that religion means obeying the powerful force in the universe (gods, goddesses, angels) and places (heaven, hell, purification) and non-human forces (mana). Talking about what religion is easy, but explaining it as an amazing universal phenomenon is not an easy task. Religion is a system of thoughts. If in the past the sword was used as a means of "expansion", it has now been replaced by terror, the sword and gunpowder.

They condemned Richard Pearl upon adopting a foreign policy based on suppressing Arabic terrorism although he did understand the true nature of the issue.

لا اله الا الله محمد رسول الله means there is no God other than Allah, and Muhammad is the only prophet means not accepting Jesus or Moses. This is the worst insult to Christianity, Judaism, Hindu,

Buddhism, etc. I heard on TV that the American Muslims are better than European Muslims. No brother! This is not true.

The US is not the only a superpower but has a brave nation too. Muslims here have manners.

The new Islam is led by Osama bin Laden who has been given the title of Sheikh (clergyman). I'm asking you Americans, here in the US or Europe, have you ever heard any Muslim call Osama bin Laden an infidel or terrorist? No, never, except for Abdullah al Motlaq who is one of the pioneer Imams of Saudi Arabia.

Al Qaida (which was created according to the philosophy of Hassan Al Bana, the leader of Ikhvan Al Muslimin of Egypt), now has new Muslim followers who follow his Koran which is more violent than the Ottoman's Koran. I believe that those Imams who ignore social manners and say their prayers at airport terminals are just showing off. They are embarrassing their own selves.

In fact, they have made our children think in a fanatical way. The American appeasement policy towards Islamic fundamentalists is not a healthy policy. When there is an epidemic, either in animal or in plant life, people try to prevent the spread of the disease. The 9/11 commission reported that the enemy is not just terrorism, but some generic evil.

Grasshoppers belong to the Acrididae family.

Moroccan or Italian grasshoppers (known as locusts) are a kind of desert grasshopper which if not removed, will destroy grains and vegetables (our food and our animals food) because they have both wings and jumping legs. Therefore, if Mr. Richard Pearl has adopted a policy, we should not criticize him.

Professor Robert J. Lieber says, "Thus in confronting the menace of terrorism and (WMD) and when values such as human rights, liberty and the rule of law cannot be guaranteed by institutions such as the U.N. and the European Union, American intervention becomes a necessity, not something about which to be apologetic. This understanding should inform our thinking not only about security, but about Europe, the Middle East, Asia, globalization and anti-Americanism as well."

Have you ever noticed that in the post 9/11 Muslims have become so proud and fundamentalist out of total despair? Muslim women not only wear the chador here in the US but they wear fashionable ones indeed. Such a shameful imported culture is fading in Europe but here in the US a civilized country they most welcome such kind of fashion shows which represent not only a primitive but a regressive culture - over the long term it has a great negative impact on the culture of American people. You, European, American, Canadian, Australian, Chinese, Hindu and other non-Muslims, should know your enemy well.

An Afghan who used to be the driver of an American fellow in Afghanistan once told me that whenever the infidel left the car, he cleaned the seat with a piece of cloth because he believed that it was filthy.

I asked him about the cloth. He replied that he put it back in his pocket. But a few seconds later he laughed and told me that he should have thrown the cloth away. Religion is a doctrine, which has been injected into the brains of some people through the use of force. In order to wipe off all these teachings we need to not listen to the religious teachers.

One can't buy a ticket to heaven by wearing Monk-ery outfit and growing beards. In India, millions of women wear the chador, in Russia most women put on scarf, as do some women in Africa, and women wear beautiful chadors in Guatemala. The philosophy for wearing these things does not lie in heaven and hell but it's for keeping away dust or protecting against strong winds.

In India millions of Sikhs grow long beards, even Russians used to have long beards but Peter the Great told them to shave them off or pay a "beard tax" to the government. Such old-fashioned beliefs don't have anything to do with heaven and hell. At the time of Muhammad, women (including Muhammad's wives) used to go out without covering their faces. The enemies used to call his wives bad names and consequently Muhammad advised his wives (through verse No. 59 of the Hijab chapter) to cover their faces.

Louis Coulan of France, 78 used to have an 11-foot long beard in 1904. Can we call him the prophet of the beard? According to Taslimeh Nasrin, only when the Koran is re-written and all prejudicial and discriminatory phrases are deleted can we call these people good Muslims. Verse No. 33 of Noor Chapter reads, "But force not your maids to prostitution when you desire chastity, in order that ye may make a gain in the goods of this life. But if anyone compels them, yet, after such compulsion, is Allah, Oft-Forgiving, Most Merciful (to them)". In the light sura verse 33 Allah says:

ولا تُكرِهُوا فتيتِكُم على البغاءِ إن اردن لِتبتغوا عرض الحيواةِ الدنيا و من يُكرِ هُهُنَ فإنَ اللهَ مِن بعدِ اكراهِهِنَ غفورُ، رحيم.

In these verses God is forgiving the prostitutes but in verse No. 80 of Al Safat he punishes those who do good.

In this case the generous god forgives three sinners: adulterer, adultress, and the compulsive.

این حیلت بازان فقیهایند شما را   ابلیس فقیه است گر اینها فقایند
گر احمد مرسل پدر امت خویش است   این بی پدران پس همه اولاد زنایند
ناصرخسرو

Chaptr Eight

A GLANCE AT SUPPOSITIONS

Religion is one of the imitative facts of society which is irrelevant to God, Allah, Lord, Bogvan or any other thing. Another practice of which the followers of Muhammad are very proud of is the act of circumcision. This tradition is a "way" or "method" which has been inherited from the past.

Circumcision involves cutting away part of the prepuce of the male organ, the penis. There is an equally ancient practice of female circumcision, which consists of cutting away all or part of the external genitalia (clitoris). The origin of circumcision is unknown, but it was practiced quite widely among most ancient societies; and it is still required among most Jews, Ethiopians, Muslims, and some other people. Among ancient Egyptians, boys were circumcised between the ages of 6 and 12, and it was probably performed on girls of the same age. The origins of and original reasons for circumcision are unknown, it may have symbolized a blood offering to the gods. Medical circumcision of newborn boys was once a routine in many English speaking countries, especially in the United States, although the practice has declined in popularity. A church festival celebrated January 1st commemorates the circumcision of Jesus.

The interesting thing is that the Turkish people, in respect of circumcision, named a pavilion after it.

We come to this result that such methods do not depend on the doctrine of this woman physician or that male professor but is widely practiced among the people in the world. In 1960, I asked a question about circumcision of girls from one of my classmates in AUB University of Lebanon. His name was Bashir Adan and he was from Somalia. He replied that girls' private parts appeared discomfortable with a clitoris so mothers cut it out and it has nothing to do with sexual arousal. Removing the prepuce (head cover or chador) of the penis in childhood, should be considered a brand of slavery. Practicing such a method does not improve the quality of it, but decreases the quantity of the penis. When this procedure as a religious requirement was introduced to Islam, Muhammad was over 40 years old. I do not forget nor forgive that painful and torturing experience.

Mohammad used to travel frequently to Iraq and was interested in Jerusalem, which was the crossroads of trade and cultural exchange in the East. He was impressed by one of the Jewish religious traditions, which was circumcision. He declared Jerusalem as the Kaaba of Muslims as indicated in the verse No. 142 of the Cow Chapter in the Koran but since his relations with Jews in Medina deteriorated he changed Kaaba and was hard on Jews since then. Jews used to be traders and landowners in the region and resisted against the demands of Muhammad. One of those Jewish tribes was Bani Nazir who were ordered by Muhammad to cut off all their palm trees and in reply to the peoples' reaction he mentioned the verse No. 5 of Al Hashr (Exile) Chapter which says whether ye cut down (O ye Muslim!) The tender palm-trees, or ye left them standing on their roots; it was by leave of Allah.

ماقطعتم مِن لِنَتهِ او تَركتُمُوها قِلمَه على اُ صُولیها فبا ذن اللہِ ولیُخزى الفاسقینَ.

Muhammad changed Yathrib, which belonged to Jews, to Medina and imposed levy or Jeziya on Jews as being non Muslims under the rule of Muslims (Ahl dhimma). Mawlana has well described the behavior of Jews with regards to ahl dhimma in the following poem:

همچون جهودان می زیی ترسان و خواران و متهم
پس چون جهودان توبه کن عصابه بر دستار کش

If the structure of religion was based on kindness and guidance instead of on swords and violence, then according to historical records, either western or eastern scholars wouldn't have blamed such a religion. Shedding blood, bombing, beheading of innocent people, etc. which has been going on until today, is a message conveyed by those swordsmen. Just have a look at the symbol on the flag of Saudi Arabia.

God is created by the fantasy of human being, which has not been seen yet.

منم چون چرخ گردنده که خورشید است جان من   یکی کشتی پر رختم که پای من بود دریا
(مولوی)

Mary Khalili Naseri, daughter of the late professor Khalilullah (Khalili) is one of the knowledgeable and kind ladies and a fan of Mawlana. In her visit to Mawlana's shrine in Konya, Turkey she called him the God of Balkh, what a nice and wise metaphor. She is an author who holds a high position in modern literature. I wish I could visit the shrine of God of Balkh or I was rich enough to build his shrine from red gold. His religion and tradition is so popular. As a good gesture we could name Konya as Molavi, God of Balkh and sun of Khorasan who also shines West and it could become the Mecca for all people worldwide. Mary writes that she has whispered this Ghazal of Molavi, which she likes most and is one of the masterpieces in poetry indicating solidarity among humans.

نه تـرسا نـه یـهودم نـه گبر ونی مسلمانم	چـه تدبیر ای مسلمانان کـه من خود را نمیدانم
نه از کـان طبیعـیم نـه از افـلاک گـردانم	نه شرقی یم نه غربی یم نه بحری یم نه بری یم
نه از عرشم نه از فرشم نه از کونم نه از کانم	نـه از خاکم نـه از ابم نـه از بادم نه از اتش
نـه از ادم نـه از حوا نـه ار فردوس رضوانم	نـه از دنیا نـه از عقبی نـه از جنت نه از دوزخ
دویـی از خود بدر کردم یکی بینم یکی خوانم	مکانم لا مکان باشد کـه مـن از جان جانانـم
که جز مستی و قـلاشی نبـاشد هیـتچ داستانـم	الله ای شمس تبریزی چنین مستم در این عالـم

One of the childish behaviors which I call tricky or political in order to stabilize and maintain Islam as a religion is saying Allah Akbar to the ears of a newborn. How far do these Arabs go to cheat and deceive in order to maintain their religion?

One of my friends had a dream in which Mawlana Jalaludin Muhammad Rumi had gone to the shrine of the Great Ferdowsi in Toos. Someone brought a baby to Mawlana asking him to say Allah Akbar to the baby's ears and name the baby. Looking at the baby and in commemoration of Shams Tabrizi, Mawlana said, "Dear Son, welcome to this world, I hope you'll become an honest person." People were surprised, but Mawlana told them: "For God's sake, don't be a xenophile. You should worship your own great figures". He was then a little bit angry and asked people, "who destroyed the glorious civilization of Egypt and the Hellenistic cultural center in Alexandria?" And finally he said to the people that he would have been so happy if they wouldn't have named their babies after Arabs.

Imam Hamid Ghazali 505-450 Hijra (1084-1030 A.D.) in support of Mawlana said to the people that verses of Koran were revealed to Muhammad within 23 years by Gabriel so similar verses shouldn't have been revealed again. In fact, if this is true then why should Ottoman have completed his own Koran and replace it with another version (tablet)? Mawlana made a lot of effort to reach the point of creation but finally, like Mansour (Hallaj) cried out that all the theories like Adam and Eve and other myths were not true. Ghazali, the great Islamic scholar says:

> One of the interesting events in the life of Muhammad is his journey to heaven. According to a tradition narrated by Ibn Hisham 1300 years ago with regards to ascension quoted as saying by Aiyasheh, Muhammad's favorite wife: In the night of ascension, the body of the prophet didn't disappear but his soul went on a journey. (Book by Ibn Hisham, volume 1, p 399). The most logical interpretation about these verses is the popular interpretation of Avicenna who says that such a journey can only be spiritual.

Avicenna (980-1037). During the middle ages, few scholars contributed more to science and philosophy than the Muslim scholar Avicenna. By his writings he helped convey the thought of Greek philosopher Aristotle to the thinkers of Western Europe, and his "Canon of Medicine" became the definitive work in its field for centuries. Born in Bukhara, Persia (now Iran), in 980, he spent his childhood and youth getting a profound education in Islamic law, literature and medicine. By age 21 he was considered a great scholar and outstanding physician. After his father's death, Avicenna left Bukahra and lived in different Persian cities for about twenty years working as a physician and completing two of his major works:

1. "The book of Healing", a large encyclopedia covering the natural sciences, logic, mathematics, psychology, astronomy, music, and philosophy. It probably is the largest work of its kind ever written by one man, and

2. "The canon of Medicine", a systematic exposition of the achievements of Greek and Roman physicians. For the last 14 years of his life, Avicenna lived in the city of Isfahan and continued his prodigious writing career. He died in 1037. In the next century, much of Avicenna's work was translated into Latin and thereby became available to philosophers and

theologians of Europe. In Islam his contributions in medicine, theology, and philosophy are still recognized as valuable."

According to Jalalin Interpretation, Muhammad the Prophet tells Ali, his son in law, and Fatima, his daughter, about his journey," Over there I saw a woman hanged by her hair and her brain was boiling. I asked the guard of Hell who was she. He replied that she was a woman whose hair was seen by aliens. I saw a woman hanged by her tongue and fire of hell was pouring into her mouth. When I asked about her I found out that she had insulted her husband. I saw another woman whose hands and legs were tied and snakes were all around her because she left the house without permission of her husband. Another woman's flesh was cut off and she was forced to eat it because she used to wear make up when she wanted to go out. Another woman whose head was like a pig and her body was like a donkey and fire was injected through her anus and ejected through her mouth. She used to be a singer.

What is dreaming?

Dream - A series of images, ideas and emotions occurring in certain stages of sleep. In her book, <u>Like Sex With Gods</u>, Dr. Bayla Singer wrote about flying. "What does taming of the air mean? Physical flight, freedom to move about in the heaven is just one part of it."

When someone falls in love with something, all he or she has in mind is dreaming about it, hoping for it to achieve his or her goals. His or her body and mind both want to achieve the same thing. A good example is the Charles Manson's symbol for good luck (the Swastika) which remains on his forehead.

Ernesto Che Guevara (1928-1967) and Leon Trotsky (1879-1940), the first one was shot and the second one was killed by an axe but neither ever denied their beliefs.

Once I saw a show on TV that a huge animal, a buffalo, got into a fight with a lion and defeated him. I was so pleased with what the big guy did. This was in my mind and I had a dream that someone threw the body of the dead lion into the sea.

Mankind can't fly but with the help of aerodynamics he was able to. There is a huge difference between experimental wisdom and narrative wisdom. If myths and narrations are not tried and tested, we can't call them experimental wisdom.

Flying in the skies (heavens) riding on a goose, cock, horse and raven is only a myth. Just like myths about rescuing Israelis from Egypt with the help of an eagle. I don't know when religious schools will stop psychological torment.

Islam, like other rites, is a crumb of the mythological process of Persian, Egyptian, Greek, Chinese, Babylonian, Indian, Chaldeans, Israelite, Roman and Christian cultures. George Sarton, in his book <u>Hellenistic Science and Culture in the Last Three Centuries B.C.</u> wrote: "The Greek genius was prolific in the invention of myths because it was essentially poetic. This peculiarity is better understood when one compares it with Semitic genius. The Muslims were more fatalistic than the Greeks and they often expressed the idea of moiré (fate) by means of equivalent words (qisma, "kismet," nasib) but they did not use the imagery of women to symbolize that idea and nipped in the bud the poetic and artistic development of that which gives us so much pleasure in the Greek arts and letters.

When Gengis Khan conquered Bukhara he together with his soldiers entered the great mosque, he converted the Koran cases into feedbags and made socks from the Korans for the horses because it was winter time. One Imam asked the great Imam "What is going on"? The great Imam told him: "Don't ask such a question because it belongs to fate". The question is this: If the holy book belongs to him, why did he do nothing to stop Gengis Khan who profaned his holy book?

Sun Myung Moon, a North Korean, had a dream of Jesus, Moses and Buddha when he was young. He is not only popular but also a millionaire. But here is the question, why didn't Muhammad come into his dream? Is Mr. Moon afraid of circumcision and the five fundamentals of being a Muslim?

Saber was a farmer used to cultivate our lands. He was such a hardworking person. When I was 13 or 14, I had a dream that he was dead and I was crying, I saw God wearing Black from head to toe, ordering me to gather Saber's bones because he wanted to bring him back to life. I gathered Saber's bones at once and brought them back to God. God put the bones together and Saber was alive. That was when I used to pray a lot and loved God. My mother told a religious man about my dream and he interpreted that I would be raised to be a good human being. But how is it that Mr. Moon became popular and a millionaire in the world of Christianity, but I didn't in the world of Islam? Maybe it was because Mr. Moon's dream was political in nature and good for propaganda.

Dr. Singer wrote, "Franciscan Monk Saint Joseph, who was mentally and physically disabled, had the power of levitation. In a state of ecstasy, he jumped into a tree but couldn't get down without the help of others. Perhaps it's because of these imaginary flights that mankind is attracted to aerospace technology.

Mr. Moon: there was a prophet who had only one follower and he used to carry him on his back. Someone asked him "why do you do that?" He replied that if he didn't he wouldn't have any followers. Mr. Moon you are so lucky to have millions of followers. There were men who cut the river and the moon into two parts, made a dead man become alive or walked on water. Mr. Moon is proud that his friends pledged to destroy Marxism and he himself pledged to destroy Darwinism, which is a war with the"whirlwind".

Mr. Shojeddin Shafa has explained that all such stories are amateur copies of "The Book of Arda Viraf". The **Book of Arda Viraf** is a Zoroastrian religious text written by Zoroastrian priests in the 3rd century (Hijra calendar) that describes the dream-journey of a devout Zoroastrian to the next world. It served as a pattern for Dante's Divine Comedy which is widely considered to be a central epic poem.

One should ask himself why those in hell were all women, no men. Isn't it a good example of matriarchy? How does a scientist evaluate such injustice with regards to specific subjects such as wisdom and justice?

It has been stated that Muhammad lost his mother after he was born and his father (Abdullah) had died before his birth. Other sources have indicated that he became an orphan at the age of six. After he was born, he was left without milk until afew days later when God brought milk to the breasts of his uncle Abu Talib.

Afterwards Halimah Sa'dieh became Muhammad's nanny. Perhaps it was because of these deprivations, separations and not having a mother during childhood that Muhammad did not trust women.

According to Verse No. 223 of Al Baqara and Verse No. 34 of Al Nesa, maybe Halimah abused Muhammad, he didn't have much exposure to women and some even believe that women had hurt him. I think maybe culture has a backward effect on mankind. As Shah, daughter of Sultana, says Arabs like their baby camels much more than their wives. They place the baby camel near the air-conditioning and sit their wives in an uncovered area.

On April 11th, 2002, a girls' school in Riyadh, Saudi Arabia caught fire. To save themselves young girls ran out without chadors but religious police forced them back into the school to put on their chadors. As a result of such disrespect for human rights, especially women's rights and being such sycophants, 15 young girls were burned in the fire. There were hundreds of girls and most of them didn't dare think to confront police, otherwise some of them could have been spared injury, but at least there were no casualties.

An interesting point to which the world of Islam has not yet paid attention is the transliteration of الله (Allah) which is comprised of double L, and adding an H in the end is wrong. To me the word of Ala made of three words not four or five. In Russia the ladies carry the name of Alla, but without H.

This is not a criticism but a reminder and there should be an explanation in the dictionary. However Allah is written with double L in English too.

Instructed by the angel Gabriel, Muhammad passed on to his followers the words or prophecies of Allah (from Al ilah, meaning "the God"). If God is called Alilah then what is Allah? Alilah means God in relation to what Gabriel passed on to Muhammad. This name was not unique in that peninsula since Muhammad's father was called Abdullah.

The Mishnah is the oldest collection of Rabbinic which is the foundation for Talmud. It says that those who cannot correctly pronounce the name of the God of the Jews as it is written, cannot go to heaven. Then why didn't Muslims pay attention to this fact? In English, not only one L but also one H has been added to Allah.

"Abul'ala Mudoudi", Leader of Al Ikhwan Al Muslimin of Pakistan, and an Arab Sheikh by the name of "Abdul Aziz Baz", due to their jealousy towards the western scholars and technology, ignore and deny facts like Static, Mechanic, Dynamic and Motion which are related to Physics. Even school children make fun of their ignorant points of view. Mr. Mudoudi, Aziz Baz Sheikh Abdul Rahman Al Sadais, I think you belong to those cave prisoners in the Plato writings.

If Imams prohibit using polio vaccines or the Vatican prohibits condoms then what is the difference between Christianity and Islam from theological point of view? Edward Jenner tried the smallpox vaccine on humans in 1796 and saved the lives of millions.

Also Dr. Babdiel Boylston and his wife Lady Mary Worthle Montagu were among those who saved so many lives but the Chancellor of Yale university, Timothy Dewight opposed the smallpox vaccine stating that it was a kind of intervention in God's creation. People called these scientists many names (Rawhead and Bloody-Bones) such as illiterate, negligent, ignorant, confused, rash, mischievous and inconsiderate and a mob howled outside and threw pebbles, rotten fruits and eggs at them. By the time the Renaissance emerged, the European philosophers diverted their attention from the supernatural to the natural like George Berkeley (1685-1753) who argued that things not perceived do not exist.

Plato (427-347 B.C.) believed that we must go beyond the evidence of our senses to find ultimate reality and truth. In The Republic, Plato writes: "We see objects as real, but in fact they are only poor reflections of ideal models, or "forms", which are eternal and perfect originals of any given object or notion". In The Republic, Plato illustrates our lack of true perception with a famous metaphor: Imagine men sitting in a cave, facing a wall, with a fire behind them. As others carry objects through the cave, in front of the fire the men see only vague shadows of the object and therefore can't make out the reality. Everyone we see is like these imprecise shadows; so, what we see as justice, for example, is nothing but approximation of the true "form" of justice.

Plato has summarized a good ruling of a state, "Until philosophers rule as kings or those who are now called kings and leading men genuinely and adequately philosophize."

Unfortunately, Mullahs are not only ruling the state in Afghanistan now but also streets are now named after such disreputable Mullahs and their incompetent relatives. 150 years ago Abdul Rahman called these Mullahs the most ignorant and destructive people. He said that what they preached was contrary to what Muhammad taught. He banned the religious trusts which caused Mullahs' economic situation to deteriorate. He assigned them to office work like the Catherine the Great of Russia did. Abdul Rahman supervised legal matters of religious courts and tested their abilities. They were entitled to receive their salary if they could pass the test and gain Abdul Rahman's trust. Throughout the history of government in Afghanistan, Abdul Rahman was the only one who could exclusively declare Jihad, meaning that not every clergy could declare Jihad willfully.

He, cut off the head of a mola amongst the Ghalzaie Pashton's tribe by the name of Perfume of the Universe. These Pashton tribes, because of religiosity and lack of social importance, are generally the cause of socio economic stagnations in Afghanistan. The fundamentalist mola, the perfume of the Universs in Ghazni province declared Jihad against the Roberts of Kandahar (Major General Frederick Roberts) a very tough English General. In the end, the mola lost 3000 of his own people in the war. Those who helped Osama Bin Laden to flee to Pakistan were pashtons and those who harbored Osama Bin Laden in Kandahar Afghanistan were Pashtons. The person in the Afghan Embassy in Washington who raised the Taliban flag was Pashton. The people who turned the Kabul international sport

Stadium to a slaughter house were Pashtons. Pashton's Taliban blew up the Buddha, our historical treasure. Those who blew up the Sarobi electricity towers and created the Kabul black out numerous times were also Pashtons.

In January of 1842, seventeen thousand English military personnel along with their families abandoned Kabul toward Jalalabad, to the East. Sadly, all of them were slaughtered by Pashtons. But in February of 1989, when Russians left Kabul to the North toward Russia not even one shot was fired.

In order to better relations between tribes, he transferred 10,000 Ghalzaie families to the north of Hindu Kush. For their income Abdul Rahman assigned them some plots of lands there. During the years of my appointment at the Agricultural Department of Badakhshan, whenever there was a dispute concerning pasture land, these people used to show me the deeds which Abdul Rahman had given them. It would have been better if Abdul Rahman would have distributed 10,000 Ghalzaie families equally in other provinces. Even today, people still criticize his move.

Muhammad Gol Pacha (Mahmand), who used to be an intriguer, was the Governor of the northern area. He lured His Majesty Nader Shah, father of Zaher Shah and transferred a great number of Pashtons to those parts. He assigned them the best parts of the land, whereas the indigenous people received nothing.

At that time, General Abdul Ghafoor, father of Abdul Rahim Ghafoorzai (chief commander) used to serve at Balkh in Mazari-Sharif. Muhammad Gol had requested him to evacuate the barracks due to other projects taking place instead.

The General refused the request and said "the fort is an historical monument and no body has the authorisation to destroy the place."

Ignorant Muhammad Gol {scum of the meat} ordred 300 workers to march and destroy the barracks. The General summoned the soldiers and instructed them that if the workers got close to the fort, warn them three times. Afterwards the soldiers were free to fire on the workers. When the workers got the message they fled the area.

At this time the king Nader shah, the General closest friend, was assassinated and Hashim Khan the king's brother, a most atrocious person and friend of Muhammad Gol took over.Taking advantage of the situation Muhammad Gol informed the prime minister Hashim khan and lied to him that the General had communication with the deposed king Amanullah. Subsequently the General was removed from his post.

I used to study at the School of Economics in the north in Tashkqurghan during the 50's. In the course of my summer trips I used to pass Samangan. My Lari driver was so cautious not to damage the irrigation ducts, since the best fertile lands belonged to Muhammad Gol Pacha- Gestapo's representative, Prime Minister Hashem Khan. Muhammad Gol Pacha was the only outsider fascist who didn't appreciate Persian, Tajik, Uzbek and Hazara tribes and didn't allocate them any land or space. In spite of the fact that he was the Governor of the north, he never learned their language. He had no understanding of the language because he had no tongue.

Manuel Komroff, in his book <u>Marco Polo</u>, writes:

> "The three Polos went on alone, forcing their way across the perilous desert of Persia. It was here that Marco contracted a dangerous fever and was led to record in his travels the great joy that they will experience when they reach the cool, fragrant climate of Balkh in Khorasan, the birth place of Mawlana Jallaluddin Mohammad Rumi. Here they remained a whole year, recovering from the illness contracted in Persia and taking advantage of the time, studied the

Farsi and Uzbek languages. By this time, Marco was twenty-one and the year was 1275.

Professor Abdul Hai Habibi was from Super tribe and was a dogmatic person who belonged to the era of Hashim Khan Gestapo and Mohmmad Gol Mahmand. I'm not surprised what the Taliban did.

Take into consideration that the Taliban did nothing wrong, they executed everything according to the Islamic traditional book as it mentioned in verse No. 73 of Repentance Chapter, "O Prophet! strive hard against the unbelievers and the Hypocrites, and be firm against them. Their abode is Hell,- an evil refuge indeed."

These people of Super tribe destroyed the achievements of Buddhists and Koshanis, shooting people in groups or declaring Shiite and Sunnis as infidels and outsiders and did all this to defend tribalism and Arab traditions.

They whipped girls, women and widows in front of their husbands, brothers, relatives and others. Shooting needy and innocent women, cutting off their hands and legs or even marrying them to foreigners.

They were not Indians, Russians, Iranians, Chinese, Tajik, Hazara or Uzbek, they all belonged to the Valanejad tribe who was supported financially by Arab sheikhs, Ikhvan Al Muslimin and Pakistanis and other enemies of humanism to commit all those crimes and atrocities on our soil.

A Pakistani hand was therefore evident at the outset of the Taliban's emergence; and, despite their denials, their complicity in the Taliban's subsequent succeses is also beyond any reasonable doubt. "Sir Martin Ewans"

We should bear in mind that Afghans used to wipe Arab marble. Ahmad Shah Masoud was killed by an Arab saying Allah Akbar;

even so, they still engraved Allah Akbar on his gravestone. Allah Akbar is an appalling slogan, which reminds one of "The Song of Chanson de Roland", dated 1100.

It was northern people who supported the succession governments after Shah Shoja was killed. Upon collapse of the Taliban, the plane carrying Muhammad Zaher, the former king, landed for the first time in Balkh and Abdul Rashid Dostom received the former king very warmly. The Pashton Taliban mercenaries during their 6 years of rule, had left a blot in the thousand-year history of Afghanistan. In spite of that, the president was again selected from amongst Pashtons and he appointed an incompetent Pashton and representative of Hekmatyar as the governor of Jozjan who massacred innocent people in just one day and injured many others. Were the people of Jozjan so incompetent that rulers couldn't appoint a governor from amongst them?

Question?

Why do some Pashtuns hate others? Because they are the wrong Pashtuns.

Arthur Kent on November 2007 wrote an article on a web that when Khalilzad served the Reagan administration in the 1980, he backed anti-Soviet Afghan's figures of his own Pashton ethnicity— despite their extremist views.He favoured fundamentalists like Gulbuddin Hekmatyar, and allied himself to Pakistan's campaign against the Afghan nationalist leader Ahmad Shah Massoud, an ethnic Tajik. Today, Hekmatyar is America's most wanted Afghan terrorists. Massoud is revered as a hero who prevented the Taliban from seizing all of Afghanistan, but whose warnings about Alqaeda went unheeded by the US.

By the time the Taliban seized Kabul in 1996, Khalilzad's geopolitical aim had not improved. As a director of the Rand corporation, he lobbied the Clinton administration to recognize the Taliban regim.

At the time, he was a paid consultant for the proposed Unocol trans-Afghanistan gas pipeline.

Then came a chance to shape post-Taliban Afghanistan, first as President Bush's special representative and later as ambassador to Kabul. Says a source close to the Presidential Palace: "He encouraged Karzai to rid his govornment of tajiks, and except for a few positions,he has succeeded.

"Khalilzad's plan was to weaken the Taliban by co-opting the Pashtun tribes and the movement feeds on for recruits and support. Stack Karzai's ruling elite with Pashtun,s the reasoning went, and the Taliban movement would fade away.But in many cases, Zal's Pashtuns were the wrong Pashtuns," says a member of Europe's diplomatic corps in Kabul."Advancing ministers on the basis of ethnicity was a mistake." Figures like Information Minister Khorram and Attorney General Sabet bear the out. Both are unbashed fundamentalists,and long time aids to the fugitive warlord Hekmatyar. While they were empowered, respected Tajiks, notably former foreign minister Dr. Abdullah Abdullah were pushed aside.

Mr. Khalilzad!

Your geopolitical idea can not cure the chronic illness of the socio-political srtucture the Afghan people, which is based upon tribalism. Therefore, the political science teaches us to have a system of federal and also secular society in Afghanistan. We want equality and neither superiority nor inferiority.

Who was Pitcher, Molly?

Pitcher, Molly (1754 -1832). The heroine of the battle of Monmouth in the Revolutionary War was Molly Pitcher. Her real name was Mary Ludwig Hays. On June 28, 1778, American troops waited on a hot, sunny field for British and Hessian soldiers to attack. One of the American soldiers was Molly's husband, John Hays, a member of an artillery unite.

Molly had come from her father's farm to visit her husband. When the battle began, she stayed and helped. She carried water from a well to the hot and tired wounded men. When the soldiers saw her they would shout "Here comes Molly with the Pitcher!"

Soon, this was shortened to "Molly Pitcher!" On one trip, she reached her husband's cannon just as he fell, overcome by a wound and the heat. After this happened, Molly took his place. She swabbed out the hot cannon and drove the charge and ball down the gun.

Molly Pitcher was born on a dairy farm between Trenton and Princeton, NJ on Oct.13, 1754. Her father was John Ludwig and when she was 15, she married Hays (a barber). He died a few years after the war and Molly later married George McCauley.

In 1822, the state of Pennsylvania voted to pay her $40 every six months for the rest of her life as a reward for her heroic service. She died on Jan. 22, 1832.

At the end of 18th century, a similar story took place in Kalakan village almost 30 kms to the north of Kabul. There, a war broke out between the Kalakan people and the English army. A hard working Tajik person from Kalakan carried water to the wounded warrior . Later, his son Habibullah revolted against king Amanullah and overthrew the kingdom.

Recently, a pseudonym from the Patan ilk, who could not differentiate between the navel and the vagina or water carrier and being a water carrier, wrote not a book but a sophistry (The Second Water Carrier) in which he made fun of the water carrier (Saqi). How is it possible that the son of a water carrier from the Tajik race could become the king of Afghanistan? He thought carrying water is an inferior job. I think such a relief duty is a much more noble duty than lying down under the Pakistani ISI, Arab Shekhs and other foreign intelligence agencies.

At the American University in Lebanon, I had a classmate (Ms. Jamila from Peshawar) from Pakistan who used to study nursing there. One day, Nazar M.Shirzai (a friend of mine from "Paghman") asked her: "Would you Pashton people like to come and join us?" She responded to him in the pashto language and stated: "Get out of here, socially you people are very behind us in life,". She added: "You people come and emerge with us." These sweet academic memories from the University do not go away, especially regarding good friends like Abdul Hamid Jatala from Pakistan, Nasruddin Bakhtari from Afghanistan, Bashir Adan from Somalia, the beautiful Iranian girl Huma Pezeshki and Abdullah Almontakh from Saudi Arabia. He, unlike the others was the most intellectual and broad minded Arab.

My teacher, Dr.Valentina D. Chesnokova, from the Institute for Nuclear Research of the Ukraine in Kiev and the beautiful librarian named Alla, from the Faculty for Preparatory in Kiev. Morni Bt. Salleh, from Malaysia in Punne India, in 1982 studying methodology and techniques for cooperative staff training in South East Asia, and Tom Hamilton, my boss and a gentleman who used to work in Laurel Regional Hospital.

I convey my best regards to them and wish them good luck any where they are.

Beautiful Points!

Although he himself was not amongst the pros, in his evaluation of the Great French Revolution the French statesman Alexis de Tocqueville (1805-59) stated "This revolution (which was the start of a new era in the history of mankind) was first founded by intellectuals who had nothing but the power of their thoughts and logic. However, not only did they destroy the age-old empire, they nullified the old social structures built by the church throughout the centuries." "We should wish for our ancient land that today's enlightenment would carry the same message for tomorrow as the French Revolution did for the benighted West". (Shafa)

Quote: Marie Jean Antoine Nicolas Caritat, marquis de Condorcet (1727-1781), who thought that the French revolution was the dividing line between the past and a "glorious future", believed that there were three outstanding issues in history: The destruction of inequality between nations, the progress of equality within one and the same nation and the perfecting of mankind.

The author of this book associates himself with the big hope of brother "Shafa" in reaching a new world for his country Iran. He wants his country to be released from the prison of Mullahs. I hoped that this message of fortune could reach the great land of Iran and the light of establishment of intellectualism there, could also enlighten the other side of Khorasan territory. The religious reform movement, after the 15th century, destroyed the solidarity of powerful churches in Europe. We are waiting for the day that the revolutionary youth of Islamic Society might attain such substantive enlightenment.

Through their intelligence service the Americans found out that poverty (economic or educational) does not depend on the Arabic terrorism movement because terrorists have a rather high-level education. Osama bin Laden is a millionaire and Al Zawahiri is highly educated. So what is the disease and which is the medicine to cure it?

Europeans and Americans have developed the deserts of Arab peninsula, have excavated oil and gas wells there and constructed highways, buildings and towers. They have saved many Muslims in Africa, Europe, Middle East and Asia, but nevertheless Arabs and Ajamis have animosity towards them.Why? Because they were under the influence of religious schools and certain ideologies. They are not taught coexistence and cooperation, rather they are taught hatred, imposter, and how to protect Arab dignity.

Arabs exclusively, and Ajams in general, are in need of the Enlightenment era which took place in the 18th century in Europe. Secular philosophers not only rocked Europe but deeply affected the intellectual movements in the world of Islam. Mustapha Kamal Ata Turk in Turkey and Shah Amanullah in Afghanistan were the followers of such intellectual movements but the cowards took away the gifts of freedom in order to promote Arab culture and tradition.

Secularism- The view, that the consideration of the present well-being of mankind should predominate over religious considerations in civil affairs or public education.

In his book, How Religion Poisons Everything, God is not Great, Christopher Hitchens wrote, "The Aztec had to tear open a human chest cavity every day just to make sure that the sun would rise." I don't know when these outdated thoughts will go away.According to Christopher Hitchens, "There were those who said that the fossils had been placed in the rock by god, in order to test our faith." I'm really thankful to Christopher Hitchens, the famous author who nailed coffin closed on old-fashioned ideas and drew a line between religion and state.

The Aztec used to immolate a person every day just to make sure that the sun would rise.

Look at the propitiatory killing in Islam under the pretext of martyrdom and elation, people kill themselves and others by the thousands.

This act does not come from the commandment of God, but rather from customs and dreams which are inherited from the past where primitive people lived under a more vicious environment.

The countless reparations which have resulted from the dream of Abraham turned to religious exaltations for billion of Muslims (Arab, Ajam and the psychological one). In-order to appease the gods, they covered and are still covering the lands with the blood of humans and animals.

I could not understand who went to Heaven and who burned in Hell. Billy Graham has claimed that all 9/11 victims have gone to heaven but he should have deducted the 19 Arab terrorists from the real victims. Maybe Billy Graham knows that those who commit Jihad will go to Heaven. According to Verses No. 72-74 and 76 of the Al Rahman chapter of the Koran: "In them will be fair companions, beautiful companions restrained in nice pavilions, reclining on green cushions and rich carpets of beauty." They 're 14 year olds and still are 14 even though 1400 years passed.

Is Islam great? If a Muslim kills an infidel or if an infidel kills a Muslim, the Muslim becomes Ghazi and either way the Muslim goes to heaven. Where there are streams of wine, milk, and honey running everywhere? Also, where are the virgin girls that have not been touched before and are waiting there for you?

Do you believe that the honey streams are moving? Where do these honey streams,

milk and wine come from? Standing nearby kids, laughed a lot when they heard the story and one of them said "our bees and our neighbors bees disappeard in one day". The other smart kid told them they might have gone up there and he added that if the milk and the wine are kept open in the opened air, one of them will convert into yogurt and the other one into vinegar. People all around them laughed very much and had a little fun.

You sheeps! How long will your head be down and your ass up like sheep on the grazing ground?

Islam says if a Muslim kills an infidel? in the war he the Muslim becomes ghazi, a stupid honorary name. This psychodynamic version as an incentive factor to conquer the world is the invention of Arab invaders which penetrated in to the cowardly Ajam's cultures.

What is worshipping?

The fervent love and allegiance accord a deity, idol,or sacred object, or other religious forms by which this love is expressed.

Religious adulators and reverent believers through flattering, lies, and exaggerations want to uplift the greatness of their lovers from implosion.Look at the Muslims the religious ties among them is usually stronger than their national sentiment. For example Jihad a non-productive pray on the basis of Arabic propaganda million Muslims being killed all over the world in vain.

In my country Afghanistan for the love of Allah, Afghanistanies ruined completly their own country I wish they would have known that the play was a part of the old great game in central Asia, but in different political version, (stability through destability).

If Hindus worship the cow, that is a productive pray because the animal provides them with every physical necessities especially in the fields of agriculture and dairy products.

When I was a kid a group of soldiers were dragging a young farmer to the court because he was shouting and cursing at Allah. The farmer who had a milking cow and she being burst up because she had been eating fresh clover. He was very enraged, yelling and shouting. He said that he prays every day and starving every year in the month of Ramadan, want to go to Mecca to become haji, pays tithes and taxes therefore, he is fad up with the oppressive and repressive policy of negligent Allah, why he did not save the life of my milking cow the only family income he said.

Muslims: black and white, Ajams and Arabs, men, and women to become heavenly, every year they go to Mecca to become haji and hajia.

Before the Prophet, peopple used to worship there in the nude, but now they put on Sari,

kiss the black stone and bit up on the white rock. I don't know what are the reasons behind of this two unorganic objects.?

Unctuous adherents know very well that, the Prophet himself prior the Prophecy had been circled Kabba numerous times.

In Islam, as a religious rite there is a funny exercise called Tayamum or desert ablution. If there is no water around, the person starts beating up on his own body with his two hands and then he or she gets clean.

Another religious rite in Islam is Halalah. If a person divorces his own wife and wants to remarry her, she has to engage in intercourse with another strange person in front of the witnesses.

Here in the US on CNN news on July 6th, a Muslim physician condemned the terror plot of a few British Muslim physicians and said it went against Islamic medical ethics. This is the first time that I hear about Islamic medical ethics and such a fundamentalist idea about medicine. I asked myself was it possible to have an Islamic medical practice?

However I thought that now that Muslims have the Islamic Atomic bomb so they should have Islamic Aspirin, Islamic Plavix, Islamic Serum, Islamic Syringe, Islamic condom, etc. A good example is that Arabs have made a pirate copy of the Red Cross created by Henry Dunant resulting in the Red Crescent. In this regard, Dr. Roshangar wrote in his book that before the introduction of Islam the Arabs used to worship the moon and they believed that the moon was a female married to the sun (who was a male) and the stars are their children. In Japanese mythology the sun is female and the moon is male. The Sumerians believed that Ishtar and Innana were the daughters of their moon god, Nanna.

In several verses of Koran God swears on the moon, e.g. verses 77 and 78 of Al An'am chapter. Not only Arabs but all the Middle Eastern people and the inhabitants of the Nile River worshipped the moon. The statutes and plates which are in the western museums now clearly indicate the above fact. For example, fasting starts and ends by spotting the new moon. Fasting was a Jewish tradition copied by Islam. To be forgiven for their sins, Jews fast on Yom Kippur which is on the 10th of Tishri, in the first month of the new year. Yom means day in Arabic and it is a Hebrew word. Muslims go on the rooftops to spot the new moon in Ramadhan. When they see the moon they hold their hands up and say prayers and wish to be blessed. If an abnormal growth appears on someone's skin, grandpa grabs a broom and holds it against the moon then rubs it on the growth and prays for it to remain if it's for goodness, otherwise it should fade away.

Please note that there is a crescent on top of every mosque which stems from supernatural philosophy since the Middle East was the center point for trade and mythology and tradesmen imported and exported merchandise from China and India. The traders used to tell their stories for the people of Middle East while chatting in tea houses or caravans and books were written based on those stories. On the other hand, because of the heat resulting from direct sunshine, it was impossible to travel in the daytime, therefore Arab caravans preferred to travel at night under the moonlight. Maybe this is the reason why Arabs used to worship the moon as their God. It's worth mentioning that the moon on the flags of Islamic countries is considered to be a national symbol.

Mawlana, in his poems 2544, he tells the story of how important the moon light is. A person was looking after his camel and he lost it in the bright day light. He was looking everywhere but he could not find it. The man was desperate, broke and hopeless and he got tired and went to sleep until the moon appeared. Once the moon appeared, he found his camel.

ز شادی امدش گریه بسان ابر نیسانی   بنور مه بدید اشتر میان راه استاده

که هم خوبی و نیکویی هم زیبا و تابانی   رخ اندر ماه روشن کرد و گفتا چون دهم شرحت

تا گم کرده خود را بیابد عقل انسانی   خداوندا در این منزل بر افروز از کرم نوری

Here, Mawlana pursues wisdom and he wants to distinguish between two different objects: lightness and darkness. He considered lightness as wisdom and darkness as ignorance. With the help of light, which is wisdom, you can see things and differentiate but in the environment of darkness (ignorance, blindness), you cannot. In the words of someone, you are a dead body. In the dictionary, wisdom means understanding of what is true, right or lasting.

The Muslim women are ignorant of social manners in the civilized countries of their residence and while wearing a ridiculous scarf (which makes them look like a baby kangaroo peeping out from the pouch of an Arab kangaroo) appear on TV and talk about Islam. This practical appearance, regardless of the time and the requirements, clearly symbolizes their primitive, cohesive and fundamentalistic culture.

لاجُناحه عليهِنَ فى ابائِهِنَ ولا ابنائِهِنَ ولا اخوانِهِنَ ولا ابناء اخوانِهِينَ ولا ابناء اخواتِهنَ و لا نِسا
ئيهِن ولا ملكت ايمائُهُنَ و تقِينَ الله انا لله على كل شىء شهيدا 55. (احزاب)

In the Koran, in verse 31 of the Noor's chapter about wearing chador, it is said:

> "Do not disclose your jewels, eyes, faces and your private places to strangers except for your parents, relatives and male servants who do not have penis and ladies like you.

It's clear now that in Islam, fathers, brothers, sisters, mothers and other relatives are permitted to look at the private places of one another. In reality, if wearing hijab is a divinity issue or a very necessary piousity commandment, this verse should have been revealed in the first or in the second chapter of the koran and not in the last chapter.

What about the physical involvements of the medical doctors in the hospitals who look in detail at the private places of the veiled ladies?

The above manifesto, as a divinity requirement, belongs to the primitive culture of special people. Whether this unconsidered subject has been mentioned in this or in another book or not, the people know how to adopt themselves with the requirements of the environment. Because the intertwined constructive elements of human behavior are one of the main factors of our social development.

I wonder why these people who waited for years behind the closed doors of Embassies to get a visa and come to heavenly countries such as the US, Europe, Canada or Australia and then they disrespect the culture of their host.

I believe that the strong generation of Arab and Ajami, men or women, are able to create an Enlightenment movement. The ignorant rivals either our own countrymen or foreigners, lock us in a cage (of superstitious beliefs) and party all night long.

To whom do I talk and who are my listeners that share my cogitation about the decisive role of the social science in our society?

Good hearted people! Kings and Emirs have created religion (the opium of the people) and by occupying our minds and bodies, have deprived us from good quality material and the spiritual pleasures of life while science and technology are blooming. It's because of this fact that continuous struggle and confrontation with the above mentioned is considered a responsibility for the whole world.

Those who fight for freedom against old fashioned ideas and lose their lives or disappear are the heroes whose names have been recorded in the history and we are proud of them. If you, the emancipators, youth die while fighting satanic old fashioned believers and your children become orphans or bereave your family or even become disabled, you have finally created a world in which we fly peacefully through free skies.

As the author of this book I would like to mention that with regards to the political system of Afghanistan, there has been a ruling class, 250 years of Durrani, as they have always occupied the highest military and civil positions. Most achievements, whether material or spiritual, have been attributed to them. Now that democracy is being implemented, their political monopoly should come to an end.

Other Afghan groups including Tajik, Uzbek, Hazara, Qezelbash, Nurestani,etc. should have the right to be considered for the position of presidency with no consideration of inherited privilege, based simply on competency (race, language, or religion).

Otherwise it would run contrary to the principles of democracy. Therefore, I'd like to ask all of the politicians in the world who believe in democratic justice and honor to break the curse of feudalism, and tribalism in Afghanistan. If democracy is not implemented, there will be no social justice in Afghanistan.

Therefore, I ask the respected and reverent generals, soldiers and others who are serving in the backward country of Afghanistan to be firm in their resolutions. This is necessary in order to bring peace and security there. Also, please do not be more apologetic and too benignant toward stupid people.

In his book "America and the World", General Scocroft writes: "War rarely solves problems". But he refrained to say that war is not necessary.

War is necessary to stop those vicious retrogressive groups who deteriorate peace, law and order in Afghanistan.

Begot Muhmend executed the policy of sectarian expansionism to the north of Afghanistan in a dishonest way, a trite action as historical event which are only attributed to this type of psychopathic ruler and those of the same ilk, enemies of liberalism, who not only cast seeds of hatred among the tribes, but also damaged the coherency of our people.

The writer believes that the settlements of the armed Pashtons together with their families and their livestocks to the North of Afghanistan illegally, was the act of the rulers of the country in order to block every relationsips of the north with the people of middle Asian neighbors, who they have common history and traditions therefore, this Stalinistic policy as a national tragedy and social injustice must be condemned in the history of Afghanistan.

We and the world have witnessed the dictatorship of the Pashton Taliban towards the inhabitants of the North. The settled Pashtons there took side with their own Pashtons Taliban including the Arab invaders, Chechenians from Russia and others.

They killed the indigenous people, burned their houses, pulled out the fruit trees and pushed out the ladies and children from their houses.

To prevent the probably attack of Bolshewiks, the Afghan government: king Amanullah and Nader shah wanted to have them as a scape goat in the North.

The Pashtons settlement to the North, in my view was, the British imperialistic plan; With the occupation of Pamir's heights in the end of 18th century by Russian's Tzar, the distance between these two imperials became narrower and narrower to the extent that 100 miles in some places reached up to 20 miles; and this situation scared the English very much because it was to the advantage of Russians to reach Indian Oceans through Afghanistan.

To block or impede the Russians advances toward India, the English imperial came up with a plan of Pashtons settlements to the North to be applied by the king Nader shah through its agent, Mohamad Gul Mohmand and their other trustees.

Durani as a Despotic regime, on the basis of language, race and religion separated these two brother nations (Iran and Afghanistan) for more than two hundred years. Some crude minded Pashton stood at the threshold of a new era, a jealous fortune era. Look at the Iranians and see how much they are ahead of us especially in the fields of art, literature and music. High quality of conception or execution, as found in the works of beauty, aesthetic value.

Since the time of Ahmad Shah Durrani, the tribal leaders in Kandahar had been exempted from paying land tax, and during the king of Nader Shah the Paktia people had been exempted from paying tax.

Be sure that these backward people are totally accountable to the miseries and the <u>non-modern</u> lifestyle of the country. Do you remember the Taliban, the contemporary international mercenaries power? In a short time, they caused more destruction than Genghis Khan did in a much longer time frame.

Washington Times dated 10.15,96 writes that the Pakistan priminister Benazir Bhutto at the United Nation was speaking about the Kashmir issues.

A journalist asked her whether the Pakistan government supported the Taliban? Benazir responded why are you accusing us? The journalist said that Mr. Abdul Rahim Ghafoorzai, the previous foreign minister, confirmed that 25 Pakistanis were captured together with five Taliban and five of them were Pakistani military officers. Benazir responded that this is something I have heard for the first time. There is no war in Afghanistan and Pakistani military personnel are not there. The citizens of Kabul cooperated with the Taliban and overthrew Rabani's government.

When she was ousted from office and was living in London, she revealed the truth and said that the Taliban was the invention of Americans.

In his book about the vulnerabilities of Iran to the East with Baluchis to the North with Azeris and some Arabs on coast near Iraq, Brzezinski writes:

> "But I think we ought to take into account this reality
> is much more complex, and not forget the relatively
> positive role Iran played in the immediate aftermath
> of 9\11 and our <u>overthrow of the Taliban where they</u>
> <u>were extremly helpful to us.</u>"

<u>President Ronald Reagan, "the film boy" بچی فیلم according to the democratic regime of Aghanistan, wanted to change the political system of the world. He wasted more than $3 Billion of tax payer money to destroy a small and poor country which was known as the eyesore of the world. Consequently, we have no peace today but a very appalling world.</u>

<u>Marc Sageman former CIA officer attributed to the upheaval political situation of Afghanistan in 1980 in interwiev with RT said: Afghanistan was not important then as it is now he added that the world with the disappearence of the Soviet is safer and he deadly is wrong.</u>

Mr. Brzezinski! A person kept a bear and anywhere he went he took the bear with him. While he <u>was on a trip to visit his older brother,</u> he got tired and went to sleep. All of a sudden, a big fly appeared and started circling around his head.

The bear got agitated and wanted to get rid of this intruder so he looked around and picked up a big stone but smashed the head of his own boss.

A poet says:

دشمن دانـــا بلند ت میکنـــد   بر زمینت میزند نادان دوست

The smart enemy picks you up, but puts you down the ignorant friend.

I think the democratic government in Afghanistan is much better and more useful to world peace than the Taliban, the mujahiddin, <u>Hamid Karzai, and others like them</u>. The borrowed parochial Arabic book, according to Hitchens, is not burned yet but the Afghan street boys are already protesting against the burning of the book. So what is the moral obligation of Mr. Karzai and the megalomaniacal Defense Minister under the leadership of another MacNaghten? Believe me, these sweethearts of the <u>U.S. lack of awareness are not capable of making a society or working for the interests of world peace.</u>

Scrupulous fundamentalists like Mr. Karzai and people around him that are infatuated with Talibanism idealogy are hardening the ground for democracy. Karzai himself is the biggest obstacle to proceeding democracy in Afghanistan and a great motive for imams in the mosques to preach against America. Now is the time to overthrow the corrupt government of Mr. Karzai and replace it with a democratic and fairminded regime. The American Congress and government would be accountable for the miseries of widows and orphans of Afghanistan if they don't remove Karzai and his regime from power.

Most American politicians acknowledge that they do not have another choice except to put up with Mr.Karzai's corrupt government. This kind of mentality is disrespectful to most highly educated Afghan people inside and outside of the country. I'm puzzled with such a new despicable model of political terminology in the 21th century.

Again Mr. Karzai himself is the problem but not part of the problem, him and around him with close relationships with pashton Taliban flaming unrest to vilify the Gen. David H. Petraeus, the coalition military commander in Afghanistan. According to the Washington Post, Monday, November 15 2010,: Officials discounted early reports Sunday that Petraeus had threatened to resign.

Is there any smart person at the top to teach these stupid street boys about the Koran? Caetany said that the Koran, as it exists today, did not come word for word from the pen of the prophet but was the result of a standardization and clean up effort ("Uthman's recension") undertaken many years after his death.

The Russian Poet- Pushkin, Aleksander Sergeevich (1799-1837) says "Koran is a beautiful dramatic book".

Pushkin missed the point he could have said that Islam is crazy glue. In 1400 years, this religion did not allow us to turn from one side to another.

My dear country men (worldwide):

Our country is a mountainous and barren land but the Mujahideen (lovers of voluptuous beautiful virgin girls of Paradise and ghulman, the young handsome teenaged slave boys) made her even more barren and deforested and, therefore, her glory and beauty once again requires the sympathy of you broad-minded people.

Friends; Darius the Great, Alexander the Great, British the Great, Russians and Indians did not destroy or disgrace our lovely country, but Arab Imperialism through Arabization, the Mongol Emperor Genghis Khan did. More recently Pakistanies, together with the Ikhwan Al Muslimin, who carried the American bazooka on their shoulders, dollars and dinars in their pockets, repeated the bloody scenes of 7th century in my country.

In my books, <u>Hindukush</u> or <u>Army of Hindukush,</u> based on the self-interested foreign propaganda that caused mass displacements, immigration and separations, I was shocked to observe such a painful tragedy in modern times; and emotionally I have shown my compassion towards those (Mujahideen) who later became robbers, kidnappers, killers, drug traffickers and contrabandists. Disturbingly, I was wrong and apologize. Such people invite Arabs as holy guests into their houses but behead the likes of Daniel Pearl.

Using plagiarized ideology, the Arabs pillaged and plundered countries just to become superior through absolutism. Absolutism was the only factor in the obscurant world of Islam for 1400 years and we cannot blame Zoroastrianism, secularism, Buddhism and others for these entanglements, but rather the successors of prophets and Islamic jurisprudents, like Imam Aziz Baz who says that the sun moves around the earth and that Onanism inflames the testicles, damages the eyesight and erodes the spinal cord.

Be smart (like Gene Autry) and be remembered for good forever.

Because of ignorance Arab-loving Afghans cannot differentiate between Satan and Angel or concepts of construction and destruction, invasion and division. Arabs blow themselves up for nothing, but the Afghan tribes do so because of abjectness and deformed spirit.

For example, America wanted to sign an agreement with the Tailban similar to the treaty of Saudi Arabia in 1945. But the Taliban, because of Verse 28 of Al Omran's chapter, denied it. Maybe Bin Ladin or the Pakistani ISI or some other sources warned them about the consequences.

گفتند که موضوع شریعت نه به عقل است   زیرا که به شمشیر شد اسلام مقرر
"حکیم ناصر خسرو قوباد یانی"

It has said that the Sharia subject is not based on wisdom because Islam is established by the sword.

My thanks go also to the brave young lady Saira Shah, who pictured the shame of Islam the excution of an innocent poor lady by Taliban in a Kabul international sports stadium with the bullet of accomplices, on top Saudi Arabia.

Around 707 A.D., the Arab Imperialism invaded my country (Khorasan or Afghanistan). The bedouins inflicted heavy casualties on us both physically and mentally. Through the non stop war, the Arabs reached Kabul. The citizens of Kabul resisted the occupiers very well but in the end, the Arabs conquered the city.

Based on verse 24 (woman's chapter) of the Koran, they raped our mothers, wives, sisters and daughters (because we were infidels). In the past 1400 years we, suffered too much from the Arab religion. During the 1960's, in President Daoud's era the democratic regime thrived in Afghanistan and Islam fled Afghanistan. But in the 1980's, Ronald Reagan brought back this evil to my country.

American's wrong policy attributed to the political changes in Afghanistan and made Islam very strong as well as vicious. This is why they are pushing the indigenous Christians out of the Middle East.

لرغونی بامیان وران سو د پنجاب په افتخار   معصوم بودا شهید شو په چاله د استکبار
فیصل زموژ امام سو ، اسامه زموژه پــلار   کابل چلی خانه سوه د عــربـــو د ناتار
سپاس بر تو برادر گرامی بزرگوار سلیمان لایق

According to the Brisard and Dasquie: "Prior to September 11th, the US government had an extremely benevolent understanding of the Taliban regime. The Taliban were perceived as a source of stability in Central Asia that would enable the construction of an oil pipeline across Central Asia from the rich oil fields in Turkmenistan, Uzbekistan and Kazakistan, through Afghanistan and Pakistan to the Indian Ocean. This would have secured, for the US, another huge captive and alternate oil resource center. The oil and gas reserves of Central Asia have been controlled by Russia. The Bush government wanted to change all that. This rational of energy security changed into a military one," the authors claim.

The authors added that: "The main objective of the US government in Afghanistan prior to the Black Tuesday was aimed at the consolidating of the Taliban regime inorder to obtain access to the oil and gas reserves in Central Asia".

The Taliban are a blot in the page of history. Fred Gedrich a foreign policy and national security analyst in the Departments of State and defense writes: "Poppy farmers, traffickers and the Taliban terror group form the main components of the drug trade", The Washington times April 4, 2008.

Zhores A. Medvedev, in his book <u>Andropov,</u> writes: "Soviet military experts might have saved themselves a great deal of trouble if they had read the works of Professor Nikolai Vavilov, a remarkable Soviet scientist and a genuine hero in the struggle for the establishment of scientific principles in Soviet genetics".

Vavilov was famous for his botanical-geographical expeditions, of which the most important was to Afghanistan in 1924-26.

He visited many parts of the country which had never been seen by Europeans and was the first geographer to make maps of several areas. He also wrote about his expedition and his description makes it clear that there was a great deal of local hostility, directed both towards him and towards other villages and tribes.

Vavilov made a further observation which is probably relevant to current problems in Afganistan: "There was a tradition of cultivating a unique, fast-growing poppy, Papaver Somniferum, from which opium is produced and exported".

It is now known that the production of opium in Afghanistan increased during the 1960s and 1970s – the remote villages in the main valleys, completely independent from the central government, were very suitable for cultivation of this crop, which also spread into North Pakistan, where government control was again, non-existent.

The Soviet invasion was not only an affront to national pride, it also disrupted the normal opium and heroin trade route. Socialism did not suit the opium traders and as the war intensified, the main centers of poppy cultivation as well as the opium and heroin trade were transferred to the northern Parts of Pakistan (which is now probably the largest center of heroin production in the world).

Machiavillianism? The political doctrine of Machiavelli denies the relevant of morality in political affairs and holds that craft and deceit are justified in pursuing and maintaining political power.

Reaching towards economic goals is more important than the heinous crimes that have been committed by the Taliban in the name of religion.

My heart goes to those gallant heroes who died for freedom but not in the service or worship of a deity, god, sacred or holy.

The five fundamentals of Islam are included in the following: Jihad, prayers, calling prayers into the ears of newborns, recitation of the Koran, cutting off hands and legs, beheadings, killing individuals by stoning, different Eids (celebrations), performing Haj, burning individuals are all factors of stability in Islam. Without these factors, religions will soon fade out.

Remember witch hunts in the 17th and 18th centuries in Europe? This era was called "The great witch craze". It caused a great concern for the Christian bishops who felt that such a movement might be a great threat to religion. Thousands of innocent people were killed and burned. People were killed under torture by the Church and a great number of women in Europe fell victim to this "phony" religion.

There is a proverb which says "The bowl is hotter than the soup". Indonesian people converted to Islam because they feared the volcano. That's why the government of Indonesia announced a one-week holiday for the Eid of Ramdhan (small Eid). There is another Eid coming, Eid-e Kalan or (bloody Eid), maybe this time the Indonesian government will announce a two-week holiday.

I don't know how and why the Indonesian people converted in to Islam since Buddhism is the most peaceful religion.

I remember some Indonesian students in Kiev Ukraine during 1963. I also remember some in Vaikunth Mehta National institute of Cooperative Management at Pune India during 1982 and some in the State University of New York at Albany in the summer Intensive English Language Program during 1985. They were very smart and open minded people. Now I do not know what their reactions would be to my remarks. Do you think religion is retarding the development of civilization?

In Saudi Arabia, because of the Ramadan holiday or holiness, they liberated the Al Qaida terrorists from prison and gave each one $2500. I don't know why Ramadan is holy. I mutter to myself that the Arabs sure have a lot of holy stuff like the holy Medina, holy Mecca, holy land (other lands are dirty!) holy Koran, holy Eids, holy war, holy caves, holy mosque, holy hair, holy cloak and other holy holy holy.

For God's sake, physically and mentally, Ramadan is a very torturous month, driving everybody crazy like Mawlana Jalalludin Muhammad Rumi, the greatest Islamic philosopher explains Ramadan.

Ramadhan is a stifling machine of life, pain in the stomach, the file of life and the junkyard.

این روزه چو غربال به بیزد جان را   پیدا ارد قـــراضه پنـــهان را

Fasting is some sort of starveling, poor in quality and inadequate. It means that if a person is fasting, physically and mentally she or he is out of chemical balance and cannot judge properly. <u>This is why Sharia Law grants indulgences to the Kings and Emirs about fasting in Ramadan.</u>

Today, Islamic religious adulators in their writing like their step brothers (the Christians) have on ill founded issues discovered many excuses offering too many indulgences to their father and grandfather.

I don't know why none of the Islamic media call it a holy month without delving into the actual content of Ramadan.

In the Koran, there are three verses which state that no one can change the word of Allah what so ever. So why did Muhammed, the king of Arabs, change the only holy land to another holy land? This rehearsal apparently potrays the veracity and inveracity of a religion like Islam.

In school, our Islamiat teachers taught us that Islamic leaders are excused from fasting during the month of Ramadan. I'm hoping that some day we all could get rid of this ugly porcupine.One year fasting in 12 years is crazy and it implies to the disendowment of a religion.

Forming the formulation and delimitation of contemplation is a beautiful adjudication: I like such formulation when Christians say that (The Bible Says). Isn't fair for lslamic Imams to say the same thing that (The Koran says?) and delete the philosophy of phantasmal, an illusionary mental image from the teaching of school curriculums.

In the Koran it has been mentioned that revelations were written on leaves and bones.

1. Bone is an oily substance on which nothing can be written.

2. Aged bones, they have many pores, which absorb color and anything written on them may smear. Aged bones will also very easily crack under pressure.

3. Leaves not only dry very rapidly, but also quickly curl up and if someone tries to unfold them, they will be in a thousand pieces. Goats and camels might even eat them. Also, the wind can easily dislocate them rain and snow wipe out the scriptures. So, how is it possible to write over one hundred thousand verses on leaves? Even so, what is the first and the last verse? It's not even clear whether the verses were written on one side of the leaf or on both sides.

4. It is said that revelations were written on objects such as bones, leather and leaves. Now, I ask the Islamic scholars to explain what happened to these objects they carried which were the Holy Scriptures and sacred scrolls? Did they bury them? Burn them? Or thrown them away? Were they sent back to heaven?

Definition of revelation on the Web:

- Disclosure: the speech act of making evident
- Communication of knowledge to man by a divine or supernatural agency
- An enlightening or astonishing disclosure

Science tells us that every kind of sound begins in a vibrating object.

If a revelation is not a physical sound, how does the communication process take place?

The above definition, (of revelation) which is not limited to scientific evidence, makes it clear that such communication as defined by science can not happens.

Sound, then, depends on three things.

There must be a vibrating object to set up sound waves, a medium (such as air) to carry the waves and an ear to receive them.

پس محل وحی وحی گردد هوش جان   وحی چه بود؟ گفتن حس نهان
(مولوی)

Mawlana Jalaladdin Muhammad – Rumi (1207-1273) about the revelation says: "Revelation is a feeling evolves from the inside and does not come from supernatural objects".

A critical case in point is the work of Christoph Luxenburg, The Syriac-Aramaic version of the Koran, published in Berlin in the year 2000. Luxenburg coolly purports that far from being a monoglot screed, the Koran is far better understood once we concede that many of its words are Syriac-Aramaic rather than Arabic. (His most celebrated example concerns the rewards of a "martyr" in paradise: when retranslated and redacted, the heavenly offering consists of sweet white raisins rather than virgins). This is the same language, and the same region, from which much of Judaism and Christianity emerged. "Christopher Hitchens"

Like Naser Khosrow (Balkhi) 1253-1325 and Baruch Spinoze, I tried honestly to reveal that religion is made by men. I believe in what Spinoze believed in, I believe in what Naser Khosrow believed in. I believed in what Albert Einstien believed in.

Now if you want to burn me up, steal my dead body or urinate on my grave, that is up to your casuistry because I told the truths.

قانون جنگل

هر جا که نگاه کردم و ماندم قدمی   افتاده سری دیدم و بی سر تنی
خنجر کین مجاهد بدرید سینهٔ کودک   از دیدن ان لرزه بیافتاد بدشت و دمنی
مرمی و خمپاره ، میریخت چو باران   رقاصه مجاهد که مست است زبنگ عربی
فریاد یتیمان بلند ز هر کوچه و خانه   از وحشت اسلام و حکم روایات قرانی
من ندانستم جهاد چه و مجاهد چه معنی   شاخ زرین عرب رفت بهاونگ عجمی
مغزسر کودکان بپاشید بمبهایی مجاهد   دستهاست فتاده بحویلی و سرها ببامی
طفل بی سر در اغوش سر مادر کجاست   کشتن و سر کندن انسان در عشق خیالی
مستند مجاهد همه از مزهٔ خون من و تو   میریزند ازاین خون از ان جام بجامی

Friends!

Jihad is an ostentatious and blatant idea about one's accomplishments, a kind of vaunt and bragging technique to achieve political objectives. This slogan is a deceptive policy coming out from a violent culture.

Jihad was made in the Arabian Peninsula (if you are under attack, you've got to resort to Jihad). The question is this: "Who attacked the Arabs? So Arabs ordered Jihad on others and perpetuated this slogan in the culture of non Arabs or Ajams (who were seen as second class). As Caetani says: "The Arab conquests during the formative era of Islam were driven not by religion but by material want and covetousness".

The primitive slogan, as a political weapon, got into each Islamic countries culture by those who have been converted into Islam by force. As Abul Qaseem Ferdowsi said one thousand years ago: "Damn on the world, damn on this time, damn on the fate, that uncivilized Arabs come to force me to be Muslim."

If a country or if a person is being attacked by an invader, does the person surrender to him without any fight or resistance? So what is patriotism and what does freedom mean? I think love, devotion, ethic and obligation force the people to fight and resist invaders in order to protect their country, pride and dignities and it is irrelevant to the slogan of Jihad. But this is the right of every individual to defend and protect themselves at any cost regardless of Jihad exultation.

> "Those who reap the blessings of freedom must undergo the fatigue of supporting it."
>
> (Thomas Paine)

وقت ضرورت چو نماند گریز   دست بگیرد سر شمشیر تیز
" سعدی "

To My Indoctrinated Friends:

I call on all my country's brave men and women, girls and boys, academicians, intellectuals and broadminded people to come together to export the imported Arab ideology (sword, jihad and liturgy) back to the Arabian peninsula.

You noble gallant soldiers have lost your freedom, pride and dignity because you have listened to the corrupted politicians, ignorant Mullahs and foreign spies. Now, you are among the most illiterate and poor nation in the world.

Karzai's conglomerate political circles playing distructive games all the time while our orphans, widows, homeless and disabled are begging and dying on the streets.

On the other hand, some coward enemies are preventing you from forming a comprehensive unity. If you are united, you are omnipotent and nobody can divide you.

Relying on pashtuns alone without including Hzarah, Tajik, Ozbek and others is a weak vision. You are proud but are you victorious?

No. You coward religion fighters are defeated, broken, and betrayed. Ronald Reagan, former President of the United States, once called you hairy people freedom fighters.

Politically and philsophicall, he was wrong. If the Berlin wall was breached, many other walls were built up. Islamic terrorists flourished everywhere which endangered the safety and security of the world even within the United States and Europe.

Instead of two super powers, now we have many super powers. Immigration, displacing, and crossing the borders and all other tragedies evolved from the destabilization of Afghanistan.

In his book "America And The World", Brzezinski cautiously writes:"our strategy in effect postulated that the only way to have stability in the Middle East is to destabilize it. Then he says that we insisted on elections among the Palestinians which produced a victory for Hamas. We made a belated effort to move Egypt towards democracy thereby probably increasing the viability of the Muslim Brotherhood there. It may emerge as a central political force in Egypt". I wish that he, the reverend Brzezinski, could have used such an exceptional ability prior to the destruction of Afghanistan.

Intellectual Afghans, boys and girls!

This is our social duty and our moral obligation to fulfill the prospects of the late king Amanulla (secularism) which was sabotaged by British imperialism.

The thoughtful idea of social changes in Afghanistan was the initiation of this great man and on the basis of his brilliant scope, secular revolution took place there in 1978. But the reactionary forces hostile to Afghanistan's prosperities resorted to the fruitful tool (fundamentalist Muslims) to overthrow the secular government there in Afghanistan.

Now, this is the time to rise up again and fight the corrupted Afghan Islamic government and form a secular system there. Because collective behavior as a social movement is the nucleus of change and the sources of such social movements and change already exist there but they need momentum as well as coherence.

Secularism is a form of thinking which was created by George Jacob Holyoake in 1846.

Marx says:"practice is the test for any theory". Because of religious influence, we were not able to put secularism into practice.

According to Emile Durkheim: This is because society cannot make its influence felt unless it is in action, and it is not in action unless the individuals who compose it are assembled together and act in common. It is by common action that it takes consciousness of itself and realizes its position; it is before all else an active cooperation.

1400 years of history does not show that Afghanistan was ruled by an Islamic government, and why now? A bunch of regressive crudest religious and other Afghanistani mercenaries and international spies destroyed our country for the interests of the foreigners.

In Peshawer Pakistan, I saw Afghan kids fighting over the intestines and feathery skin of the chickens. Seeing this made me very sad and it was the equivalent of pouring salt on an open wound.

You hairy fallible Afghans creatures are neither freedom fighters nor defenders of the motherland but mercenaries and servants of foreigners especially of Saudi Arabia.

I wish you realized who the winner really was.

Through the incentive of foreign propaganda machines, bribery and the instruction of Pakistanies, ISI G. Wardak used to blow up the Surubi electric towers. Now he says the Duran Sir Mortimer's line 1893 is illigitimate.

Brave Generlas who used to serve and still serving for the interest of international intelligent agencies, can tell us that in the past of one hundred years did we have any governing post or any police head quarter beyond our border on those claiming areas called Azad Pashtonistan in inside Pakistan's territory ? Only in 18th century, the elder brother of Amir Dost Muhamad, Nawab Abdul Samad Khan, once he was the governor of Banu and Kohat.

Quote: The Russian foot was therefore already well in the door when in 1955, a further crisis occurred in Afghan-Pakistan relations.In March of the year, for credible internal reason, Pakistan amalgamated the provinces of west Pakistan into "One Unit." The idea was to strengthen national cohesion by giving the West and East wings of the country equality of representation in the National Assembly.

Afghan eyes, however, were on the consequent demise of the North West Frontier Province. Even though the tribal Areas were not involved in the amalgamation, they chose to see it as a deliberate move to prevent the emergence of ' Pashtonistan'.

Rioting broke out in Kabul, Jalalabad and Kandahar.In Kabul the flag was burnt at the Pakistan Embassy, and in the two other cities the Pakistani consulates were sacked. The Afghan consulate in Peshawar was then attacked in retaliation, diplomatic relations were broken, the border was closed and the countries prepared for war.

In the year of 1955, I used to work at Morrison-Knudsen company in Kandahar in the field of soil sampling, my boss was Mr. Mc Bee; that year Prime minister Mohamad Daoud summond the reservists to go to war with Pakistan. This tense situation concerning security, made the Americans very agitative, and Dr. Shold Buck? A chemist got angry and said that "what is Pashtonistan, Pashtonistan, and Pashtonistan? He added that hafe of Kandahar, hafe of Jalalabad, and hafe of Paktia is Pashtonistan".

According to the philosophy of Mr. Shold Buck, if the adherents want to form a hafe Pashtonistan please do it if you could, and live us alone.

In reality the issue of Pashtonistan is neither a national, nor international and even a tribal issue but some sort of jealousness, and complexities, of a few adventurous, narrowminded minority, and imposter people.

Now I think such a wrong Pashtonism movement policy without strategy and planning was not merely a political disaster but also direct interfering in internal affairs of another independent country. In the past century, the rest of our people were tortured because of the Pashton's transcendency.

Professor Rabany, another prelate, runagate General said that the movement of Ikhvanulmuslimin (Islamic Brotherhood) is not a slogan but strategy. While in Badakhshan, his native place, fifty percent of women die during childbirth.

Mr. Rabani! The movement of Islamic brotherhood is not strategy but rather a slogan (like Allah-Akbar).

Strategy is the science or art of military command as applied to the overall planning and conduct of large-scale combat operations. In other words, it is a plan of action resulting from the practice of strategy.

The Islamic brotherhood movement is neither food nor medicine or a safe road to reach a safe and sound home. Look at the Badakhshan roads and see how dangerous and risky they are.

Mr. Rabani, you and your colleagues are talking from the state of necromancy but not from the age of reason and sciences which is why you are acting indifferent. Neither of us knows which one came first, the egg or the chicken, but we know about the priority of nature and scripture.

Religion is not a physical necessity of human beings as we can live without religion but we cannot live without food.

"Fundementalists never say that they are wrong, because they admit that god is wrong". (Jimmy Carter, former President of the United States)

It is said that there in Moscow, a motion picture based on mujahideen crimes all over the world (especially in Afghanistan) was on display. The Russian government asked every country to send their own representative to observe the show.

As the show started, people suddenly fled the hall except for one person, a mujahid from Afghanistan, the people were amazed and got eye to eye and said to each other that he was such a brave person? The only one who could enjoy the show to the end. But later on, they found out that he had fainted.

He was not merely scared of the show, but he was ashamed of what he did to his own people. He covered his face with his hands while he was crying and he looked at the congregation and said: "I'm sorry! I did not do it, foreigners did it."

To Afghanistan Peace Council!

به انجمن اشتی گرای عففانستان

بنا به نیاز منطق پیچیـدن و درگیـر شدن پیـرامـون پدیـدۀ بسیار ابرو ریز که مزۀ تلـخ انـرا همه مـردم بی سپـر ما با گـوشت ، پـوست ، و استخـوان خـویش چشیـده اند راه انـدازی نه تنها خـانـانه بلکه بسیار کـودکانه است که هرگز ثمـر شیـرین نخـواهد داشت.

افـزار بیـرونی (طالب) الـوده با فـرهنک تازی که این اسم زیبا شایستۀ انها نیست یکجـا با مسلمـانان خبیث و کشـورهایی دشمن به میهنمـان یـورش اوردند وطن ارام مـا را نا ارام ، شهر هایی اباد را ویران ، زن ، و مـرد مـا را تـازیـانه زدند ، دست و پا بریـدند ، بـرخی را سر از تن جدا نمودند ، راه اشتی را با انها پیش گرفتن خیانت بمادر میهن است.

قمـاش مردم عـربزده بروی خشـم انین وارداتی مادری را هر دو چشمش را کـور هـردو پایش را قطع و هـر دو دستش را از شـانها جـدا کردند بـودهایی نـازنین بامیـان که انها ابـروی هنر اسیا و خـراسان زمین بودند گـرد گـرد کـردند بگفت و شنید پرداختن با چنان مردم که تنها به سیمـا اورگانیکی اند ولی در زات سخت تر از سنـگ خارا هستنـد دلالی گـرافیک است.

چقـدر درد اور است ؟ دولتی که بـرای ارامش و تجویز بیگـزند سازی ان اضـافه از چهل کشور جهان و ده ها هـزار سپـاهی با توپ ، تفنگ ، تکالوجی پیشرفتۀ یک ابر نیرو که شب و روز در خدمت اقـای حـامد کرزی هستند گروپ بیخـرد و عربزده را بزد چند کس دزدان و ادمکشان میفرستد تا انها را به سرنـوشت ما که ایشان پیشتر امتحان خـویش را بـرای مردم ما و جهان داده اند باز دیگر حاکم سازد.

اقای کـرزی این ته و بالا دویدننهایی شما بگفتۀ مولانا " گندم کشت کردن در چاه است " با بزبان دیگر باد کردن کاه بیدانه ، خنده اور است اسم مـردم بی معرفت و پلید از مغـز کـج این قلندر قنـداری زدوده نمیشود؟ پالیسی نا رو حامد کرزی دشمنی روشن با مـردم متـازی از طالبان ، گـام کـج بسـوی نیپوتیزم است که ان با هیـچ یک کته گـوریهایی در دسپلین پزیـرفته سـر نمیخـورد.

انهایکه به سیمـا ادمند ولی هنـوز انسـان نشده اند یا بـزبان دیگر پوست پوست مغـزشـان لک است که اتـومهـایی روان در ان رخـنه کـرده نمیتـوانند انها گـوش خـــر هستنـد چنـانکه مولانای بزرگ میگویند:

گوش خر بهتر بود از گوش کر   گوش کر بفروش گوش خر بخر

هـر انـدازه که ما بالای تن مـرده خـاک بیاندازیم بـویی ازاری ان فـروکش میکند همچنان در بخش دیگران هـر انـدازه که از راه رسانه هایی سخن پراگنی کمتـر از اینمـرده خـواران نام ببریم و خشمگین شویم به باور نیـرومند از ارزش ایشان هـر روز سایده میشود .

همچنان در مکاتب اگر جنبشی بسود نگرش بلند ، علیه بنیـادگـرایی و طالبان که ان انگیـزۀ بیـرونی دارد براه بیافتد روان و تن بنیادگـرایی هنـوز بسیـارتر سـایده میشود.

های هموطن! سـد سال زندگی در بند استعمار برابر است به یک دقیقه زندگی با طالب که تن و روحت در تصرف انهاست برتری دارد بپا خیزید بپا خیزید ، حـامد کرزی ایـل پـرست را که او مکتبی را نخـوانده است از کشور بیرونش کنید.

اقای کرزی اردو را هوشدار دادند که افسـران در سیاست خـود را اغشته نسـازند که چنـا ن راه انـدازی بی پایه و دیکتـاتـورانه مـرا بسیار خندانـد ، این اقا تا حـال نمیـداند که سیاست یک پدیدۀ طبیعی است و ان صـرف نه در میـان انسـانها بلکه حیـوانات هم تمـرین میشود .

بـرای نمونه اگر نرگاو نیـرومند ، اسپ با ماهیـچه ، قـوچ با بازو درون گله شـود دیگـر حیوانات ناتـوان از انها رم میخـورند یا اینست که او بـفـرار میگزارند شیر ، پلنگ ، پشک ، شغال ، روبا و دیگر جوجـه های خـویش را با دندانها گـزیده انها را بجاهایی بیگـزند تر کوچ میدهند که انهم گـونه سیـاست است ، من به اینـاورم افسـران که انها پاسبـانان اصلی در اوردن ارامش و نگهبان خـامه رو کشـور هستند از دیگران کـرده بـاید زیـاد تر سیاست بفهمند حتا که انـرا همیش به تمـرین هم بگیرند.

اقای کرزی!

بـزرگـان گفته اند که خرکاری هم دریای علم است ایا شما میدانید چرکگیر ، ذمجی ، ارغمجی ، چلبر ، لجام ، و کلگی چیست؟ اینها چیزهایی نامبرده همه پـاره هایی سیاسی هستند که چسان میتوان یک حیـوان را ارام و از ان بهـره بـرد؟.

The German novelist, Thomas Mann once penned the line, "There is nothing that is not political. (Thomas Mann, The Magic Mounain,1942.)

وی میگوید " انجا هیچ چیزی نیست که ان سیاسی نباشد."

شما با این سازگار نخواهید بود، بگزارید یک کمی روشنی بالای ان بیاندازم. فکر کنید که سیاست دارای استراتیژیست که انرا برای انجام هدفی بکار میبریم. بهر رنگی که شما بمرام خود برسید، هر گاهیکه یکی دوستتان عضو خانواده بخواهد چیزی را انجام بدهد، ان میتواند سیاسی باشد. اگر ما این تعریف را بکار میگیریم سیاست بخش بزرگ هر کدام ما و شما را میسازد.

در حقیقت، هر کدام ما در طبیعت موجود سیاسی هستیم. اگر اکادمیک سخن بزیم ، سیاست هنر و دانش است که حکومت را میچرخاند. اغلب ما ، چه اگر ، ماییلیم سیاست فرصت طلبی ، تدبیر انجام دادن کاری ، یا کجروشی است.
گفتار آقای کرزی مرا بیاد عبارت دینیات مکتب ابتدایی هفتاد سال پیش میاندازد که میگفت " بحث و تتبع در حد زات بار تعالی خاج از حدود شرع مجاز نیست ." وما که به مفهوم ان زبان در انوقت پی نمیبردیم ، انزبان پوچ هم گونه ی سیاست مذهبی است.

تماس مان هنر و دانش سیاست را چقدر زیبا شناسایی کرده است " بهر روشیکه شما بهدف خود برسید "
دانشمند علم سیاست Harold Lasswell میگوید سیاست انست که کی چه میستاند ،
چه وقت ، و چتور. هر گاهیکه یک پوزیشن شرطی " چتور" باشد ان شما را یاری میدهد تا چیزی را بدست بیاورید ، با تعریف لاسویل ان سیاست شمرده میشود (چیزی قابل بحث که اغلب بتور عموم یک مطلب پزیرفته شده در دسپلین میباشد).

سیاستهای اریستائل یونانی یک کار فلسفه سیاسی است. اعلامیه که رسیدگی در اخلاقیات ضرور سیاستها را دنبال میکند، و هردو کارها به نظر میرسند که بخشهایی بزرگ رساله ها ، یا شاید لیکچرهایی ارتباطی باشند، که با فلسفه انسان معامله میکنند.

اصطلاح سیاست نباید مقید ، شرطی ، و محدود بشمار فعالیتها گردد ، بلکه بعادات کلاس بشری که مطلب مشترک دارند .
کسی میگوید:
دانشجویی در دانشکدۀ بالای تنگ نظری بنام گزینشهای سیاست مشروع Legitimate political options. (برای مثال سوسیالیزم علمی که درون اجندا نیست خشمگین بود.)
من از درک و درد این دانشجوی با احساس سخت پشتیبای میکنم و از دیگران میخواهم در همچو گردهمایهایی بویژه علمی (ساینس) اگر موضوع مورد علاقۀ دیگران بموجب تنگ نظری یا ملاحظات دیگر از مطالب اجندا انداخته شده باشد اشتراک نکنند یا بضد ان احتجاج نمایند.

بود هنگامیکه دسپلین راجع بقانون و حکومت بود. پسان پژوهش جنبش اجتماعی شامل ان میشود .
باز وقت امد که ان مطالعه ی موثریت پالیسی را در بر داشت. و راجع به رای دادن. و راجع به فیصله کردن و گزینش معقول. اکنون علم روانی اجتماعی عملکرد من و تو یا (عمل متقابل) را در ان اغشته کردند. این چیزهایی که ما انرا سیاست مینامیم .
David Easton میگوید سیاستها "بخش ارزشهای امرانه برای دسپلین است. "

Gallants (cowards and ignoble mujahideen) who are proud that with the support of American bazzoka, Saudi Arabian money and under the supervision and guideline of Pakistani ISI, defeated the democratic government of Afghanistan which resulted in the complete destruction of the infrastructures of the country.

Therefore, for the triumphs of the foreighners interests, brave mujahideen indiffferently celebrate their failures every year. We are further witnessed the day of the 16[th years] of celebration (the exhibitionism generals) by a small incident fled the stage, except mullah Rabani and his clown friend Subghatullah Mujadidi.

A story about the bravery of a military General.

A king invited another king to visite his country and he assigned a very beautiful girl in his services. When the king returned back home, he suddenly declared war against the hosted king. He, the king, asked the fighting General: "what is this all about?" The General politely responded that: "the king wants that girl".

The king asked the General: "why he did not say anything about it when he was here?"

The king hands over the girl.

On their way back, the General camped and lodged in tents in an open area. The general kept the girl in his own tent. After a few minutes, a voice was heard which said: "the lion is coming the lion is coming". After hearing this, the general jumped out of the tent naked with a sword. Running after the animal, he killed the lion and came back but his thing is still up.

The other night, when the girl was in bed with the king, the king heard something strange and his thing promptly shrank. This scene made the girl laugh loudly and the king got very nervous and asked her to tell the truth. When the king got the message, he said to himself really he was a brave general and married her to him.

Hi, my country intellectual men and women! For god sake, get up and fight the backwarded fundamentalists and Islamic brotherhood movement in the country. Otherwise, due to the pleasantness of the environment, they get stronger day by day and it helps to bring back the Taliban (bubonic plague) which is an Al Qaeda movement.

Recently, mullah Rabani said: "The movement of the Islamic brotherhood is not a slogan, rather than strategy" and this is a good example of the bad and subversive political organized religion in a society.

Please, please get away from religious people and do not pay attention to their fake stories. Please listen to the remarkable voice of reason before you hit your head against the sharp object. In the course of history, human miseries have been mostly evolved from the philosophy of religious divisionism.

Thanks to the brave scientists and because of their tireless efforts, we live in a different world today. The internet, for example, revolutionized the world as well as its thoughts. The internet promoted freedom all over the world. In less than a minute, we can see the Madonna show in America, Ali Lizee in Paris and Sima Bina (the jewel of Khurasan) in Australia.

My special thanks go to the wonderful surge of Italian Renaissance 1860, of which revolutionized every aspect of our life.

If the responsive out-standing thinkers and brave scientists are afraid to tell the truths, do we have access to free speech, or free thought and free inquiry to-day?

> *Is it a small thing to quench the flames of hell with the holy tears of pity - to unbind the martyr from the stake – break all chains – put out the fires of civil war – stay the sword of the fanatic, and tear the bloody hands of the Church from the white throat of Science?*
>
> *Is it a small thing to make men truly free – to destroy the dogmas of ignorance, prejudice and power – the poisoned fables of superstition, and drive from the beautiful face of the earth the fiend of fear?*
> *Robert Green Ingersoll."Thomas Paine" (1870)*

When I was at school, in the first or second grade, the arithmetic teacher made us memorize the multiplication tables. Now, I know that those tables belong to the 14th Century Abbaco schools in Italia which Machiavelli graduated from.

In Conclusion:

This book (<u>Secularism In Afghanistan</u>), which I now offer to readers, is a translation from Farsi into English. Respected reader, pardon me if you cannot read the Farsi portions of the book because the translation of poetry is a hard task.

The contents of this book, which is based on facts and fictions, are excerpted from credible documentation sources. The main idea of this book is to change the religious behavior of Afghan people toward a better understanding and a better life because the imported Islam religion is a big obstacle to the system of modernity and openness in the Islamic world. In order to get rid of such stupidity and superstitions, we have got to fight irrationalism with rationalism and reason.

Religion, from its birth, is a totalitarian movement and can be seen when one looks at the Islamic regimes in Iran, Saudi Arabia, and Afghanistan. For the smallest infringement of a footling object, regardless of the human rights principles and values, a Mullah (on the basis of discarded thoughts and small tongue) puts you to death. Secularism, however, is a lack of such authorities and egoism. With regard to this religion as a sin must be condemned.

A scholar said: "The political conflicts and wars remained essentially the same during this period and later but the religious conflict was deeply modified." Therefore, I'm optimistic this change will occur in Afghan society if the new Afghan generation enmesh themselves with the realities.

Secularism, as a quality condition to the governing system of a country, is a vital issue and it should be taught in every school, especially in Afghanistan. This is the right of every political party and individual to motivate the people to bring change to the state constitution.

Secularism does not disband or abstain the religious movement but limits the power of religion in the political arena.

If religion, because of some considerations, moves toward fanaticism (as it is today) then clearly people turn to secularism or to a peaceful religion like Rumiesm, Buddhism and or Zoroastrianism.

Religion is the enemy of science and technology, but secularisn is not; religion is against the freedom of thoughts but secularism is not; religion forbids teaching Darwinism but secularism does not; religion condemns wearing condoms but secularism does not;

religion denies the polio vaccination but secularism does not.

secularism is not an obstacle to the religious movement but religion opposes the secularism movement; secularism does not impose circumcision but religion does;

religion divides the societies but secularism unites the people.

Quote: "Religion prosecuted and condemned the first atheist Anaxagoras (fl. 480-450 BC) in history for his free thought".

For their abhorrent religious exaltations maledicted Taliban, illegitimate violated and abusieve kids, and cut-off the heads of the innocent people with dulled knives from behind and front, despite such heinous crimes the Taliban and their adherents are still enjoying freedom under the institutions of Sheik- cracy of Mullah Karzai.

Nothing is greater than to break the chains from the bodies of men-nothing nobler than to destroy the phantom of the soul.Robert Green (1833-1899) the Magnificient.

Countinuous stories of superstitions as a domain form the source of lies, fear and punishment after death never go away unless to find a way out of this miseries.

Did we forget the tyrannies of religions in the past by Arab imperialism, the Turks, recently the mujahidin (the Reagan freedom fighters) and the

Taliban (the invention of C.I.A). who gave birth to Alqaeda and other Islamic terrorist factions?

Therefore, I'm asking all Islamic reverent broadminded leaders not by the name of religions but secularism to come together and form a secular united front. Creation of such a comprehensive association mentally and physically makes you very strong. In these circumstances, you not merely repress the fundamentalist movement but repeal the imperialism unfounded pretensions and also pave the way for more noxious imams to come to U.S.

Afghanistan, Iraq, and Iran were secular states but all of them have been replaced by Islamic regimes because of taking vengeance and retaliation.

The secular system was confirmed by many Islamic thinkers like Muhamed bin Zikria Razi, Mansour Abolghasem Ferdowsi, Jalaluddin muhamed Rumi, Omar Khiam, Haafiz Sherazi, Nasir Khisraou and others almost one thousand years ago.

Secularism is the belief and a patriotic feeling to fight superstitions and diffusion of values, strengthening solidarities and friendships among the different groups. Secularism is not against any religion or any creeds.

As much as secularism gets strength the more religion becoming sentimental and modernized, secularism is a model differs from other political systems and differenciates between good and evil, old and new.

Therefore, Islamic countries have no other choice except to resort to the age of reason. The more toward openness and freedom, the more prosperous the society would become.

To have good radio talk shows, good television shows, sagacious Imams in the Mosques and other reasonable speakers in our educational institutions are very important to shed more light on our dissonant documents (which induce regression and ignorance).

Today, religion as a low commodity in the market is loosing its grip on society and this compels us into the direction of prosperity and glorifying environment.

Quote

Thursday, August 6, 2009

America is becoming more secular slowly. In a survey released by Trinity College of Hartford, the ARIS 2008 the headline in part is "Non religious on the Rise". Finally!

The Bright Liberta Posted by Allen Smal.

History teaches us that both Islam and Christianity, in the process of history, tried to kill and colonialize countries through religious expansionism plots. I think this is the time to say goodbye to both of them and refer to Mawlana Rumi's belief (secularism).

Mawlana Jalaluddin Mohammad Rumi, the great philosopher who is the founder of secularism in Islam.

To my kids and to my friends! Do not pay the exorbitant tithes or taxes to the Mullahs and do not let them to read Arabic tawdry words on my dead body or on my enlightening grave because their gruffly, voices hurts me the most. Please do not lament after me, but laugh, dance, and be happy, remember I was a gift of the nature and go back to my origin.

I was born in a country in which Islam's pilloried ideology was imposed on her, destroyed our culture and our way of life. I'm sorry if I'm offending anyone about the piffling theology, but it is my right to say no to religion. I'm proud to die secular because the Great philosopher Mawlana Rumi, told me to do so.

I wrote this book in secrecy because my kids and my friends, on the basis of religious indoctrinations, are cursed and thought that some abominable thing would have happened to me (even the enlightened woman who translated this book from Farsi to English was afraid to have her name in the book). I appreciated their concerns and told them that my head is on my own body and it is the obligation of every righteous and erudite person to tell the truth as Christopher Hitchens writes: "God did not make us, we made God." Religion, he explains, is a distortion of our origin, our nature and the Cosmos. We damage our children and endanger our world by indoctrinating them.

Before the collapsed of the Soviet Union, communism was the enemy of Islam and capitalism, now, however, it is Secularism and Atheism. Fundamentalist, Tayyib Erdogan the prime minister of Turkey, says: "you can only be a Muslim or a secular, A human can't be a secular and a Muslim at the same time and he added that secularism is a big lie and a secular people can not be Muslim."

Another lunatic from the same color Injem Choudary a Musilm with Hindu face warns America and says "Islam is coming to your back yard." I'm not sure what academic of thought did they finish?

In Deepa Kumar: During the era of the Cold War, the United States viewed radical nationalism and communism as dire threats to its influence. After an initial period when Washington tried to win Nasser, and the Iranian secular nationalist Mohammed Mossadegh, to its side and failed, it developed an "Islamic strategy" whereby Islamist groups, helped by Saudi Arabia, would be cultivated as bulwarks against radical nationalism and communism. During the 1950s, the United States would use the Muslim Brotherhood in Egypt against Nasser, and group of clergy in Iran against Mossadegh.

Let us ask who strengthened Islam and the Islamic brotherhood. Several assassination attempts on Nasser attributed to national secularism and the leftists.

If there is freedom of religion in one billion spoiled Islam, for sure would be left there only a thousand of Muslims including Mr.Choudary and Prime Minister Tyyib Erdogan.

It was America because of its national interests made Islam very deceitful and arrogant.

Islam is alive because of Christianity and without the presence of Christianity, Islam will disappears among one day I am the witness of the moribund Islam in Afghanistan in 1960. But Saudi Arabia together with America and others to suppres of the democracy movement in Afghanistan revived the dead Islam globally.

Deepa Kumar says: In a previous on Islamophobia, we challenge this "clash of civilization" thesis ("Islam and Islamophobia," ISR 52, March-April 2007). This article set out to look historically at the phenomenon called political Islam and to explain the conditions under which it comes into being. It will begin by the bunking the notion that the rise of Islamist organizations is the natural outgrowth of Islam, and instead point the historical de facto separation between religion and politics in Muslim majority societies.

Additionally, it will show that for at least the last two centuries and up until the last few decades twentieth century, the dominant trend in the "Muslim world" was toward secularization. The turn toward Islamism in last three decades of the twentieth century was the product of particular economic and political conditions. Moreover, these conditions are not dissimilar to the ones that enabled the rise of other fundamentalism in India and the New Right in the United State.

The essay then outlines the particular historic conditions that have enabled the rise of political Islam. These include the active role played by the U.S. in posing Islam and political Islam as an alternative to secular nationalism and the left; persistent imperial intervention and domination; internal weakness that led to the decline of secular nationalist and various left parties, creating an ideological vacuum that Islamists were able to occupy, economic crises and its exacerbation under the neoliberal era,which present an economic opening for Islamists and their charitable networks.

ISR "International Socialist Review" Issue 76, march –April 2011 (Political Islam: a Marxist analysis)

Now you tell me who radicalized Islam and why? Prior to 9\11, Choudary was an opened minded person but now he is a charlatan because the western power provided a pleasant environment for the fundamentalists to grow and fight communism.

A quarter of a century of imposed religious war and deprivation of socialization in the family turned the Afghan children to primitive and isolated people. A rigid religious environment brought them up to be ignorant, harsh and very heartless human beings. Hamid Karzai is one of them and his religious police arrested girls for "moral crimes" and subjected them to intrusive "virginity tests". They also killed Hanifa Safi, head of women's affairs in Laghman province, a woman "known locally for going out without her head being covered." (The Huffington Post September 17,2012)

The brutalities of the the mujahidin and the vicious actions of the Taliban, the fruit of the conspiracies of international coalition under the banner of Islam, is great or Islam is in danger. My country, Afghanistan, was physically and mentally destroyed.

I respectfully disagree with the philosophy of reverent Marvin E. Gettleman who in his book "The Middle East and Islamic World Reader" notifies of Islam's golden age regardless of the shameful history of Islam the killer.

Around 750 AD, the Bukhara in central Asia was invaded four times by an Arab commander, Qutaiba Ben-e- Muslim, to impose the Arab's provincial religion "Islam" on the people. Any time he conquered a city and left, the people reverted back to their own tradition of Zoroastrianism.

So the Qutaiba does not know what to do? Finally he reached to a decision that every household has to share their home with young Arabs to dwell in alongside with the families and oversight the people until they become accustomed to the Arab's religion, otherwise the transgressor she or he on the basis of the witness testimony would be persecuted. (1400 years after, Shujaudin Shafa page 407.)

C. Wright Mills. A sociologist in Sociological Footprints in his essay "The Promise," writes: "we do not know the limits of man's capacities for supreme effort or willing degradation, for agony or glee, for pleasurable brutality or the sweetness of reason. But in our time we have come to know the limit of human nature are frighteningly broad".

Mr. Mills is right because we saw the power of the social media in staging issues like religion in 1980 in Afghanistan. In this way, the media could have sabotaged the trust and the cohesiveness of the people with the democratic government. In the end, people because of parochial Islam religion, butchered one another. Fathers gunned down their sons or pushed them down from the top of the mountain.

Religious supremacy on the basis of authority of higher beings in Afghanistan our young generation for almost thirty years have been deprived from the taste and the beauty of life. As Karl Marx says: "life is not determined by consciousness but consciousness by life."

The Quran says debating about Allah is forbidden because you do not have such knowledge to reach to the bottom of the reality. Since debating and criticizing for solving a contentious and obscured issue, logic is the pivotal principle of the subjects.

Philosopher Durkheim says: "religion is a system of ideas, corresponding to some determined object. This object has been conceived in a multitude of ways: nature, the infinite, the unknowable, the ideal, etc, but these differences matter but little".

Quran is a plagiarized book, look at the word of kanoon, means law in Arabic but its Greek word 'kavwv.'

We know religion is for one person but secularism is for all, religion cannot preserve equal rights but secularism does.

On October 9\ 2012 – 14 year old Pakistani activist Malalai Yusufzai a brave human being shot at the head and at the nick by Taliban because she was preaching secularism.

Secularism is a political system of government and unbiased from religious influence. Secularism removes the barriers of classes and fights illiteracy, ignorant, starvation, diseases, superstitions, and others.

Some body says secularism is religion respectfully I reject that idea, if it is so why we are insisting on separation of church and state. We cannot bring people together under the banner of religions but we can make secularism internationally.

Religion commits burning, stoning, cutting the throat and dismembering the body but secularism condemns these heinous crimes. Today we suffer too much of fanaticism "bogeyman."

Quote in Emille, for example, he issues the reproach that, fanaticism dare to counterfeit it and to dictate crime in its name.'2

In the draft of the one social contract, the so called Geneva Manuscript, he refers to "the furies of fanaticism," which, if unrestrained by philosophy and laws," would cover the earth with blood and destroy the human race.3

Rousseau starts by reiterating his view that religion is necessary to maintain citizens' obedience to the state.15 He explains this necessity in terms of demand states make on citizens to face death. Without a belief in after life, no one could rationally face death. Thus, in a state without religion rational citizens would shirk their duty like cowards, leaving only lunatics to fight the state's wars.

In Rousseau national religion is good, he argues, in part because under it "to die for one's country is to be martyred."18 National religion can thus serve the function he projected in the first paragraph, i.e. to deploy the psychic energies of fanaticism in the service of the state, transforming religious into civic fanaticism. The association is made even clearer when, in the sixth paragraph of the draft, Rousseau turns to what is bad about national religion. It is bad not simply because, from the standpoint of the "true theism" embodied in the Gospel, 19 it is "based on error and falsehood," 20 The telling danger is that, ' when becoming exclusive and tyrannical it makes a people bloodthirsty and intolerant to the point where it lives only for murder and massacre, and believes it performs a holy act by killing whoever does not accept its gods and its laws."21 National religion is bad, that is, because it inevitably makes its citizens fanatical.22

Rousseau on Fanaticism, Patriotism, and the Dynamics of Pity (Zev Trachtenberg Department of philosophy University of Oklahoma)

Yes. Fanaticism is ugly. A while ago, Mohammedan's fanatics, because of the "Film of Innocence Muslims" and the burning of the Quran, went crazy and many delusional people have been killed. As a result, they left behind their wives to become widows and their lovely kids on the street to beg.

In 1220, Genghiz Khan destroyed the cities of Bukhara and Samarkand (Uzbekistan). He made from the cases "Sanadiq" of Qurans feedbags for their horses. From the Qurans, he made socks for his own horse because it was winter time. But no body went on strike and terror. Why?

To me, this film of Innocence of Muslims displays a love story. What is wrong with that? If the brave Muslim's fanatics are ashamed of this aesthetic, please efface this excellence craftsmanship and romantic legend from the beauty of the book.

يآيهاالنبىُ لِمَ تُحَرِمُ مآ احَلَ اللهُ لكَ تبَتغى مَرَضاتَ ازوَاجِكَ واللهُ غُفورُ، رحيم (1-66)

O Prophet,why dost thou forbid (thyself) that which Allah has made lawful (Halal) for thee ?Seekest thou to please thy wives? And Allah is forgiving,Merciful.

I'm sorry because you the lovers got no sensing and -not feeling to tell what is taste and what is the beauty, love and hatred, pleasure and pain. Why are you weeping, crying, and killing yourselves and others for the diversion and worldly enjoyment of your only lovely Prophet who loves the love? Such a beautiful romantic historical love in a polygamy environment in a primitive society is very unique.

This Verse is said to contain a reference to the Prophet,s conjugal relations with the Mary, the Coptic lady, which, it is alleged, being discovered by his wife Hafasah, the Prophet swore not to have anything more to do with her.

In the interpretation of Hussaini Shah Wali-Ullah Dayhlawi says: O Prophet, because appeasement of your wives why are you prohibiting the thing which Allah made Halal lawful) for you? But regardless, assuring of his Allah how is it possible the Prophet, swears to his wife Hafasah not to have any thing more to do with Mary?

Why should I be apologetic to the stoned culture wherein ironic nail does not get through it? This policy under any situation exhibits the weakness understanding of a person who renounces the historical event and prefers ignorance over intellect.

To me, nothing is holy except for my mother, my teacher, and my ass. She took me to school for six years and brought me back home sound and safe.

Let us make Muslim people a little bit happier and stronger to tell them that your God, has not only 99 names but one hundred names.

Quran 2. 286, Allah is called "Mowlana" it says:

انت مولانا فالنصرنا على القوم الكفرين .286 -2

You are our God (Allah) then succeed us over the infidels.

Also in Quran in chapter 55, I found two Verses 19 and 20 that talk about the barrier of the Suez canal.

مرج البحرين يلتقين (19)

19. He has made the two seas (the Mediterranean and the Red sea) to flow freely –they meet:

بينهما برزخ لايبغين(20)

20. Between them is a barrier which they cannot pass.

The Suez Canal, connecting the Mediterranean and the Red sea. The construction on the Suez Canal began in April 1859 and was completed on November 17, 1869. The barrier between the two seas which is mentioned in the Quran was removed. If he (Allah) was able to make the two huge seas, why was he unable to remove the small barrier between the two seas?

*Also in 25-53 Koran says: And he it is who has made the seas **to flow** freely the one **sweet, very sweet, and the other saltish, bitter.** And the two (oceans) he has made a barrier and inviolable obstruction? Here Allah mentions two oceans but he forgets to tell between rivers and oceans. Furthermore, he puts barriers among rivers and oceans not to merge with each other because the drinking water becomes tasteless and bitter.*

*Naturally, all the rivers empty into the oceans but not the oceans in to the rivers and no body has the power or the knowledge to avert the flow of the rivers.The writer did not know that the oceans are naturally confined by the barriers and they **cannot flow.***

In Koran, clearly has been mentioned the name of the Euphrates river which flows into the Persian Gulf, one is salty and the other one is sweet. But the translater to unthought the muslims and abstract the non muslims, counterfeited to mention the name of the Euphrates river in English transcription?

Euphrates or Farat in Persian (2,800km) originates in Turkey, from a spring in the Taurus mountains entering Syria then Iraq and then empties into the Persian Gulf.

Religion does not merely confuse me but Allah too in the above stories once he complains from the barriers and in other place he himself creates the barriers?

*Also, in 25-52, Allah says: So obey not the **disbelievers**, and strive against them a mighty striving with it. In such a circumstance, perspicaciously whom do you blame? The soldier or the commander? Sure common sesnse tells us that the one who disrespects and hates the people, disobeys ethics moralities, law and orders and divides the human kind?*

The English translaters of kuran because of fear or shame refrained to use the word of infidels but disbelievers. Such tawdry tautology utterly not perverting the society, but it is a big contempt to the humanities.

Look at the verses below, Allah created man from different objects:

1 – خلق الانسان:

In chapter 55, in Quran Verse 3, it is written:
1-He (Allah) created man, why not human beings or human kind, or Islam to be differentiated by religions?

2- خلق الانسان من علق :

2-In Quran ch 96 verse 2, Allah says he creates man from a clot?

Based on the above manifestation, isn't the red skinned race the product of divine enveloping biotechnic?

3- خُلِقَ من مأم دافق

3-In Quran ch 86 verse 6, it says he is created of water pouring forth

4- خَلقَ الانسان من صلصال كالفخار:

4-In ch 55 verse 14, Allah says he created man from dry clay like earthen vessels

In chapter 53 Verse 43, it is written: And that he it is who makes (men) laugh and makes them to cry so why you (muslims) killing the artists?

In 1972, German archaeologists discovered the dotless quran from the Sana Mosque in northern Yemen. Because of it's sensitivity or other factors, it has been kept in secrecy for sixty years. This new quran says those who sacrifice themselves in the way of Allah will go to heaven and will be offered white grapes. In Othman's quran, however, the white grapes have been replaced by Hur (روح), which means virgin girls. This is a big blow to the Islamic world about the authenticity of today's quran . I think this is the time for gallant sagacious Islamic schoalrs from all over the world to face the reality of this very important historical discovery regardless of what the consequences would be as it is said that this quran is the first and the oldest quran (it was written seventy years after the death of Muhammad).

Islam a branch of theology of the Middle East methodology founded by pillaging, spoiling and killing. Now, Islamic fanaticism is spreading through the use of oil wealth all over the world, especially in Pakistan against Shiaiesm of Iranian revolution. This is a very dangerous development against world peace.

Speaking of conscience in Emile, for example, he issues the reproach that "Fanaticism dares to counterfeit it and to dictate crime in its name."2 In the draft of On the Social Contract, the so called Geneva Manuscript, he refers to "the furies of fanaticism" which, if unrestrained by "Philosophy and Laws" would cover the earth with blood and destroy the human race.

Listen to this fiery love poems, an anthology have ever written about love story in Kabuly language by "Bahaar Saeed" a highly educated and opened minded lady.

And Iranian lady, Forugh Farrokhzad in 2oth century.

Waw their convention and their exceptional audacity as a sharp sword being put to the nick of the thick skinned fanatic.

> Pour my perfumed fresh hair around my shoulders.
>
> let my two hands encircle your neck up to my arms.
>
> Squeeze my hot perfumed body against your chest tightly.
>
> for the sake of my poems I.m naked in your embrace to night.
> Come go to bed with me to neght.
>
> "Bahaar Saeed"

بروی شانه هایت ریز عطر ، تازه ی مویم
بدور گردنت پیچد ، دو دستم تا به بازویم
به تنگ سینه ات بفشار جسم داغ و خوشبویم
به شعرم بهر اغوشت خودم عریانترم امشب
بیا در بسترم امشب
" بهار سعید"

I whispered in his ear these words
of love
"I want you, mate of my soul
I want you, life giving embrace
I want you, lover gone mad"
"Forugh Farrokhzad"

فرو خواندم به گوشش قصهٔ عشق
ترا میخواهم ای جانانهٔ من
ترا میخواهم ای اغوش جانبخش
ترا ای عاشق دیوانهٔ من
فروغ فرخزاد

I am naked, naked, naked
Naked as the hushed stillness
Between words of love and
My scars are all from loving
From loving, loving, loving.
I have steered this island of
Agony over the ocean,s uproar
Above volcanic violence, and
Falling apart was at the heart of
That wholesome being whose least
Atoms gave birth to the sun.
"Farrokhzad"

من عریانم ، عریانم ، عریانم
مثل سکوتهای میان کلام های محبت عریانم
و زخم های من همه از عشق است
از عشق ، عشق ، عشق.

من این جزیرهٔ سرگردان را از انقلاب اقیانوس
و انفجار کوه ها گذر داده ام ، و تکه تکه شدن
ان وجودِ متحدی بود که از حقیرترین راز
زرّه هایش افتاب به دنیا امد.

330

این چند فرد شعر روای استم شن در سطر زیبای و بلند زی
مزار فضان و عاشق و مرز راعی در د ، زم برایت که برو آرد
ست گرایان لگ پرست مانده میرود .

Bear in mind that these two talented and brave open minded ladies borned the same year 1935; removed the barriers of the traditions relevant to religion in two religious societies, Iran and Afghanistan are appreciated all the time for their courage and great services in the field of "the finer arts" of poetry, painting, music, sculpture, freedom of

thoughts, creation of beauties and happy environment.

Mr. Akhond! When you sit on a commode that is also part of art you feel very relax, but you condemn the love poetry which carries our pains away.

Dr. Ahmad karimi Hakak – in his small book "Remembering The Flight" about outstanding Iranian poet Forugh Farrkhzad writes:

However, this very openness proved more shocking given the traditional and patriarchal character of Iranian society. The response was swift and violent:

In many tabloids she was depicted as a woman of loose morals, and her poems- indeed her life was subjected to male fantasies cloaked as biography or interpretation.We can only guess at the effect of all the sensational accounts and sexual innuendoes on the young women and aspiring poet.

Reuters July 11, 2012 on web writes:

Violence against women has been steadily increasing in Afghanistan, according to the country's independent human rights commission, and *activists blame this on what they say waning interest in women's wrights of President Hamid Karzai's government.*

Mothers cradling babies and school girls in uniform shouted "death to the man who killed our sister!", days after Reuters obtained a video of 22-year-old Najiba being riddled with bullets to cheers of jubilation from a male crowd just over an hour's drive from Kabul. As it said the important measure of social justice is equality, and yet inequality in a misogynistic society not only exists but growing.

Now the time is right for Khurasani, Irani and Pakistani women to come together to form a revolutionary movement to fight to free themselves from the grip and tyranny of religious backwarded fundamentalism and push more forward to a more democratic and secular society.

It is obvious that polygamy is a very irritating practice. First of all, it not only institutionalizes inequality among the wives but jealousy too. Second, the wives are always subjected to abuses weather verbally or physically and the children start crying and running to their own mothers. This is a very tragic scene, strife, bitter conflict and squeamishness about polygamy all the time exists between the families. Sometimes it ends in death, broken noses and separations.

In Afghanistan, young King Amanullah who for the first time compiled our National constitution also abolished polygamy (may peace be upon him).

Quoted: Hume proposes that feeling, not thought, informs us that an object is beautiful or ugly, or that an action exhibits virtue or vice: "the very feeling constitutes our praise or admiration" The feeling or sentiment is itself aesthetic or moral discrimination.

Unfortunately, the Islamic religionists with their small tongues and big mouths do not feel what is art, discrimination and indiscrimination.

Look at the mentality of Hamed Karzai. Any time a suicide bomber blows himself up and kills many people, he says this is against Islam and he does not know what humanitarianism is?

Where are the thinkers and the border breakers of traditions (Rumi, Sadee, Khiam, Hafiz, Aqbal, Forugh Farrokhzad) and thousands others. Those who for their audacious talents related to human sexuality and physical intimacy as a sinners were convicted by an imitated theology called Arab's religion (Islam) to come and see that theology is dead.

Today the Darwin's powerful thought evolution revolutionised all aspects of our life, even the technology. With the push of a button, you see a lady covered up from the head to toe. With the push of another button on the shore, you see a beautiful naked lady lying on the sand.

After the collapsed of the democratic regime in Afghanistan in 1993, the Afghan fanatics saturised in superstitions destroyed the wine making factory and let the smart donkeys eat the grapes. Ha-Ha-Ha. Our grapes "Vitis Vinifera" are very similar to European grapes which are very suitable to make wine.

Around year 1969, the ministry of planning in Afghanistan made a smart economic decision to build a factory that has a production capacity of 13 thousand tons of grapes to process wine. Relevant to this economic project, a Russian delegation including specialists in wine making came to Kabul.

The ministry of agriculture and irrigation assigned me to join them to study the variety of grapes for wine processing. We started to under take this project from Logar in Charkh, Parwan, Ghazni,Dawlat Abad in Balkh and in the end to the valley of Pirooz Nakh-cheer in Samangan province. Here, the people grow only one kind of light black grape that they call Saw-ebi grape (this is almost one inch long). At the main time, we observed that not donkey but donkeys were eating grapes and we were all amazed.

Seeing this made me laugh but an Armenian lady specialist in wine making almost cried. The Russians referred to me to find out what is this all about. The poor people hopelessly responded to me that they do not have marketing and are also away from the city. This pity sound brook the heart of every one. This was a civilized time and no body rejected the establishment of the factory for the processing of wine because Islam was death in Afghanistan.

At that time, we were a free country and had a smart government with and iron fist. This government preferred reason over religion and the Saudi could not meddle in our internal affairs. I'm hoping this will happen again soon.

When mujahidin "Ronald Reagon's freedom fighters" and the Taliban (the creation of the CIA), took over, religion triumphed over reason and this avenging policy changed our civilized society to a fanatical one which Rousseau links to" deceit and cruelty."

Today in Afghanistan, according to the Arabic book, drinking alcohol in an Islamic state is Haram. In other Islamic states, however, drinking wine is Halal? In the Quran, there are three notices about the drinking of wine:

1.16- 67 in Quran says: And of the fruits of the palms and grapes, you obtain from them intoxicants and goodly provision. There is surely a sign in this for a people who ponder. Up there the interpreter used tricky word goodly provision, wherein it means that from the grape and palm you make wine it is your decent" Halal" food if you use your wisdom properly, in this scripture is not mentioned any things not to drink wine.

1. *In 4\43-O you who believe, go not near prayer when you are intoxicated till you know what you say, nor after sexual intercourse- except you are merely passing by-until you have bathed. And if are sick, or on a journey, or one of you come from the privy, or you have touched the women, and you can not find*

water, betake yourselves, to pure earth, then wipe your faces and your hands. Surely Allah is ever pardoning, forgiving.

2. *In this scripture if wine as a toxicant was forbidden so it should be avoided from Mentioning it in Quran, specially when it said "when you are intoxicated from wine.?"*

3. *In 2\219 in Quran says they ask thee about intoxicants and gambling. say In both of them is a great sin and (some) advantage for men, and their sin is greater than their advantage. And they ask thee as to what they should spend. Say what you can spare. Thus does Allah make clear to you the messages that you may ponder,*

In the last scripture says: yeas there is some risk and some benefit but never said do not drink wine. Yeas with the gambling we do not have a problem but with wine you go in to jail or go under sever punishment.

Therefore, on the basis of these three promiscuous notations I edict that selling, making and drinking wine in the Islamic nations is not prohibited. If you glance at the craftsmanship culture of poetry in Iran, central Asia, India as well as Pakistan, the main component of their poetry is wine.

Abu Abdullah Rudaki Samarkandi 874-999 is the one and also the first poet who wrote poems in the Pahlavi language and he writes about the importance of wine:

اگر مَی نیستی ، یکسر همه دلها خرابستی
اگر در کالُبد ، جان را ندیستی شرابستی

"If there is no wine there is not happiness, if you cannot see spirit in the body that is the wine."

Avicenna (Arabic Ibn Sina 980-1037 a philosopher from Balkh) says when he got tired of too much studying, he stopped and drank a glass of wine to refresh and get his strength back.

Recently in August, 2012, DR. Asghar Ali Engineer an Indian religious scholar, visited Kabul and he found out how ignorant the mullas there are. In his written note, he complained too much about the well being of the women there.

He says in Badkhshan province a woman said to me that Ulama tell us that we are naqis al aql and naqis al iman (our reason and our faith is weak and defective) and it is written so in Quranic status.

I told her no such thing is written in the Quran. On the contrary, entire discourses about women are right based in the Quran and entire discourse about men are duty based in the Quran.

One sees outside Kabul totally wrapped in burqa' from head to toe and their eyes also cannot be seen.

Iqbal Lahoori a great poet about veil wrote:

ای ز خود پوشیده خود را باز یاب
در مسلمانی حرام است این حجاب

Hi veiled lady you got to finde out who are you,
in Islam putting veil on is Haram.

And also mawlawi "Rumi"says

یکی دَم دست را از روی بر گیر
که در دنیا، بهشت و حور خواهم

Please take off hands of your face for a second, because I want heaven and pure one in this world.

I also met Deputy Minister of wakf and Haj Affairs Mawlawi Abdul Hakim Munib, who was former minister in the Taliban government. This is the same man who asked the United Nation to build a new stadium to fire bullets into the heads of innocent ladies and dismember their bodies.

Alas, is there any experienced sniper who can blow up the heads of these two dishonest and ignorant people (Hamid Karzai a street Kandahari boy and the killer, Hakim Munib the same ilk.)

Thanks to the brave lady Kira Davis she on her video February 23, 2012 said mostly, President Karzai, I'm sorry that we don't have a leader with enough balls to tell you to kindly take your fake moral outrage and your terrorist sensibilities and shove them both where the sun don't shine: and I'm not talking about those caves you use to house Taliban allies.

DR. Asghar says on his way to Badakhshan among the ulama I, said about the women relevant to naqisal aql and naqis al iman (defective in reasoning and lesser in faith) women are in possession of same faculty of reasoning and have equally sound faith as men, perhaps more. This is merely cultural belief and have nothing to do with Quran.

This upset some ulama and became restless to reply to me. One alim came on stage and made emotional speech and accused me of being ignorant of Quran and hadith. I was advised not to reply and instead Mawlawi Ataurrehman came and spook and told the' alim that you have misunderstood Dr. Engineer. Later on many younger ulama came to me and told me we agree with you and believe in gender equality. It gave me relief that there are some ulama who accept gender equality.

I spook in Urdu ex-tempore as I had no time to write a paper. First I tried to remove the confusion that only liquor has been prohibited in Quran. In fact all that produces inebriation are haram (prohibited) including narcotics. Liquor is called khamr in Arabic and which means some thing that covers. Liquor thus is called khamr as it covers up our understanding and reason. A piece of cloth is also called khimar as it covers our body.

Narcotics also produces inebriation and hence is khamr. Liquor is called umm al khaba'is i.e.mother of all evils and Quran asks us to refrain from it.

There was no problem of narcotics when Quran was being revealed but one, through analogical reasoning (in shariah formulation analogy has been widely used and in fact, is one of the sources of shariah law), can easily conclude that narcotics are as much haram as alcoholic drinks.

In fact all over world (except some Islamic countries) alcohol is sold and marketed whereas narcotics are strictly prohibited and its possession even punished severely, even through death in countries like Singapore, Malasia etc. No such punishment is given for drinking alcohol. It clearly shows that narcotic drugs are far more harmful than alcohol.

Thank you very much Dr.Asghar. You as a thinker and good hearted person did a great service and opened the eyes and ears of the ulama in Afghanistan especially on two very sensitive issues: women's rights and the consumption of liquor in the Islamic world. These unfortunate and ignorant people do not know the importance of economy, values of life, greatness of education and the role of freedom and democracy in society. These organisms, the Allah lovers, must know that we need change, diversity and the necessities for survival. Religion is nether food nor medicine or shelter to save the life. In Durkheim religion is a system of ideas corresponding to air.

What is food-1- material usually of plant or animal origin, containing or consisting of essential body nutrients, as carbohydrates, fats, proteins, vitamins, or minerals that is taken in and assimilated by an organism to maintain life and growth.We can see the foods, food got weight and taste, by food we can reproduce and survive. The effect of food psychology is very grave.

I have a story by a witness "Ishan Bavah" about a mouse who supplied walnuts for himself because winter was ahead. In Badakhshan (Afghanistan), there is a village called Zardew and the produce of that village are walnuts. A mouse was running up and down to supply walnuts to his house. When the mouse ran after another walnut, the kids sitting around rushed toward the home of the mouse and robbed all of his walnuts. When the mouse with another walnut in his mouth got into his hole promptly, he got out, jumped up into the air and dropped dead.

<u>Mr.Engineer Sahib Asghar!</u> We ignorant people because of the Arab imposed religion, Islam, are stabbed all the time from behind. The struggle for the freedom of in Afghanistan was not an easy task, it took all 19th century era to implement this decent movement. But allies under the pretext of Islam is in danger or Islam is great resorted to plots and created the mujahidin (the mother killers) and the Taliban (the women killers) the Leviathan, not only to overturn the democratic movement in Afghanistan but to also suppress the women's freedom and progressives and leftists too. Now, the revival of such beautiful movements are a crisis. In a land locked country like Afghanistan, in eighty years almost teen its leader have been killed or went to exile is horrible and we are still losing more democratic faces, more understanding and more brave ladies everyday.

I personally do not blame the mujahidin or the Taliban for the savageries they have committed in Afghanistan. Rather, I blame the allies and the billions of dollars that have been spent and the loss of a million lives all in vain.

Let us not forget the ferocities and savageness of the Arab lover who killed the Rawa young leader, Meena (1956-1987) Actress Benifsha, Hanifa Safi. Head of women's in Laghman province, actress Donya Porkar and thousands of others.

In Afghanistan, because of the wrong interpretation of Quranic Verses donkeys are eating grapes and people go to bed hungry.

I wish some other good hearted Islamic thinkers follow the path of the great engineer Asghar and make these backwarded people be more tolerant and educated. Also, tell them that your loving book is not a supernatural one but a plagiarized one. Otherwise, the chronic ferocities of these stone aged people will not fade away because these white capped people now have an establishment called "Afghanistan Academic and Islamic Research center."

First, we have to know what academy and research means?

My friends religion is not knowledge and does not need research or an academic center.

Let us find out in the dictionary what knowledge is and what research means?

Knowledge 1. The state or fact of knowing. 2.Familiarity, awareness, or understanding gained through experience or study.3. The sum or range of what has been perceived, discovered, or learned. 4. Learning erudition: men of knowledge. 5. Specific information about something.

Research- 1.Scholarly or scientific investigation or inquiry. 2. Close and careful study. To study thoroughly.

The science today makes the dick bigger but religion by removing the prepuce" the head cover" shrinks it?

There is a Russian anecdote that says: three ladies and three men spent one night in one hotel, in the morning the French lady got up and started looking under her pillow, the Russian got up and went straight to work, and the third one who slept with a Jew was crying, her close friend asked her what is wrong with you she replied his penis was "mocho choquioto.".

Russians in the field of humoring are very advanced. One day, my Dean of Faculty of Agronomy in Agriculture Academy in Kiev Ukraine, relevant to agronomy subject gave me a question and said that the atomic weight of Oxygen in the Soviet Union is 16 and how much is it in Cuba? To me, it was a confusing question but then I thought that maybe it is a political question. After a long pause, my answer was eight. Upon hearing that, he laughed a lot and he gave me a very good mark.

Hi Afghanistanies white capped Akhonds. Two years ago, your brothers in Egypt buried three hundred healthy pigs, the creation of your Allah alive. And Hakim Munib the Kandahari killer who blew up the Bamian's Statutes, Alqaeda caused the tragedy of 9\11, and the massacre in Baslan school in Russia, these and another heinous crimes have been committed are the most important ingredients of your Islamic research center?

If you are really a human being and believe in your Allah the creator, why do you hate the creation of your creator Allah, "the pig?"

In Afghanistan we have almost eighty varieties of grapes but because of the Islamic religion, the Arab's culture, we cannot process them into wine. We know Islam is imposed up on us and we have an Arab witness in Kabul call him (the king of the two swords). In the Quran, there are eleven Verses that say Islam is only for Arabs (Saudi Arabia). A country rich in oil in the Middle East is also one of the states of the United States.

What does it mean Saudi Arabia? It means that this country belongs to only one family and not to the people of the Arabian Peninsula. The country belonging to one family in the Middle East is the most accomplice enemy of democratic movements in the Islamic countries all over the world.

As Rachel Bronson notes: "it was Saudi Arabia, with its vast fortune and very real foreign threats, that altered the global course of political Islam. In doing so, it received the tacit approval of the United States."56 This role was accentuated even more after1979 when the Soviet Union invaded Afghanistan and the Iranian Revolution deposed the Shah. This is why America loves the Saudis the most and lesser the Israeli.

Saudi, the Wahabi eagle, with American eyes in the long run one way or another will hurt America. This is why Choudary says: "Islam the backward coming to your backyard."

The oil money from a country 95% sand and the beautiful poetic tradition according to reverent Christopher Hitchens as a Sidr honey, attracts converting flies from everywhere. An Iranian Nationalist and an arabized fanatic, Hassan Abbasi, says do not attack the enemy but attack the strategy of the enemy.

Islam, political Islam and secularism

Deepa Kumar writes:

An argument that has become almost commonsensical today is that the parties of political Islam are a natural outgrowth of Muslim societies. For instance, an introductory book on the world's religious published by Oxford University press in 2007 has a time line in chapter on Islam that begins with the birth of the religion and ends with the events of 9\11, Madrid bombing, and the London transit bombing. The logic is straightforward- Islam leads to (violent) political Islam an in a simple and unproblematic way.3

In this section, we debunk this notion in two parts.

First, we lay out the historic separation between the religious and political spheres in Islam. Second, we outline the trend toward secularism over the last two centuries.

The architects of the idea that religion and politics have always been intertwined in Islam are the right-wing ideologues Samuel Huntington and Bernard Lewis. Lewis, in a now famous titled "Roots of Muslim Rage" sets out his arguments as follows.

He begins by pointing to the historic separation of religion and politics in Christianity and then states that such a separation has not occurred in Muslim societies, which have not seen the equivalent of the enlightenment, the philosophical and scientific movement in the West that militated against Christian dogma.

Lewis argues that whereas Muslims at one point admired the West for its achievements, this" mood of admiration and emulation has, among many Muslims, given way to one of hostility and rejection."4 He goes on to add that this "is no less than a clash of civilizations- the perhaps irrational but surely historic reaction of an ancient rival against your Judeo-Christian heritage, our secular and the worldwide expansion of both."5

If the Islamic scholars like European thinkers are enough reasonable, but not cowards to separate religion from politics they have to know they are in state of dogma and have not accomplished any thing good in Islam history.

For Lewis, this is not a clash between Islam and Judeo- Christianity alone; it is a clash between the religious East and the secular West. As he notes, whereas Christians and the West were able to separate religion and politics, "Muslims experienced no such need and evolved no such doctrine." 6 As he put it, "the origins of secularism in the West may be found in two circumstances- in early Christian teachings, and, still more, experience, which created two institutions church and state; and in later Christian conflicts which drove the two apart." In contrast, there was" no need for secularism in Islam.' 7 In his book What Went Wrong published shortly after 9/11, Lewis develops these arguments that, "The notion of a non religious society as something desirable or even permissible was totally alien to Islam."9

At primary school, our religious teachers taught us wonderful stories about the greatness of Moses and Jesus. We loved them as a prophet very much and the main time the Jewish people who used to live in Afghanistan.

Bear in mind that our poetry craftsmanship are full of stories of Moses and Jesus but everything changed very rapidly because of the establishment of the Jewish state in 1947. Then the Arab imams, especially the Saudi, by hate speeches against Jews in mosques and other gatherings related to the Palestinian cause changed the attitudes of Muslims relevant to Jewish and Christianity all over the world then on the Muslims love less Moses and Jesus.

It was the great mistake of the United States to support the Islamists street boys to bring down the democratic regime in Afghanistan. Thus, with the help of its allies in the region (Saudi Arabia, Egypt, Israel, and Pakistan) it pumped billions of dollars into the training and arming of the enemies of Afghanistan. This was a golden age for the Pakistani to build up his Islamic atomic bomb and for Saudis, "the American milking cow in the Middle East the ideology to radicalization in order to hate the Jews, Christians, and Shiah and love the most Pakistani and the Pashtun tribes.

The strange thing to me is that why the Saudi, the American's allies, do not allow the other American allies, the Israelis, to visit Saudi Arabia (their native place).

<u>*Why Ibrahimic religions confusing us by using hyper bole?*</u>

Muhammad son of Abdullah not to get killed so in 622 B.C secretly in the darkness of the night fled from Mecca to Yethrib and named this episode, Islamic hijree calendar.

We have to find out what is emigration and what is fleeing? Fleeing means to swiftly pass away, as from danger but in case of emigration you tell every body around you that you are moving to another state or to another country, so to me this is not logical to call it Islamic hijree calendar (emigrating calendar) rather than fleeing calendar.

Second what is pilgrimage? Prior to Islam there in Arabian Peninsula was a custom, that every indigenous person at least once in their lives perform pilgrimage which it was based on idolatry and that custom after 1400 years still is continued there.

Ex 20: 3-4 (NIV) "You shall have no other gods before me. You shall not make for your self an idol in the form of any thing in hevean above or on the earth beneath or in the water below. God destroys idol; He is the great iconoclast.To Socrates if the art is a gift of gods then they might not have been iconoclasts?

According to the report Dr M.A. Fared WHO Regional Malaria Adviser 9, April 1956 as the large majority of pilgrims are poor, or middle- class people, and as many of them are old and infirm, one can imagine the effect of such rigorous and strenuous trip, the severe climatic conditions and the lack of environmental sanitation facilities on the Well-being of the pilgrims.

Germs of pestilential diseases are liable to be carried by the mass of pilgrims numbering sometimes hafe a million and now because of economic openness one million, and this has always been a potential source of severe epidemics, afflecting not only the pilgrims but also spreading to there origin.

I think in case of collapsing of Saudi kingdom and emergengce of a secular system there the door to pilgrims might be closed or reconsidered.

Ibrahimic religions, a collection of methology of the Middle East, evolved from the Jewish culture based on monotheism but not with different gods, different prophets and different books. This divisive development proved that religions plainly are a fabrication and it might be good news for the expansion of atheist association in the 21th century globally.

I respectfully disagree with the agendum of young, beautiful and brave lady Ann Barnhardt except on one thing the Islam attitudes a crumbing ideology. In quran in Abraham chapter verses 5,6,7 says Allah told Moses bring forth thy people from darkness into light it meams that Allah is also the Jewish god?

I'm alarming the free world that religion is not a good stuff and Islam is the most political subversive ideology, the materialist opportunistic policy of the West under the pretext of the national interest endangering the beauty and taste of the Western civilization a gift from the free gallant thinkers. Freedom for religion is better or freedom from national religion? In the course of history, Islam was the shoe horse of the Western countries especially Great Britain and later America. Now, the west has to pay the price.

Quote: But I think we ought to take into account that this reality is much more complex, and not forget the relatively positive role Iran played in the immediate aftermath of 9/11 and our overthrow of <u>the Taliban where they were extremely helpful to us.(Brzezinski)</u>

Brothers and sisters, those who believe in freedom and in humanism have to fight the pathogen "Saudi Kingdom." Or according to the former defense minister of the UK, drop the Neutron bomb on Afghanistan and Pakistan to pacify the region.

Do not pray to the empty air because every thing evolves from the living Earth. This is why muslims in their five times praying (heads down and the asses up) kiss the earth more than fifty times everyday. They have no time left for them to think about the importance of humanism and what taste and beauty are.

تصاویری از شاه افغانستان با بانوی اول و اعضای حکومت، در ضیافت های رسمی و اولین پارلمان افغانستان حدود یک قرن پیش.

Religion is the negative part of human culture but because of its holiness, it is not fluid and is resistant to intellectualism as well as political reforms. Religion and wealth are both a social disease and cause alienation among societies.

Quoted:

Socrates (469 BC – 399 BC) believed the best way for people to live was to focus on self – development rather than the persuit of material wealth. He always invited others to try to concentrate more on friendships and a sense of true community. To Socrates, poetry, mysticism, love and even philosophy itself are the gifts of gods. But he refrains to include fabricated issues like religion and prophets as gifts of the gods. In his agendum, conversely, he relies too much on virtue, ethics and logic rather than gods.

Epistemology and empricisim provide a foundation to disbelieve transcendentalism as Marx says: "human beings make history and they are their own creator".

347

Socrates's assertion that the gods had singled him out as a divine emissary to provoke irritation, if not outright ridicule. But conversely, he in another place claims to have been deeply influenced by two women besides his mother and one of them was a witch. He, Socrates, pointing at something strange (demonic sign= satanic sign) an averting inner sign. Socrates heard only he was about to make a mistake but in Islamic history, such a sign called revelation a manifestation of divine will or truth.

My friends!

Towards the end of 2004, I paid a visit to "Banu-e-Andarab" in the province of "Boghlan" in the north of my country, Afghanistan. I had the opportunity for the first time to visit a girls' school there. The teachers and students warmly received myself and my entourage, including Professor Dr. Muhammad Afzal Banuwal, a professor at Kabul University and the girls received us very well and sang songs.

During the six years of religious tyranny of Taliban, they couldn't influence the girls' school. In the end, I contributed a little money for the school, a part of which was distributed among the students and the other part was saved to be spent on stationary.

I felt so oppressed by what I observed, and began thinking about how I could help the school, which was in very bad shape.

Although I'm not a journalist or professional author, or a politicion I felt the responsibility to write a book and contribute to the economic, social and artistic well-being of the school; some of the income from its sales will go to provide them with a library, a small museum and crafts teacher.

If that income is not enough so that I could help the school financially, I reach out to the world's aid organizations to assist the girls in that school, because they cry out for your help.

Education and interaction of groups in daily life is the essential issue for recognition of realities and truths, and disprove of superstitions. The present situation in Afghanistan under Karzai, shameful leadership is a disaster for the Afghan nation and to the world. Therefore, I propose a few things to lead the Afghani people to a more prosperous and fairminded envioronment.

1-Bring about changes to the national constitution of Afghanistan. 2. Standardize the schools curriculum relatively consistence to the schools curriculum of central Asian countries to wash out the dark age mentalities of our young generations 3. Change the present imposed theocratic regime of Afghanistan to a democratic and more represented one and evacuate more constructive sets to the more experienced and opened minded ladies of the previous democratic government, otherwise diversities and changes through the leadership like Karzai and alike him reminiscence of the middle age is impossible in Afghanistan. 4. Strenghten the values of women's organizations. 5. In the future, political leaders do not let a deviant and insufficient person like Karzai usurp political power in Afghanistan. 6. Data gathering evidences show that Farsi-Dari language because of its historical role in the regions got the quality to become the langauge of communications in the country but not the Taliban tongue the node of the sugar cane.

نا برابری بازار تربیت و پرورش در صفغانستان بنا به زیر دستی ایل پشتون در جامعه در دراز مدت که همه امتیازات روانی و تنی به اوشان داده میشد روشن که میتوان انرا ستم نژادی نامید چرا که دسته هایی دیگر زیر نام ایل کمترین از جهان خورد و نوش کنار زده شدند.

Pashto in dictionary: An Iranian language that is the principal <u>vernacular</u> language of Afghanistan and parts of West Pakistan. What does it mean <u>vernacular</u>?

Vernacular 1. The native language of a country or region, esp. as distinct from literary language. 2. The nonstandard or substandard every day speech of a country or region.

Substandard 1. Failing to meet a standard; below standard. 2. Considered unacceptable usage by the educated members of a speech community.

Nonstandard 1. Varying from or not adhering to the standard. 2. Of pertaining to, or indicating a level of language usage that is usualy avoided by educated speakers and writers.

If the above remarks because of obscurantism or some other negative considerations can not be implemented in a backward country like Afghanistan we got to resort to Revolution; because the present government of Afghanistan unlike the previous one is a backward, misogynistic and very rligious state which opposes intellectual advacement and political reform,we got to make a wise decieion between necessity survival and supernatural (talking to air).

Every society made of a particular structure, and needs different approaches to changes shaping the condition of life and changing the mentality of a society for good you make the history beautiful.

Today we live in another century and every body observed the very interesting 99% occupy movement all over the USA.And this is a pivotal of classical social clashes for equality and justice.

In the end, my best gratitudes go to my daughter, the lovely and dedicated lady who helped me to start and end this book. Without her comprehensive efforts, the mission could not have been accomplished.

With the hope for a better tomorrow and Universal peace.

"Zardushtian"